Tales from the Symphony

Tales from the Symphony

Perspectives from African American Musicians

To my dear Neighbors and their baby girl.

Robert Lee Watt

Robert Watt

2024

ROWMAN & LITTLEFIELD
Lanham • Boulder • New York • London

Published by Rowman & Littlefield
An imprint of The Rowman & Littlefield Publishing Group, Inc.
4501 Forbes Boulevard, Suite 200, Lanham, Maryland 20706
www.rowman.com

86-90 Paul Street, London EC2A 4NE

British Library Cataloguing in Publication Information Available

Library of Congress Cataloging-in-Publication Data

Names: Watt, Robert Lee, author.
Title: Tales from the symphony : perspectives from African American
    musicians / Robert Lee Watt.
Description: Lanham, Maryland : Rowman & Littlefield Publishers, 2024. |
    Includes index.
Identifiers: LCCN 2023056438 (print) | LCCN 2023056439 (ebook) | ISBN
    9781538194737 (cloth) | ISBN 9781538194744 (paperback) | ISBN
    9781538194751 (ebook)
Subjects: LCSH: African American musicians--Employment. | Discrimination in
    the music trade--United States. | Music and race--United States. |
    African American musicians--Interviews. | Instrumentalists--United
    States--Interviews. | Symphony orchestras--United States.
Classification: LCC ML3795 .W38 2024 (print) | LCC ML3795 (ebook) | DDC
    784.089/96073--dc23/eng/20231208
LC record available at https://lccn.loc.gov/2023056438
LC ebook record available at https://lccn.loc.gov/2023056439

Contents

Acknowledgments

Tales from the Symphony

I am more than pleased to have enlightened my curiosity about the African American classical musicians, who are performing or have in the past performed in major American Symphony Orchestras. I will be forever grateful for those African American Classical musicians who shared their stories with me over the past year and a half. It is my sincere hope that this book will serve to enlighten and inspire the younger generations of African American Classical musicians that are up and coming and attending the top musical institutions today.

I am also deeply grateful to my dear lady friend, Mariana Drove (*And her baby Yorkie, Pixie*)

for the generous and invaluable assistance in the delivery of the book's manuscript and other technical items.

I hope that this book serves to shed some valuable light on an institution that has been too long a cloistered item in the music world.

Prelude

This book is a series of stories told, in conversation with the author, by African American instrumentalists who are currently performing or have in the recent past performed with a major American symphony orchestra. Their stories are part of an unfortunate and little-known history from more than half a century ago, when African American classical musicians were absolutely denied entry into symphony orchestras in these United States, regardless of their talent, musical proficiency, or their love and passion for the music.

The history of African Americans being denied entry into major American symphony orchestras would not necessarily be known to the present-day Black Lives Matter movement. However, the nature of its powerful present-day protests would have surely been welcomed by those African American classical musicians over half a century ago to confront head on that unique brand of racial exclusion in American symphony orchestras.

However, the Black Lives Matter movement certainly caused the entire world to focus on an age-old problem still very present in these United States by *screaming loudly* about the George Floyd murder and, for the first time in history, prompting the entire world to *scream loudly* along with them that Black lives do indeed matter. Many will never forget that amazing moment in American history, where it felt like the entire world was engaged in protest over a single racial incident that hopefully prompted a deeper examination of racial issues in some of the other more cloistered and socially elite areas of American life like the American symphony orchestra.

One must realize that racial discrimination in symphony orchestras pales in comparison to the hardcore version that is this country's birthright, the hardcore, historical discrimination that prompted the formation of a global movement like Black Lives Matter. The privileged, cloistered world of the American symphony orchestra and its peculiar racial issues may not even appear on the radar of the Black Lives Matter movement, but I'm sure if they were aware of it, they would surely sweep it together with all the other racial injustices they stand against.

However, it is the purpose of this book to shed light on a field of music that has always been, in and of itself, cloistered and, for the most part, denied from all but a certain segment of our American society. This book sheds light on the experiences that those African American instrumentalists who managed to get hired by a major American symphony orchestra endured from more than half a century ago.

The book also hopes to enlighten those loyal symphony patrons about the inner workings of this celebrated institution and art form, which they've held for so long in such high artistic esteem.

Those loyal patrons who would surely exempt this art form from any and all accusations of racism or exclusion of any type, even though for many decades symphony orchestras were referred to as, "The Men." *The men* because they were, in fact, only men, white men. The only women hired by major American symphony orchestras over half a century ago were harpists. And as progressive, liberal, and shall I say angelic as that might have seemed to the symphony orchestra male psyche in those days, many of the major concert halls still had no female restrooms backstage.

As time moved on, women other than harpists gradually began to get hired by major symphony orchestras—violinists, violists, cellists, flautists—and it was almost proverbial that these women were, with few exceptions, exclusively Asian. Then a small group of Asian men trickled in and after a short while, Asians in general became the largest minority presence ever so slowly emerging onto the all-white symphony orchestra mosaic. If one were to look hard and carefully, one might possibly see a few Latinx musicians.

Today, as I recall watching it ever so gradually unfold in my symphony orchestra years, let's call it, *the peoples of color numbers*. The highest number of peoples of color in American symphony orchestras were clearly Asian, a handful of Latinx, and finally, bordering on damn near highly unlikely, African Americans. The *peoples of color numbers* are also quite obvious when thumbing through the eighty-six pages of the current International Conference of Symphony and Opera Musicians directory, which lists the personnel of the major orchestras.

The book also hopes to answer an age-old, annoying question that most Black people constantly ask Black classical musicians, especially those musicians playing in symphony orchestras: "So what's it like playing music up on that stage with all a them white folks?"

For Black classical musicians in symphony orchestras in these United States, it was only recently that the nearly twenty-seven major American symphony orchestras showed barely 2 percent African American instrumentalists, men *or* women, in their ranks. This small percentage of African American symphony orchestra players, this 2 percent (actually, 1.86 percent according to the League of American Orchestras), are often mentioned in conversations about the number of African Americans *actually playing today* in America's major symphony orchestras, but who *are* these musicians? What are their stories?

These were questions I kept asking myself. So in the past year I had the honor of sitting down with most of them in conversation. Their stories range from amazingly brave, confronting head on all the historical racist residue and its moral monstrosities, to simply unbelievable. They navigate, almost humorously, the thousand unnatural, racist shocks that all colored flesh seems heir to, living in these United States.

Former Cellist of a Major East Coast Symphony Orchestra

Author: So where are you from Sir, the South?

Cello: No, I'm a Northerner. . . . I don't have any racial experiences or any experiences with the South. All my experiences with music teachers and schools were always positive. No one ever uttered a word of racial discouragement to me, ever.

Author: Even in your early years?

Cello: No, never, not one time. The first real racial encounter I ever had was in the Congress of Strings Orchestra, where I was principal cellist at age seventeen. However, said racial encounter was by no means negative or uncomfortable.

Author: Congress of Strings had an orchestra?

Cello: Oh yeah, these were young string players from all over the world. They met in Michigan where we all had to audition for the orchestra.

They made me principal cello, because in those days I had everything as a player, an incredible bow arm, I had the best sound, just everything. Plus, the other cellists couldn't do what I did. They just couldn't. So, they picked me for principal cellist and of course they invited me to play a concerto with the orchestra, at the end of the season. So, I played the Haydn D Major cello concerto. A rather difficult concerto for someone my age . . . or any age.

Author: Of course, of course . . .

Cello: So after I played the concerto, my stand partner in the Congress of Strings orchestra said, "Boy, you played that concerto as well as Feuermann." I said, "as well as Feuermann, really? The greatest cellist, who ever lived?" Afterwards, everybody in the orchestra came up to congratulate me. I was very nervous while playing though. I used to sweat a lot in those days. During my performance, I thought if I got any wetter, I might start screwing up badly. As I recall, I didn't play my best that night, but I guess it was good enough, because everyone was very complimentary, saying things like, "Oh my God, you have such technique and a wonderful sound." On and on, saying this and that.

All I'm saying is that, up to that point I had yet to experience any negative racial confrontations about being a classical musician.

Case in point, after that Congress of Strings concert there was a great party. I was dancing with all these white girls!

I had never even touched a white girl before in my life, until that Congress of Strings party. So, to be honest, dancing with those white girls that way was really my first real racial encounter, you might say. Like I said, for what it was worth, I honestly enjoyed that particular first racial encounter. However, up to that time, I had never experienced any kind of negative, racial discouragement.

Author: And this was high school?

Cello: No, I was in junior high school.

Author: Oh really, that young?

Cello: Yes, so the very first time I experienced any kind of negative racism was during my senior year in high school. It was when I entered the Merriweather Post Music Competition. Merriweather Post was the owner of the newspaper and the judges for the competition were made up of people from the Chicago Symphony.

Author: I see . . .

Cello: So all the judges said I won the competition hands down and nobody else came close. So, when Merriweather Post heard that a Negro (term used at that time) had won her competition, she lost it. She said, "A Negro won my competition? Oh, no, no, no, no, you can't let him have this . . . I can't have a Negro winning my competition, you pick somebody else! You can't pick him!"

Oh, it was a big scandal around school. My teacher told me what had happened with the competition and of course, everybody knew about it. It was a really big deal. I was so angry, because that was the very first time, I had any kind of negative racial matter brought to my attention that was connected to me.

Author: And did they actually choose someone else, in your place for the competition?

Cello: Yes, they picked someone else.

Author: Damn . . . amazing!

Cello: Yes, they did . . . so I told my teacher, I wasn't going to practice anymore, because I had practiced really hard for that competition. And they're telling me that race was why they turned me down? I didn't want to practice anymore! My teacher tried to console me, saying I shouldn't stop practicing because I'd only be hurting myself. So I didn't practice for about three days and eventually, of course, I returned to practicing.

So that was the first time I had experienced any kind of racial matter in music. I mean, I was first cellist in the youth orchestra of Chicago, first cellist in Congress of Strings, so I had a lot of encounters with white people.

Now the way Chicago was set up, we lived on the Southside, what we called the middle-class Black area. But we could always go downtown, which was the racially neutral part of Chicago. When I first joined the youth orchestra in my freshman year, I knew about racism, because I went to a Catholic high school. It was all white and I was the only Black person in the freshman class, but I don't recall any racial problems.

Author: A Catholic high school?

Cello: Yeah, a Catholic, all-boys high school called Brother Rice. Across the way was Mother McAuleys, an all-white girl's Catholic school. Now we knew we had to get on the same bus as the white girls from Mother McAuleys, to get to school . . . and we also knew we dared not talk to any of those lovely white girls. Certain things we just knew, back in those days. You didn't talk to white girls! I only dated black girls. I didn't talk to any white girls back then. You just didn't do that.

Author: But you said you were dancing with white girls at the Congress of String's after party.

Cello: Oh yeah, but that was at the Congress of Strings.

Author: Oh, and only at the Congress of Strings.

Cello: Only at the Congress of Strings and only with the musician white girls. But outside of that cloistered environment, at home, in Chicago, when I was going to school, I would never even talk to, much less touch, a white girl.

Author: Amazing, sad, sad . . .

Cello: But, in my social life, on my own time, on the weekends. I went to a certain place, an Episcopal church, to their monthly functions and dances to meet Black girls, which had nothing to do with my all-white Catholic high school.

So, as I said, downtown Chicago was sort of a racially neutral area of the city, which is where I met for the youth orchestra of Chicago in my freshman year. People were always very friendly, the white girls were very friendly and one day, after a rehearsal, some of the white girl string players took me to a violin shop downtown. So, there I was, walking around downtown Chicago with all these white girls and they weren't even thinking about that as an issue. They were taking me to all the violin shops, and we were all trying out cellos and stuff, damn! So, I had asked myself, should I be walking around downtown Chicago with all these white girls? I'm not supposed to be doing this, am I?

Author: So what happened when you were trying out the instruments in those violin and cello dealers with all those white girls?

Cello: Oh, when I asked to try out a cello, people were very friendly and gave me a cello to try out; we interacted very well. Never once did I have any kind of racial push-back from any of the violin or cello dealers for being there or for being with all those white girls, never a word.

Author: Interesting, interesting . . .

Cello: Like I said before, the very first time I experienced any kind of racial pushback was from that Merriweather Post competition and that was not from musicians. It was from Marjorie Merriweather Post herself. The owner of that competition and the owner of that newspaper. I was dumbfounded because music had always been an absolute path of joy for me. Of course, I knew in general that there was a separation of the races in this country, because in my senior year of high school, I transferred to another school, closer to where I lived, and that school was half white and half Black.

However, at that school, there was one fellow who was a star of the basketball team, a "pretty boy," one of the best-looking Black guys in the school. He went out with a white girl, and we all asked him, "You're going out with a white girl?" That was unthinkable in those days!

Author: And what year was that, exactly?

Cello: This was 1963. That was unheard of, a Black guy going out on a date with a white girl. Black guys only dated Black girls. I didn't dare go out with a white girl in those days. That was just unheard of! But he went out with that white girl, and we just couldn't believe it.

Author: Where did he take her on their date?

Cello: Oh, I don't recall but, he went out somewhere fancy with her. Then, he was the star of the basketball team and carried a certain racially neutral status that the rest of us didn't, I guess.

Then of course, like I said, we all knew as students that there was a racial line of demarcation in the country, but none of my music teachers or anybody I encountered ever said a word about race. And all the people I met in the Chicago symphony were always very friendly, but then I was around them all the time. I played concerti around Chicago Musical College, Chicago Civic orchestra, and I was an usher at Orchestra Hall. Also, during that time, I had just played the Dvorak Cello concerto with the NBC Symphony on television at age sixteen, so people knew me.

Author: Ah! What . . . really?

Cello: Yeah, in my sophomore year in high school I played that concerto with the NBC Symphony. I have a recording of it . . . and at my age, that was pretty good.

Author: For sure, my God! Who was conducting then?

Cello: Ah, Joseph Galluccio was conducting at the time. But I must say, everyone was always very friendly, welcoming, and helpful. Not a word or hint of any racial micro-aggressions or push-back. Of course, then, my father started taking me to Chicago Symphony concerts when I was about twelve years old. So yeah, that's when I first met some of the Chicago Symphony players. Also, around that time I was soloist with the De Paul University Symphony, I played the Boccherini cello concerto at age thirteen.

A lot of the Chicago Symphony players filled out the string section of the De Paul University Orchestra. And all those Chicago Symphony players and the De Paul Symphony players were all very friendly and helpful to me. I didn't receive any racial tension or push-back at all unless I was just naive. I don't think so or I would've known. So, like I said, my first run in with real racism was with that Merriweather Post Competition.

So, then I went on to the Chicago Music College as a regular university student, where I had a wonderful cello teacher and I got to solo with the college orchestra.

Author: And who was your teacher?

Cello: His name was Karl Fruh, who was considered the Leonard Rose of the Midwest. He had been my teacher since high school, and he had been a former member of the Chicago Symphony. He was also a big cheese in the Chicago studios. He did all the commercial work in town.

He was such a wonderful teacher and personality, always encouraging, pushing me here and pushing me there and recommending me for just about everything. But my very first cello teacher was my father, and my second teacher was Hans Hess.

Author: Oh really, your father? Okay. And of course I've heard of Hans Hess.

Cello: Yes, my father was my very first cello teacher. He was a conductor, cellist, and supervisor of instrumental music in the Chicago school district.

Author: Is that right? Now I see why you were so advanced . . . and cocky too. [Laughing]

Cello: [Laughing] He was a PhD, a very learned man. I studied not only cello, but he taught me music theory, solfege, and conducting.

Author: Okay, impressive . . .

Cello: So by the time I got to university, I had studied most of the music theory that they were teaching. I told my theory teacher that I knew a lot of what he was teaching already and that I had too much practicing and performing to do and no time for those elementary theory exercises he was having us do.

We had a course on the Neapolitan 6th chord. I said, "I know all about the Neapolitan 6th chord it's on the 4th degree of the scale with a lowered 3rd and

6th. I don't have time for these stupid exercises." I learned that stuff when I was eight years old from my father.

I learned all that business while riding with my father in the car as a kid. The clefs, the keys, solfege, I know all that business and I'm not doing it again. I don't have time for it.

We had an assignment where I had a parallel 5th by mistake and the professor pointed it out. So, I told him, "So I missed the parallel 5th, big deal! I'll just take the final exam now. I have too many concerts to play and too much practicing to do. I don't have time for your class." I was not popular with the theory teachers.

Author: I bet you weren't . . . [Laughing]

Cello: I said, I'll just come and take the final exam.

Author: Oh really?

Cello: I told the professor that I didn't have time to come his classes.

Author: And did you pass the course?

Cello: Oh yeah, I passed, but the teacher said, "You got a C, because you didn't come to class. Who do you think you are?"

So, when I went to Roosevelt College as a freshman, I had already done four recordings with the NBC Symphony, so I was well known and going to school was sort of a comedown for me. Sitting there was hard, I'd say to the teachers out right, "You don't think I know that? I know that already! You think I need to hear that again?" I said that in front of the class to the teacher. Of course, he said again, "Who do you think you are?"

Author: Oh boy! Cocky, cocky . . . [Laughing]

Cello: So I snapped back at him, "haven't you seen me performing on NBC Television? What do you mean, who do I think I am? Don't you know who I am?" Oh, I was an obnoxious kid . . . really obnoxious.

Author: Sounds like it. [Laughing] Oh and I'm sure he loved that, coming from a Black kid in those days.

Cello: Oh for sure, so the teacher asked me, "Why do you have to be so arrogant? You're so arrogant!"

So, as I said before, I never got any racial push-back, even though I was a very obnoxious Black kid. Case in point, when I soloed with the Roosevelt College orchestra, the conductor was Morris Gomberg. I had this good friend who played oboe and studied with oboist Ray Still. So as the soloist for that semester, playing the Saint Saëns cello concerto, at the first rehearsal, to show you how obnoxious I was in those days. I had my friend, the oboist, carry my cello in for me. I was dressed up in a fancy suit with an ascot and smoking a pipe.

Author: Ha! A pipe and an ascot? [Laughing]

Cello: So like a slave, my oboist friend carries my cello up on stage, I interrupt the rehearsal by walking up to the conductor telling him that I'm here and ready to rehearse the concerto and was he ready?

Author: You said that to the conductor?

Cello: Yes, I said that to the conductor.

Author: Holy shit, I don't believe this. [Laughing]

Cello: So the conductor said to the orchestra, "Oh well, I see our soloist is here. I guess he's going to let us rehearse with him." So, I said to my oboe friend, "would you please take my cello out of the case?" So, he takes my cello out of the case . . . [Laughing] and hands it to me, like a flunky.

Author: [Laughing] So please tell me that your oboe friend was part of this whole scheme?

Cello: Oh yeah, we orchestrated the whole thing. You know, we were in our first year of college and just crazy.

Author: Yeah, yeah, I remember those days and that mentality. Insane!

Cello: Yeah, I was very obnoxious. . . . I was pretty bad. So, I sat down, and we rehearsed the concerto with Gomberg. Oh, my father knew Gomberg when he went to that same college in the 1940s. My father never talked about race, but the first time he did, he said, "I remember old Gomberg, that God damn white bigot!"

So that was my first year at Roosevelt College, and that same year I entered the Michaels Award Competition. I practiced very hard for that, which was a competition for all instruments, piano, vocal, cello, et al. So, I played Saint Saëns and the last movement of the Kodály, unaccompanied Cello Sonata. Boy, that last movement is a tough one! I also played the Prelude of the 6th Bach Cello Suite. The committee was made up of Frank Miller, principal cellist, and the entire first desk of the Chicago Symphony string players.

However, a pianist won the competition, playing the Rachmaninoff 3rd piano concerto. So, I thought, okay that's how that goes, that's fine. That competition was on a Saturday and that very next Wednesday, while I was living at home, attending the Chicago Music College of Roosevelt University, the phone rang and my mother called me saying Frank Miller was on the phone. I thought, *Frank Miller, of the Chicago Symphony is calling me?* So I picked up the phone and he had this strange way of talking. "Hello Earl, this is Frank Miller." I said, respectfully, "Hello Mr. Miller" (I admired him so much). I was also an usher at Orchestra Hall and Frank Miller would see me ushering people into the hall at all the concerts.

Oh, one of my important tasks was to usher in Claudia Cassidy, the famous music critic of the *Chicago Tribune* every Thursday night. So Frank Miller knew me well and of course, he had seen me on NBC playing the Dvorak cello concerto.

So, on that phone call, he said he really liked my playing at the competition and that he wanted me in the Chicago Symphony and that I should play for Mr. Martineau on that Saturday. It was Wednesday then and I told him that I didn't know much orchestra repertoire. He said, "That's okay. I know your playing and I know you. I assured Mr. Martineau that you'd be prepared each week, but I want you in the Chicago Symphony." So, I said, "Okay, Mr. Miller, I'll be there on Saturday." I was feeling in shape, because I had just played the Saint Saëns with the Chicago Music College orchestra. He said, "Make sure you play something very flashy. Play the Saint Saëns and play the last movement of the Kodály, unaccompanied cello sonata." So, I said, "Okay, Mr. Miller that's what I'll do." So, when I got there to play, I started the Saint Saëns and Maestro Martineau stopped me and said, "That's too fast, play it a little bit slower."

Author: Martineau said that?

Cello: Yeah, he said I was playing it a little bit too fast. So, I thought to myself, I'm gonna play it Leonard Rose style, who plays it much slower and very rhythmic. So, I thought to myself, *Okay, Earl, Leonard Rose style, Leonard Rose style.* So that's what I did. Then I went on to play the last movement of the Kokály unaccompanied Cello Sonata. Maestro Martineau said, "Okay, very good!" So, Walter Hendl was there, who was the assistant conductor of the Chicago Symphony, he put something in front of me to sight read.

So my teacher said, "Now Earl make sure you look at all the flats and all the sharps and take some time before you play." So I looked at all the flats and sharps, key signatures, and tempo markings.

Author: And that was your sight-reading test?

Cello: Yeah, that was the sight-reading. . . . I don't recall what it was though. So I did what I could with it, and they all said, "Okay, alright!" Martineau thanked me and asked me how old I was. When I told him I was eighteen, he said, "Oh, you're so young, my goodness! Thank you very much though." So that was that . . . and all I heard from my teacher was that Martineau kept saying I was so young. Perhaps too young?

After that I went every Saturday to play with the Civic Orchestra of Chicago training orchestra and to a weekly repertoire sectional lesson with Frank Miller. We went through all the orchestral repertoire and Mr. Miller said, "My, you're a really good sight reader, really!" Of course, I always got there real early to go through all the music. We usually met at 10:00 AM, and I always got there at 8:00 AM to look over the notes. I mean really, you can't sight read Ein Heldenleben or Gurrelieder, that's crazy. But he thought I was sight reading, but I had practiced the music before, so I was always prepared. We did that for a whole year.

Soon after that, the personnel manager of the Civic Orchestra, which is the training orchestra of the Chicago Symphony, said, "Earl, see if you can get into a lesser orchestra and I guarantee you'll be in the Chicago Symphony next year."

So, I started to think about what he said and sure enough an opening came up. It was in the National Metropolitan Opera Touring Orchestra conducted by Robert La Marchina. So he auditioned me. He had me play Dvorak and Schumann cello concerti, Rococo Variations, and in the Dvorak concerto, he had me play all the difficult passages. After hearing me, he said, "Oh my goodness, you're really a virtuoso! Can you read?" And I said, "I can read," and he hired me on the spot. I was eighteen.

That audition was around February. I was in my second year of college and that job didn't start until the following September. Just then, an opening in the Saint Louis Symphony came up. I happened to be visiting a friend of mine who lived in Saint Louis. While visiting him I decided to audition for the symphony. They had me play the entire International Music Excerpt Book One, in addition to the Dvorak and Saint Saëns cello concerti. It was a long audition.

Author: I should think so, the entire excerpt book? Crazy!

Cello: But you know, when you're that young, nothing bothers you.

Author: Of course . . .

Cello: They were very impressed, but after a while, I didn't hear anything back from Saint Louis, so I thought, *what the hell?* Two weeks later I told my teacher I didn't hear anything from Saint Louis and maybe I should go on the road with the touring orchestra job I'd just won. I didn't want to go back to school. I hated school and couldn't do that anymore.

So my teacher told me to write to Pittsburgh and Minnesota. Minnesota didn't have a vacancy, so I wrote to Pittsburg, and they did have a vacancy. So the personnel manager called me back and said there was a vacancy and that I had a very good resumé, and it was great that I was a soloist with the NBC Symphony and that I came highly recommended. However, the manager didn't want me to audition for Mr. Steinberg unless I was really good. "He's been auditioning all kinds of cellists, and he's turned them all down. So, I don't want you to come here to audition for him unless you're really good. Now tell me, are you really good?" He asked me that on the phone. [Laughing] So I said, "Yeah, I'm really good." I had a lot of confidence in those days.

Author: I see, I see . . . [Laughing]

Cello: By the time I was about to audition for Pittsburgh I had just turned twenty and that was 1965. So the audition was arranged, and I took the train there at night, Chicago-Pittsburgh, arrived there in the morning and freshened up in the train station.

Author: Wow! Without any sleep?

Cello: Yeah, again, at that age, it didn't bother me. So, I had my audition appointment with Maestro Steinberg at the Pittsburgh Towers or some fancy place where he lived. When I got there, his wife greeted me, and said he wasn't there.

Author: No, really?

Cello: I said, "Oh my God, he's not here?" And she said, "Oh I guess he'll be along soon." So I asked her if I could warm up and she gave me a room that sounded really nice. I have this routine warm up that I do. I always warm up on the Prokofiev Cello concerto ah . . . the E minor. I always needed about half an hour to warm up in those days.

Author: Really? You needed an entire concerto to warm up?

Cello: Yeah, but, just one movement, usually . . . so what happened was apparently Steinburg came in, without my knowing, while I was still warming up on the Prokofiev. And I heard him say to his wife in the other room, "That's my cellist. That's what I'm looking for, that's what I want!" So he came in and introduced himself to me.

At that point we had a formal audition. I started playing the Dvorak Cello concerto and there's a big left-hand shift in the first movement and I'll never forget the look on his face when I made that big shift. He looked over at me surprised, as if to say, who is this guy? I had developed a system that made it impossible for me to miss a shift. I could not miss a shift. I had a lot of confidence in myself in those days. (Perhaps a bit of arrogance too.) [Laughing]

I finished the first movement and told him that I have the whole concerto prepared if he'd like to hear it. So, I played some of the second movement and some of the last and he said, "My, you really have a feel for your instrument, don't you? My goodness!"

Author: So, he was really impressed with the shifts that you were making so easily?

Cello: I guess so, I mean, you can always tell if somebody genuinely likes how you play.

Author: Of course, sure . . .

Cello: Then Steinburg opened up one of the excerpt books and asked me, "So what's this piece?" I said, "That's the Symphonie Fantastique by Berlioz," and he said, "Very good."

Author: So, he wanted to see if you could recognize just the notes?

Cello: I think so, but remember, I had practiced all the excerpts for a couple of years and knew them all even without the titles . . . and yes, I could recognize them just by the notes.

Then he said, "Do you want to break your arm now?" I said, "Sure what's next?" Then he put up the Brahms 3rd Symphony. It has a very technical part in the last movement that really works the bow arm. And he said, "Oh, very good" then I played, Don Juan, Beethoven's 5th, and a few other excerpts. Then, to my great surprise, he said, "Well, do you want the job?" I said, "Oh yes!" And he said, "Can you handle the job?" I said, "Oh yes!" He went on to say, "Well this has all worked out so well, I'm so happy. I have to get in touch with Sidney Cohen to get a contract for you. It will take me a couple of hours to do this."

I told him I could go and take a look at the city and come back in a few hours. So I left my cello there and went to a movie and then went around the city of Pittsburg to get familiar with it. Two and a half hours later I came back, and he had a contract for me. I signed it on that day and that was it. That was 1965.

Author: And those were the days before the idea of screens and formal auditions committees. In those days everybody auditioned for the conductor, and everything was wide open to any kind of discrimination too.

Cello: That's right . . . so after signing the contract I took the train back home and the next day I received an overnight Telex giving me the performance schedule for the Pittsburgh Symphony's concert season and when I should report for work. My father was very excited that I'd gotten a job. Then of course, to me, in all my arrogance, I said, "Well, it's good, but it's not the Chicago Symphony." Remember, I'd been going to the Chicago Symphony since the Fritz Reiner days. Fritz Reiner, Chicago Symphony, Fritz Reiner, Chicago Symphony. To me that was the epitome of music. And, of course, I was just a spoiled brat back then . . . no question about it.

So, when I got to the first Pittsburgh Symphony rehearsal, I didn't know exactly where I was going to sit in the cello section. So, the personnel manager came to me and said, "You will be sitting 3rd stand, outside." Not in the back, but 3rd stand, outside, okay not bad! So, that's where I started. The first rehearsal was, Schöenberg, Pelleas und Melisande.

Author: Oh! Fun!

Cello: A friend of mine who was in Chicago Symphony told me I'd better look that Schoenberg part over, because it was a tough piece. So, I got to Pittsburgh four or five days before the first rehearsal and got the music from the orchestra library. I worked on it because you can't sight read that piece. So, I was prepared. But Schoenberg, Pelieas und Melisande, oh my goodness, you can't sight read that.

Author: Oh God no, it's quite difficult for horns as well.

Cello: So at that first rehearsal there was a cellist in the back of the section who was about eighty years old who had played with the New York Philharmonic for thirty years and fifteen years with Toscanini. I could feel him watching me play and he finally said, "Oh I can see you're a real cellist, look at that vibrato you have . . . and your bow arm. I can see why Steinburg hired you, you're a real cellist. I can see the way you vibrate, you're a real cellist." The cello section, in general, was very respectful. I never had any racial push-back; people were very friendly.

Author: In the orchestra in general?

Cello: Yeah, very friendly, very respectful.

Author: Good to hear . . .

Cello: So my experiences were very good in Pittsburgh overall. I had a good time playing there.

Author: How long did you play with Pittsburgh?

Cello: I was there for four years.

Author: Oh! Only four years . . .

Cello: The only reason I left Pittsburgh was I still had this drive to be a soloist.

Author: A soloist, really?

Cello: Remember, so many of my father's students had become important composers in the Chicago recording industry. I was able to think about a career in that town, because I knew a lot of people in the industry as well. Many of the students that I went to school with at Chicago Music College were playing and becoming big in the recording studios. Then, of course, many of them also knew me from playing in the Grant Park Symphony in the summer. Oh yeah, I'd go to Chicago in the summer to see my parents. Oh, by the way, that Grant Park audition was one of the toughest auditions I'd ever taken, even tougher than Pittsburg. Good Lord! But I got the job. I was only in Pittsburg one season when I got the Grant Park job for the summer.

Pittsburg didn't have a summer season for the entire orchestra. They only had an eighteen-piece chamber group for their summer season in upstate New York.

Because of my connections in Chicago, I was told that I could make a fortune playing in the studios. Of course, my teacher, Karl Fruh, was big in that industry. So, I thought to myself, *If I played in the Chicago studios and pursued that, I'd have more time to practice and pursue my solo career and still make a fortune.*

Because in the studios, if I did three sessions a week, plus residuals, I'd make more than I ever could playing in the Pittsburgh symphony in one week. So, I started thinking, since all the musicians wanted me there in the studios, my teacher wanted me . . . and remember at that time there were only three cellists that did all the studio work in Chicago. So, if I pursued the studios, it would've been my teacher, myself, and the assistant principal cellist of the Chicago Symphony who did all the recordings. So I decided I would take that route. That's the only reason I resigned from the Pittsburgh Symphony.

Author: To be a recording artist in Chicago?

Cello: Yes, to be a recording artist in Chicago.

So, I went to Chicago, and I worked with my teacher, Karl Fruh, and Leonard Chausow, from the Chicago Symphony, and he was on the committee when I won the audition anyway, so he knew me very well.

Author: So, there were only the three of you doing all the studio recording work?

Cello: Just the three of us . . . and even some of the studio composers were composition students of my father's, so everyone knew me. So, the whole thing worked out very well for about two years and then the musical styles started to change.

Author: In the record industry?

Cello: In the phonograph recordings, the musical styles started changing and the work started being less. I was working with people such as Maurice White of Earth Wind and Fire, you've heard of him, haven't you?

Author: Yes, I used to work with him as well in Los Angeles.

Cello: So I worked with him all the time. He was their drummer then. Then suddenly, all that studio work dried up and I ended up playing all these ballets, which I hated. They didn't pay much, and the work was hard. I didn't leave the Pittsburgh Symphony to do that kind of work. So I was very unhappy and the thought of moving to Los Angeles and playing more unreliable studio work didn't appeal to me either. So then, I needed work. Remember, I had sued the New York Philharmonic by then so I thought, *Who the heck would want to hire me?*

Author: What? . . . Really? Tell me more.

Cello: Yeah, the lawsuit I mentioned happened after I had auditioned for the New York Philharmonic in 1967. The original audition was on a Tuesday, and I couldn't make it that day so the personnel manager of the New York Philharmonic asked if I could come on the following Saturday. There were twelve other cellists present on that day, but I was the only one playing in a major orchestra.

So, after I auditioned for Leonard Bernstein, all the people that worked backstage for the New York Philharmonic audition, telling the players when and where to go on stage, seemed to be looking at me in an odd and strange manner. I didn't know why at the time, but perhaps it was because I didn't know anyone in the New York music world and perhaps, along with being Negro, I appeared a total stranger to everyone. But I answered the cello audition advertisement in the Union paper like everyone else.

However, when I finally got to play, I did so for a very long time. In fact, I thought it was a very full and proper audition.

After all the other cellists had played and the audition was done, a cellist from Boston said to me, "You know, you played the best audition by far today."

Some weeks later I got a letter in the mail from the New York Philharmonic saying that I wasn't hired.

It was 1969; times were changing fast and suddenly Negro musicians became Black musicians. So that's when I decided to sue the New York Philharmonic for racial discrimination along with another musician, who joined the suit later. I went to the New York Human Rights Commission. They, however, investigated me by asking musicians around town if I was really the quality of person and more importantly that quality of a musician to sue the New York Philharmonic.

In reality, Leonard Bernstein said I played very well, but that he preferred someone else. So, he should not have been considered racist just because he preferred someone else.

So, the human rights decision on my lawsuit was made in November of 1970 after extensive testimonies were gathered from many prominent people.

They found that the New York Philharmonic engaged in a pattern and practice of discrimination with respect to the hiring of substitute and extra musicians and that the complainants are within the class affected by this pattern and practice.

Secondly, although the evidence found the complainants indeed well-qualified musicians, they didn't prove their case in regard to permanent employment.

The New York Philharmonic began to hire Black substitute and extra musicians. However, I was told by many musicians that I would be blackballed in New York as a musician because of the lawsuit, so I left the country.

When I came back from Europe, they were still holding a job for me in Antwerpen, Belgium, but I wanted to think about it first. I finally decided I didn't really want to live in Europe, but I really needed a job, so I came back to the United States.

I honestly thought after that lawsuit, I would never have to play in a symphony orchestra again. Until work slowed down in Chicago. Suddenly I thought, *What am I going to do now?*

Steinberg was furious with me for leaving the Pittsburg Symphony. They called me in three times, trying to get me to stay. Get this, they had me drive with Steinberg in his private car, with him and his girlfriend (his wife had died), for a Pittsburgh Symphony tour, from Pittsburgh to New York City.

To hopefully get us to bond more and perhaps help him persuade me to stay in the orchestra, can you believe that? He was so angry with me. He said, "You're going to Chicago to play Jingles and record dates? You're leaving here to do that?" Oh, he was furious with me!

Author: Do you think it had anything to do with your being Black and your leaving would thereby lessen the diversity or were there other Blacks in the orchestra at that time?

Cello: Oh no, there was a Black violinist and there was the orchestra pianist, but I found out that I was the first Black player to actually get a contract.

Author: I see, I see, okay interesting.

Cello: So I had sealed my fate with Pittsburgh and could never go back there, but I still needed a job. That's when Milwaukee came up. I knew the first cellist there since I was twelve years old.

Author: Who was that?

Cello: Ah! Harry Sturm, who knew about my playing in Chicago studios, and he asked me if I wanted the cello job in Milwaukee. I told him that I could use a job and he said, "Well Kenneth Schermerhorn is the conductor." So, the audition was scheduled. Then my teacher said, "For Milwaukee, really prepare for it, don't sluff it off." I really practiced hard, and I wanted to do well, especially because I'd known Harry Sturm for so long and wanted to play well for him and of course, I didn't want to embarrass myself.

So, when I arrived at the audition, of course, there were a several other cellists. Harry was there, Schermerhorn was there in a tennis outfit looking super cool, then he was extraordinarily good looking anyway. I think a Union rep was also there. So, I played all the usual stuff, but I must say, I was quite nervous.

Author: You, nervous? No . . .

Cello: Yes, I was nervous. Also, at that time I really needed a job. Remember, I was getting older . . . twenty-seven, so things weren't so easy for me anymore. Things were more serious then and I didn't want to go home and live with my parents, you know. Well, I wasn't really nervous, but let me put it this way, I had never felt that way at an audition before.

Author: So, you were more nervous than you thought you'd ever be.

Cello: Yes, more nervous than I thought I'd be. I was surprised at myself. So behind me was a mirror and after I played the Dvorak, I looked in the mirror and thought to myself, *You know, you play better than this, what's wrong with you? You really need this job. You really need this job.*

Then they had me do sightreading. The Brahms 3rd symphony again. They had me play through the entire part, all the movements and then Midsummer Night's Dream.

Author: Oh, okay . . .

Cello: That was hard, but I had been practicing that music, so I did okay. But you know, I had a way of playing when I was nervous. Something I'd worked out so when I'm nervous, I can still play alright. Next, they had me play Don Quixote and I thought, *Why are they having me play Don Quixote? I'm not auditioning for principal. I just need a job.* I didn't want to play principal.

Author: What was the position? It wasn't for principal, was it?

Cello: No, Harry Strum was the principal, and he was also the personnel manager. So, they had me play a few other things like Beethoven 5th and that was it. Then I had to go sit outside the room and wait. While I was sitting there, I thought, *what's gonna happen?*

Then after a while Harry came out all smiles and said to me, "Welcome to the orchestra!" I thought to myself, *Oh my Lord! Thank God!* I was so relieved. And you know that orchestra was not the Pittsburgh Symphony, but at least it had a nice salary, etc. Oh, I found out later that they actually wanted me to be assistant first cellist.

Author: Oh really?

Cello: Yeah, they said that the assistant first was leaving to become a professional golfer.

Author: But that wasn't the opening you auditioned for?

Cello: No, but the assistant first was leaving in a few weeks. So, they had me sit on last chair, that was the vacancy, but any time the assistant first was gone, I went up and sat on the first stand with Harry Strum. So, I told Harry that I didn't like sitting on the last stand, but what I really wanted to do was go back to school.

Author: What, wait . . . you wanted to go back to school? For what?

Cello: Not for music, but a degree in psychology and political science.

Author: Really? Really?

Cello: Oh yeah, I wanted to be an educated person. I felt like I was uneducated.

Author: Oh, I see . . .

Cello: Yeah, so I went to the University of Wisconsin full time.

Author: Full time, for real?

Cello: Oh yeah, I had a full schedule. Hell, I only slept five or six hours a night.

Author: How many weeks did the Milwaukee symphony play?

Cello: Oh the orchestra had a forty-four-week season.

Author: Oh, almost a full year season.

Cello: Oh yeah, it was a full schedule and Schermerhorn wanted me to play a concerto with the orchestra and all. Once the orchestra was playing this very difficult work with a difficult cello part, and I just barreled into it. He stopped conducting and started smiling and all the other cellists were asking me how I was playing that difficult part. Oh, he was my biggest fan, always pushing me. He wanted me to play assistant first cello, he really wanted that.

Author: I see, sounds good . . .

Cello: But like I said, I couldn't play assistant first and be a full-time student at university. That would've been too much pressure.

So, I ended up playing on the third cello stand and went to University of Wisconsin full time and got a degree in psychology and political science.

That's when the hankering came up to move out to Los Angeles to play in the studios. Because the guys in Los Angeles were after me all the time to move out there and play. They said, "Hey man come on, you need to move to LA, we've got all this work." They were playing with Earth Wind and Fire as well . . . oh they were after me all the time.

Author: Well, they were right, there was a lot of work out in LA, especially in those days.

Cello: So I took a leave of absence from the Milwaukee Symphony and went out to Los Angeles. That's when I met you.

I joined the musician's union and that very evening, I got a job playing at the Roxy Theatre. Then I met the contractor, Bills Hughes, and suddenly, I was recording all over the place. Oh, just then, there was that big strike in the music industry and after the strike, I was getting forty calls a week. Of course, I could only do ten or fifteen, because many of them were on the same day at the same time."

Author: Forty calls a week?

Cello: Yes, I was getting forty calls a week. Mostly because I'd played in the Pittsburgh Symphony, and I knew Ray Kramer and Eleanor Slatkin.

Ray Kramer was the biggest cellist in the studios at that time along with cellist, Eleanor Slatkin and they got me on all the studio calls.

Author: Okay, so what year was that?

Cello: Yeah, I skipped over a lot, so let me back up a bit. So, when I auditioned for the Pittsburgh Symphony in 1965, I won the audition that July and started playing with them in October 1965. While I was still in the Pittsburgh Symphony, another audition for the Chicago Symphony came up in December of 1965. There was no screen; Martineau was there Frank Brouk, principal horn, Frank Miller was on stage showing me where and what to play.

However, I never heard anything back from the symphony. I did hear that the concertmaster of the Chicago Symphony told a few of his students that I had won the audition, but that they were not hiring Negroes.

Author: And you never heard back from the orchestra?

Cello: No, I never heard anything. Nothing. So, I let it go and talked to my teacher about it and he said, "Don't let it discourage you. You just keep practicing and don't pay any attention to that." So, I let it go . . . but I must say, I didn't feel good about it. It bothered me a lot, but I managed to move on.

So that summer, that June, I auditioned for Grant Park Symphony conducted by Irwin Hoffman. He gave me quite a difficult audition, but I got the job, even though they had me play a huge amount of music. I got the call the next morning that I had won the audition. So, I played a summer season with Grant Park.

Let's see now, it was September of 1966 and I heard that the Chicago Symphony had another cello audition in October of 1966. They never filled the position that I had originally won, and didn't get hired, because I was a Negro. In fact, the principal French horn of the Chicago Symphony, Dale Clevenger, was very outspoken about it, calling it overt racism. I met him by chance at a music dealership in Chicago and he brought up the subject of my second cello audition for the Chicago Symphony. He also mentioned the fact that the board of directors, after hearing I had won the audition, stated outright that they didn't want the image of a Negro in their orchestra. He told me the audition committee and the music director thought I was extremely good and should have been offered the job.

Author: You know Dale Clevenger brought the story of your cello audition up to me, when I was doing a master class with his horn studio last year. He wanted the students to understand how racist the Chicago Symphony Orchestra was in the 1960s.

Cello: No! So, they had another audition in October 1966, and I was told they were trying to reach me. When they reached me, they told me the audition was on a Sunday, but the Pittsburgh Symphony had a concert on that day. We were doing the Mahler 2nd. So, I had to get permission to get off that day to take the audition in Chicago. When I talked to the personnel manager about it, he said, "Well, you'll have to talk to Dr. Steinberg about getting off for that day." So, I had to go in and see Steinberg.

Author: Really? Oh, boy!

Cello: So I told him that I had an audition for the Chicago Symphony. He really snapped back at me, "You wanna audition for Chicago? But didn't you just audition for them back in December?" He remembered the exact date too. But I reminded him that I didn't have to get off from my job in the orchestra to take that audition in December, because that was a free day.

So, Steinberg said to me, "I'm going have to hire someone to substitute for you that entire week and you're going have to pay them for that entire week. Does this job mean that much to you?" When I answered yes, he flinched! I'll never forget that. So, then he said, "Just to show you that I don't mean you any ill will. If I can engage another cellist to replace you, I'll let you off for that week." So, they hired another cellist. I had to take the entire week off and of course, everybody in the orchestra knew I was taking the Chicago audition.

So, I just went back to Chicago and practiced the entire week until the audition. When I arrived at the audition, there was a screen. I had never seen a screen before . . . and I had never played behind one either.

Author: What? They didn't have one when I auditioned in 1970 . . . well, they tried to have one, that is, there was a screen hanging from a fly that only went to my waist and somebody on the auditions committee was pissed! "I ask you what good is this God damn screen, I can see he's colored, for Christ's sake! What the hell are trying to do here?" So, you're talking four years earlier, in 1966, that they had a screen? Hmmmm?

Cello: Yes, in 1966, the audition was held in the Fine Arts building in a hall on the tenth floor that I knew very well. I had played many recitals there growing up as a kid. So, I went on stage behind the screen and of course, Frank Miller was there adjudicating. I played the Boccherini Cello Concerto, 2nd and 3rd movements, which is very rhythmical. I guess that was what they were looking for. The committee stopped me in the middle of the movement and just then, Frank Miller starts playing the piano. Then they told me to tune with the piano and continue with the 3rd movement. Then we started with sightreading, oh boy! They had me sight reading the Nielson 4th Symphony.

Author: Nice, well not easy, though.

Cello: Difficult! So, I did my usual sight-reading routine, I looked at the key signature, looked for the difficult spots that stood out, etc. Then they had me play all the standard things that I already knew. Oh, there were a lot of other cellists there too.

They had everybody play and of course, they had us waiting for quite a while, until finally, they came out and said, "Two people made it to the finals." Me and a guy from the Minneapolis symphony.

Author: Okay great . . .

Cello: So it was me and a white cellist from the Minneapolis Symphony and there was no screen for the finals.

Author: I see . . .

Cello: I got the vote of everybody on the committee in the preliminaries. I got every vote! So, in the finals, I played some of the same pieces, the Boccherini again, Flying Dutchman, Ein Heldenleben, Beethoven, Coriolan Overture, I knew that cold and Beethoven's 5th . . . the finals weren't so bad. The preliminaries were actually harder. So, when the other finalist played, he couldn't sight read the Flying Dutchman, but nobody can sight read that anyway. Then to my surprise, the other finalist actually said that my Boccherini was really beautiful. That's what he said. That was quite unusual for a competitor to admit that don't you think?

Author: Absolutely, to admit anything . . . very unusual.

Cello: So Frank Miller came up after the two of us had played and said to me, "It's so nice hearing you again and thank you so much for coming." And then, nothing.

So, I had to return to Pittsburgh with no results from the audition and then of course, everyone thought, I just didn't make it.

Author: But you still didn't hear anything from the Chicago Symphony?

Cello: No, I didn't hear anything . . . again. So, a few weeks passed and still no word about the Chicago Symphony Orchestra cello audition.

So as time went on, in December the Pittsburgh Symphony and the Chicago Symphony were both on tour for the New York Festival. We were both playing in Carnegie Hall and both staying at the same hotel. I happened to be walking through the hotel lobby, and who do I run into? Half of the players from the auditions committee of the Chicago Symphony cello audition. They were all just standing around chewing the fat. And when they spotted me one of them said, "Hey, how are you doing . . . do you know what happened at your audition?" I said, "What do you mean, what happened?" "Do you know what happened at your audition?" "I said no, I never heard back from them, so I guess I didn't make it." They said, "What do you mean you didn't make it? No, you won the audition!" Then they started explaining to me what happened. They said that I got the vote of every person on the committee—Martineau, music director, wanted me in the orchestra, Frank Miller, principal cello, wanted me in the orchestra, but the board of directors heard that I was a Negro, and they did not want that image in their orchestra.

So, the board of directors took a vote as to whether they were going to have their first Negro in the Chicago symphony. Now the board was made up of twelve members and I lost it by one vote. They said, "you almost got the call to be in the Chicago Symphony cello section. The auditions committee tried everything they could to get that vote redone, but to no avail."

Author: Wow! That was then, these days the board of directors would have nothing to do with the orchestra hiring.

Cello: Right, but back then the board of directors had all the power, and the committee could not get that vote recast. The committee said they were so sorry they couldn't help and felt really bad for me.

Author: That's amazing you never heard back from them though.

Cello: Yeah, I had to find out in the lobby of a hotel that I had actually won the audition.

Author: So, who got the job then?

Cello: Oh, they didn't hire anybody. So, what happened then, we were in December, they had another audition for the job they didn't fill . . . the job that I won and couldn't be hired because I was a Negro. So, in May of 1967, they wanted me to come back and audition again. Now, wait a minute, get this! At that time, I was on tour with the Pittsburgh Symphony in the deep South. The day they wanted me to play that audition, again, I was playing at Ole Miss University in Mississippi. Can you imagine? The worse place any Black man could be.

So I said to my father when I was back home in Chicago: "First of all, I've already auditioned once, and won! Why do they want me to come back there and go through all that again? I already won the audition . . . they should get that straight with their Board of Directors."

Author: What the fuck? But they never officially notified you that you won the audition from the last time. You found out by chance in a hotel lobby?

Cello: Well, actually, Ray Still was on the committee and told me at the time of the audition, that I had won.

Author: But no one from the symphony officially contacted you about it by mail or otherwise?

Cello: No, no one contacted me by phone or anything.

Author: My God! That was so sloppy and unprofessional.

Cello: I also told my father in May of 1967 that I would have had to get off the tour with Pittsburgh to come and audition on that day. Then I would have had to go and ask Steinberg to let me off again.

Author: Whooo!!

Cello: He would've thought I was out of my damn mind. I couldn't do that again! Secondly, we were on tour, I had no way to prepare for an audition, because we were traveling every day. Plus, Martineau already said I'd won the audition and I should be in the orchestra. Why should I audition again? They knew how I played, the first time, what were they trying to do? Did they want me to come back there so they could find something wrong with me? Is that what they wanted? So, they could say, "Oh well he played well before, but this time he didn't play quite as well." In the meantime, my father took my case to the musician's union.

Author: Oh, really . . . okay.

Cello: He took the whole thing to the union. Frank Miller verified that I had won the audition and should be in the orchestra and he wanted me in the orchestra. But they had filled the position with some white guy.

So, when the union approached the Chicago Symphony management saying I should be in the orchestra, they said, "Oh, we'd love to have him in the orchestra, but we've already filled that position, so we don't have any vacancies and besides, that position was way in the back of the cello section. If your cellist could just be patient, we'd love to have him audition in the future for a position that's more toward the front of the section."

Author: What the fuck!! Really?

Cello: The point here is, they could do anything they wanted back in those days, and nothing could be done about it. The music director had total power (except in some orchestras, the board of directors) and if they wanted a certain player or didn't want a Negro, they could say, forget the committee and put that person in the orchestra . . . or not. Then on the other hand you can't make a generalization about all orchestras, they're all slightly different, but at that time in history, 1965–1966, it was quite a different world.

Second Trombone of a Major Southern Symphony Orchestra

Trombone: One of my first experiences dealing with the racial thing in my orchestra (You're gonna love this story), one of my former colleagues came up to me, and this is after the Super Bowl, when Doug Williams was the starting quarterback for the Washington Redskins, torched the Denver Broncos. I don't know if you follow football or not, Bob . . .

Author: Ah! Not too much . . .

Trombone: So, Doug Williams was the first Black quarterback to win a Super Bowl.

Author: Right, I recall . . .

Trombone: So after the game a former colleague of mine came up to me and asked if I watched the game and I said of course I watched the game. So, he said, "Yeah and a Black quarterback won the Super Bowl!" Letting me know that he now finally believes and understands that a Black quarterback can be a quarterback in the National Football League. He was obviously, at the same time, surprised, but his subtext was, "Aren't I wonderful and progressive for finally acknowledging that fact to you."

Author: A pat on the head for him.

Trombone: Yeah, he was trying to impress upon me how much he had evolved by finally acknowledging that a Black person could be a quarterback in the National Football League.

So, I walked away from him without saying a word. That was the worst thing I could've done to him, but it was the best thing for me.

There was one rather ugly incident I recall when we had a Black conductor who was conducting an education concert and in a rehearsal the music had a lot of meter changes, 5/8, 2/4, 3/8, etc., and he got off a few times. So he had to stop the orchestra and start over, stuff like that. So one of my colleagues said, not to me, but in earshot for those in the back row. "Why don't you go back to conducting gospel music!" So, I turned to him and said to him, "You know what you said was racist?" And it was like someone punched him because he didn't think

23

I was going to say that. I just got hot all over. I was so enraged that he would say something like that.

Author: But he expected to get away with it?

Trombone: Exactly . . . so he looked at me and said, "I'm so sorry I said that." About a week later he and I were in the lounge during the concert and weren't needed for the first half. So, he said to me, "I can't believe after all these years that you would say something like that, that I was racist. As long as you've known me, I can't believe you'd say that." So, I looked at him and I said, "You know, we've had all kinds of conductors, Italian, German, Polish, you name it, we've had them on the podium and in a rehearsal they've all made mistakes. But I never once heard you say to any of them, why don't you go back to conducting polkas? Or to a German conductor, why don't you go back to conducting beer songs, or to an Italian conductor, why don't you go back to conducting Italian arias?"

Then he went on to say, "Well, ah, some people say that when you got into the orchestra . . . you didn't win an audition." So, I asked him, "Well who won the audition? Who won the audition?" So, he said, "Well, there's this one guy, and the reason he gives you a hard time is because he thinks it was unfair how you got hired." I told him point blank, that I took a national audition, did this guy, your friend or whoever he is, did he take a national audition? I was there with all the other candidates, was he there? I talked with the people on the auditions committee, and they told me why they chose me. So, this friend of yours, who didn't take the national audition for this orchestra, needs to shut the fuck up!

Author: So, the person who made those remarks about the Black conductor, and telling you about his disgruntled friend, he didn't audition either?

Trombone: That's correct! Not in his day, there were no formal auditions, he was appointed in 1964.

Author: Appointed? Oh, 1964? Okay, no wonder.

Trombone: Yes, during an earlier time, in the days when players were some-times hired by word of mouth. So, if you don't call those individuals out, especially the older appointees, such racist hyperbole will never end, as you know.

Author: Yes! And a guy his age would not be used to being called out on racial issues. He was most likely never around Black people and certainly had no Black friends to check him on his racist remarks. So he was spoiled by his white privilege. He had to be totally clueless to believe that what he said about the conductor, in that regard, was the truth and was his perfect right to express it and never be called a racist.

Trombone: Also, down here in the Bible Belt, some of the players in the orches-tra like him, when they teach a Black student, for example, they consider it their Christian duty to teach these kids, who in their minds, will never amount to very much anyway and are beneath them. It's pretty sick.

Author: Really? I had never heard of such a thing, but how racially noble of them.

Trombone: And also, down here in the South, if a classical musician thinks you're beneath them, well that's okay, but if they fear you are on par with them or better, watch out!

Author: Yes, I know. I've been there. We had a new principal years ago who came into the orchestra like "The Great White Hope" talking down to each player in the section about what he felt about the horn section and its players. He had the nerve to say that he was going to help each player, even though he had serious playing problems that got him almost fired from his previous job. Oh, and he had the nerve to say that all the criticisms he made were meant to be helpful.

Trombone: Oh my, how condescendingly thoughtful of him.

Author: When he got to me, I must add, he had just heard me play a famous chamber work and he was quite complimentary and/or threatened by my playing. So, he started out the conversation with, "This is between you and me." I told him I'd be the judge of that. When he said that, I knew I had a problem. The head of management at that time was quite hell bent on dividing the players against each other as a management style, and this fool walked right into it as a prime management lacky. He started out telling me that I had been exposed to so little and that I didn't know about Myron Bloom and that I hadn't been exposed to James Chambers and the Conn 8-D style of horn playing.

Now this was all conjecture on his part. He never had the brains to ask what I had been exposed to; he was just going to stand there, in all his prejudice and white privilege, and tell me. He went on to say that I had a chip on my shoulder about being Black and that I was defensive.

So I stopped him and asked who he'd be talking to about me and who was it that told him that he was the one to straighten me out. He still insisted that our great talk was just between us.

He was going to improve the section, even if it meant getting some people to retire and that he wanted my respect.

That I was the only one in the section who had a chance to become the right kind of horn player.

I told him that he was going to have a difficult time coming into the orchestra talking down to everyone in the horn section. Especially since I knew he'd been chosen by management to fix certain people like me. Like I said, he was the perfect type of personality and management lacky to volunteer to do so. He went on to tell me how he went to Jacobs on Chicago Southside to fix a playing problem he had that almost got him fired from his last job. He had the nerve to tell me that, "It was all Black down there" and how he got beat up. I said, "Really, you're telling me that Chicago Southside is all Black. And you went down there by your white self with your horn? And you're telling me this, because?" It was obvious he wanted me to know that he had a reason to hate me if I didn't play ball with him. We became mortal enemies to say the least.

Trombone: God! So sad to hear that kind of stuff. You know, I can only imagine what it was like for you in those early years in the orchestra.

Author: Yeah, but you know it was all worth it, to see so many other young, great Black brass players come along since my time.

Trombone: Let me tell you about another thing that happened several times with our orchestra board members. They would say lame things like, "I'm glad you're here . . . and are you part of that talent development program for minorities, is that how you got in the orchestra?"

Author: And board members would ask you this?

Trombone: Yes, I was asked that . . . and you know, you would think that board members would have a little more insight into what was happening in their own orchestra that they annually raised money for . . . or just orchestras in general. It was shameful, shameful!

Author: Wow! Did you thank them and sing Kumbaya together? I had a similar thing happen to me when the Philharmonic had their Minority Development Program. The orchestra gave a concert at a well-known church in the Black community. There was a woodwind quintet from the development program, and there was a Black horn player in that quintet. They performed on the first half of the concert. On the second half of the concert, I played a Mozart Horn concerto with the Philharmonic. Now I don't recall whether there was a written program, but at the end of the concert people from the audience thought I was a student in the Minority Development Program and started complimenting me saying things like, "Wow! You played great maybe you too will be in the Philharmonic someday, good luck."

Now perhaps the confusion was because I was the soloist, and they didn't see me actually playing in the Philharmonic during the rest of the concert. However, it was hard to believe that Black people could confuse two completely different looking Black men. It was quite the disappointment.

Trombone: Ah! Moving on, there was a woman who was a substitute for an ailing string player and we became normal friends, so I thought. Come to find out, she wanted a relationship with me. I don't know what you think about relationships in the orchestra, but I was not interested.

Author: Ah! Ya don't want to have a girlfriend in the orchestra. Taboo number one. My teacher warned me about that when I was still in Boston. And he said it a manner that was crystal clear, "When ya get out there in Los Angeles remember this, Bob: 'There are no women in the orchestra.' You get my drift? You don't want that; it's a disaster no matter how you look at it." Yet people still did it in my orchestra. We had a few of those taboo relationships in our orchestra, and it was indeed a disaster. Somehow, they always ended up in a disrupting, embarrassing bitch fight. I mean in the middle of a rehearsal sometimes.

Out of the blue, in the middle of a symphony you'd hear: "Well, fuck you, bitch." "Well no, fuck you!" Totally interrupting the rehearsal and it always seemed to happen when we had a guest conductor.

I recall hearing that I was not very popular with many of the single orchestra women, because I stayed away from them, and I kept my female business outside the orchestra. Because of that, one of my good friends in the orchestra came to me and said he'd heard a description of me from some of the single orchestra women that I might not want to hear. I told him I was curious. "Ah, okay, Robert, are you sure you want to hear this? Well, this is what one woman said: 'You are an arrogant, Black son of a bitch, good horn player, goes his own way, lady killer and thinks he's God's gift to white women.'" So, I said, "Really? [Laughing] . . . okay, that sounds about right."

We had one woman in the string section that all the men thought was so attractive, mainly because of her chest size. Now in those days, we had a few religious people that didn't play the National Anthem, so they would walk out before we played it. No big deal, no one had a problem with it. Well, one woman apparently did. One morning, in the middle of a rehearsal, she stood up and started playing the National Anthem on her violin, using double stops and all. While she was playing, she yelled at one of the religious women, "Now . . . walk out Sally, walk out! Walk out, bitch, walk out!" The conductor froze in the middle of the piece, and it seemed the entire orchestra froze along with him. Finally, the personnel manager came out and led her off stage, leaving everyone in shock as the orchestra went on break.

Trombone: Really? That is hard to believe.

Author: Yeah, I think that was quite a shocking experience for the entire orchestra to see someone suddenly lose it like that.

You know, there was another distasteful element about being in an orchestra, and I don't know if you experienced such a thing and that was the orchestra wives.

Ah! They had no filter. I always hated when they showed up for events or came on tour. They were such an unsavory bunch.

Let's see, there was one really unfortunate incident with an orchestra wife that I really resented. As I recall, the orchestra was in Italy, around the early 1980s; after a concert in Florence, there was a fantastic reception for us. I got engaged in a very fun conversation with a group of young Italian women who wanted to practice their English on me. I left the women for a minute to get drinks and one of the orchestra wives, whom I barely knew and had ever said two words to, grabbed my arm hard and said, "Now you behave!" I looked at her like she had two tails, as I jerked her hand off me, I said, "Don't ever touch me and who in hell are you to tell me to behave? Now, please get this through your head! You don't tell me what to do! I don't know you and don't care to know you, so please mind your business!"

So, what do you think brought that on? Have you had anything close to this kind of insult happen to you from any of the orchestra wives in your orchestra? I mean, the very fact that she truly believed she had the authority to seize me by the arm and talk to me that way was truly outrageous.

Trombone: My God, I should think so . . .

Author: You know, I was forced to ask many questions: What, in fact, about my behavior did she disapprove? Was it simply my personal and joyful social interaction with those Italian women that prompted such a toxic reprimand from her? Perhaps jealously? But how could that be? I didn't even know her name.

Could she have actually imagined that I was out of my Black American element and in a totally, far above my social paygrade, white social element, that is, Europe for the first time? Did she actually think, armed to the hilt, with her lily-white assumptions (even though it was my sixth trip to Europe) that I was in a situation where I might not have known how to behave with a half-dozen Italian women surrounding me in Europe? Was a Black American male, representing a high-class white American institution, the Philharmonic, enough to cause her to feel deputized by racist American culture, to check me, by pulling me aside? Or was she reminding me of my racial caste in these United States by insisting I not embarrass her and the orchestra with my American, Ghetto Blackness, way overseas in prestigious white Europe? So, you behave?

Trombone: My God! That was insane . . . infuriating! Thankfully we didn't have many events with orchestra wives and I for sure never had such a thing happen to the extent. However, I would answer yes to all the above questions, even though I don't see what behavior she was really objecting to so strongly.

Author: My point exactly and believe me, you are quite fortunate not to have experienced the orchestra wives' phenomenon.

There was another incident that happened on a different European tour. Now I don't recall if that woman was an orchestra wife or an extra musician along for the tour music. She was seated next to me on the flight over and she started to tell me, in a very excited tone of voice, what I was going to see and experience in Europe.

She went on and on about how different everything was in Europe. That the streets were super clean, and all the cities were perfect, with no bad ghetto areas, like the United States.

She went on about how great the food was and how the Europeans really loved Americans, especially musicians. Then she slapped me on the side of my leg and said, "So are you excited, Bob? You're gonna love it, I promise!" I looked at her like she was crazy and said, "After five previous trips, I'm not nearly as excited as I was about my first trip to Europe." I asked her how many times she had been to Europe, since she seemed to know so much about it and she said that was her first trip. She looked quite embarrassed, as I sarcastically asked her if she had any more exciting tidbits to tell me about Europe before I took a nap.

Trombone: Why is it always that same lame prejudice, that unconscious assumption, that they know more than we do.

Author: Yes, it was a sad moment in time.

Trombone: Now I have an interesting story about one of my former colleagues in the orchestra who used to do a 5K run with me. He was a string player and one of those guys who was born in the South and got into the orchestra in 1964, when the players were appointed and didn't audition; he's still in the orchestra.

Author: He's still in the orchestra?

Trombone: Yes, so he lived in a small southern town where they still reenacted battles from the Civil War, every year. He was very proud of his confederate heritage. Apparently his great-great-grandfather fought for the confederacy with Robert E. Lee and got shot in the leg with a lead musket ball, which he still owns and actually brings into rehearsal every year to show the musicians. During one of our rehearsal breaks he started getting emotional and kind of whining about how Black people are always complaining about what they want and how they suffered in this country, especially during the Civil War. [Whining] "But I just wanna say, my ancestors were poor white trash and lost their farms, loved ones and everything during the Civil War, so they suffered just as much as Black people." He said he understood that slavery was horrible, but people must realize that white people suffered during that time as well, but nobody talks about that do they?

Before I could open my mouth, the other white people in the room jumped down his throat. They just harangued him to the point where I had to jump in and rescue him, because they were going to tear him a new one. Saying, "How insensitive can you be, what the fuck are you talking about? You don't know a damn thing about what Black people went through! You don't have a leg to stand on when it comes understanding what it was like for people who were enslaved! They were cut off from their heritage, denied the right to learn how to even read, the women were raped for centuries, they were brutally beaten, families were broken up!"

I had to tell everybody that he and I ran together and were friends, but that he should understand that Black people knew back then that it was rich white folks who took advantage of his poor white trash ancestors. So, things cooled off after I spoke, but they were ready to carve his ass.

Author: So, I guess one learns how to negotiate the landscape of an all-white orchestra after a short while, because an orchestra is like a small town in a sense. After my first year I was comfortable with the reality of the job. I knew who and what to avoid and realized very soon that everyone was not going to be equally comfortable with me. I had a reputation of, as they put it, going my own way.

There were always a few people who just didn't know how to relate to me. Those coming up to me asking stupid racist questions, thinking they were relating instead of pissing me off. The worst situation, where I had to actually get physical, was with the older orchestra men wanting to pat me on my ass as a greeting. "Morning, Bob, Boy!" After a few of those I started grabbing wrists and twisting arms causing them to ask, "What's wrong, I can't touch you?" And I would have to say, "No you can't, unless you want me to touch you up street style." I hated that sense of entitlement that those older white men had, thinking that they could lay hands on me if they chose.

I remember a crazy situation outside the orchestra when I was supposed to be off for the week and there was an emergency in the horn section. They called and asked if I could come in for the second rehearsal of the afternoon. Well, I was up in Malibu working my show horse and had to come in at the last minute. On my way to that rehearsal, I had to stop briefly at the post office in Santa Monica. While in line at the post office, still wearing my tall riding boots and tight breeches, this old white man asked me, "Sir can you tell me why all dark people have this hump in their ass?" Amazingly, this old fucker actually had the nerve to reach out and try to touch my ass. I slapped his hand away hard and said, "Don't try to touch me, asshole!" I was furious. I yelled at him saying that I got my hump from fucking white women and the entire line turned around looking very alarmed. I really lost it. I know that was outside the orchestra, but have you had this happen to you in your orchestra, this patting on the ass greeting from the older men?

Trombone: No, I never experienced that, but I recall your telling me about that years ago.

Author: Oh, really? But you know it's also a dominance move, that is, to see what one can get away with, especially one who is intimidated by you and your Black presence. So, we have to remember that this attitude and sense of entitlement and quasi-ownership can be traced back to slavery. Imagine the horror that white slave owners experienced. Having total control of a person who looked totally different, who had amazing color, amazing body attributes.

That fact had to be overwhelming for some white slaveholders. Can you imagine all those beautiful Black women scantily clad, in chains being paraded through these American streets? Ah! Don't get me started.

Trombone: But do you know what's interesting about your situation? Two things: You came out of the 1960s when the country was going through the blood bath of the Civil Rights Movement, and you landed your job in the 1970s.

The country and the entire world were really in a different place for you. Then when I came along in the 1980s it was because of the turbulent 1960s and 1970s that the 1980s were easier to live with for me.

The turmoil from the 1960s and 1970s was still there, but it wasn't as in your face, so to speak. And the other thing that was interesting about your situation was simply living in LA.

When one thinks of Los Angeles and Hollywood, one can't help but imagine copious, mind-boggling, diversity. But that wasn't the case, listening to you, it just wasn't that way.

Author: No, you're right and I didn't realize how divided and segregated the city was until I'd lived here for a few years. A musician friend of mine that I interviewed said that certain cities in LA were like Sundown towns: Culver City, Glendale even Inglewood, which is mostly Black now but, where he was almost attacked by a white mob at a bus stop. Yeah, LA was not the liberal heaven that Hollywood portrayed on the television and movie screens. Oh, and some of the most ruthless police chiefs and police brutality, which was well documented in the Black community, hence the 1965 Watts riots.

So, what else ya got? Tell me something crazy. Come on, tell me a story. [Laughing]

Trombone: So when I joined my orchestra in the mid-1980s things were not perfect. There were a few things, but not on the magnitude that they were for you, in your day. Oh, there was something that used to irritate me when I was playing first and the conductor addressed the trombones, he wouldn't look at me, he would look at the rest of the section as if I wasn't there.

And then, when someone else was playing principal, one of the white guys, he would then look directly at the principal.

Author: Yes, yes, I've experienced that and it's one of those micro-aggressions that is so micro that if it wasn't for the fact that it happened so consistently, you could almost dismiss it as imaginary or oversensitive . . . and God forbid, you tried to talk to a white person in the orchestra about it. You would surely be accused of being too sensitive.

Trumpet of a Major Midwest Symphony Orchestra

Trumpet: Hello, nice to talk to you. So where are you from?

Author: Where am I from? I'm from New Jersey.

Trumpet: The reason I asked that is I think it has a lot to do with your perceptions of things. How you see yourself as a minority, what sort of music programs you were surrounded with when young and your family life in general.

All of these elements contribute to your choices toward having a career in classical music. I grew up in Boston and I'm from Cambridge, Massachusetts, and I must admit, it had a great influence on me as a musician.

Author: So, you believe where you were from had a lot to do with your choices as an African American, in choosing a career in classical music?

Trumpet: Yeah, growing up in Cambridge, Massachusetts, which compared to other places was a pretty diverse city, being near Harvard University and all. So being a minority was never that big of a deal to me. I never felt like I was the only one of so many. In fact, I grew up in a large ethnically diverse family. I'm one of ten kids. My folks adopted six of us from all around the world. They adopted me first. So, I have a Native American brother, a Vietnamese brother, a Cambodian sister, an El Salvadorian brother, and four other siblings who were biological from my parents, and they are white. So, all my siblings that I grew up with were different, yet we were the same in the sense that we were one family. And my parents have friends who did the same thing, adopting multi-racial and multi-cultural children. So, we hung out with them a lot. We had a whole network of this diversity. And that's what I grew up with, that was my ethos, my sympatico. I didn't think of using the word minority. What's a minority? And I grew up in Cambridge too, which, by the way, was very progressive at the time.

Author: And of course, having Harvard University there helped create that progressive climate, as I remember in my days as a student there. So, tell me something about your career journey as a trumpet player.

Trumpet: Yeah, when I auditioned for my present orchestra job, the audition process was interesting, because they had a screen up for the preliminaries and when they removed the screen, there were four of us who had advanced to the finals. So, for that segment they said they'd like to have the four of us just stay on stage together.

They set each of us up with a chair and stand and had each of us play separately. They went on to tell us the reason they preferred this arrangement was they wanted it to seem as fair as possible, because of me. Because I was a minority and they wanted everyone to see the process, especially the other candidates.

Author: So, the candidates could hear each other.

Trumpet: Yes, so we could hear each other instead of having each candidate wait in a separate room until called. To have the candidates stay on stage was new ground for me. I'd served on committees before, and we never did such a thing. They said because there was a minority involved, they wanted to have it as open and fair as possible.

Then when they got through with the audition itself, they told me I had won the audition. Maestro said, "Congratulations, we liked many things about your playing," and he mentioned some things I needed to work on and then he said to me, "I wanna tell you that, people are gonna say you got the position because you're black. But I want you to know, that you got it because of your ability."

Author: Okay, good for him . . .

Trumpet: And that . . . I was shocked by that . . . I was taken aback for a minute. At no point in the process did I even think . . . because of where I came from, because of my own perception of myself in the field of classical music, that race would even be an issue. Then it dawned on me of course, that's exactly what it was.

Author: Your take on this whole thing is quite refreshing, based on, as you say, your background and upbringing.

Just to tell you a little story about your orchestra, in 1965 a Black cellist auditioned and won the position and was going to be hired, but the board of directors stepped in and said, "They didn't want that kind of image in the orchestra," they took a vote on it, and he lost. He never got hired. Of course, these days the board of directors have nothing to do with the hiring of orchestra players. That was a different time.

Trumpet: Yeah, you know what struck me recently. There's a lot of talk about diversity and getting more people of color into orchestras. There was an article in the *New York Times* by the writer Anthony Thomasini about how audition screens should come down. There was a whole controversy about that.

Author: Really? When was this? Hmmm?

Trumpet: A few months ago, right at the height of the Black Lives Matter movement. There was a lot of push-back about that article, because people were saying, "We need to keep the screens up." We need to keep things as fair as possible, we're not quite there yet I don't think.

Author: Ah, yes, yes, I read that article. Somewhat naïve I thought. One can't just will with an edict, fairness, and equity.

One must look at the history of the symphony orchestra in this country and realize that it's going to take a long, patience-taxing time to correct the insular, cloistered, racially biased institution that it was for most of the twentieth century. There was a time when orchestral candidates actually went to a conductor's hotel room to audition, and a decision was made then and there. Some orchestra players were simply appointed. So, in those days orchestral hiring of players was wide open and free to discriminate in any way desired.

Trumpet: The screen is not so much the issue as the tiny candidate pool of African Americans or people of color showing up to auditions. I've been on so many committees, man, and I haven't seen one African American. It's not like there's a whole pool of candidates out there. The screen I always felt is to keep people from hiring their friends, their spouses, or their students.

Author: Exactly, which I assume, was one of the types of discrimination the screen was meant to prevent.

Trumpet: One of the grave experiences for me was back in the early 1990s; the New York Philharmonic had a policy that if you were Black and auditioned and didn't make it to the finals, you were automatically advanced to the finals. I auditioned for assistant principal, like I said, back in the early 1990s. I didn't advance to the finals, went back home, and then got a call from the personnel manager of the Philharmonic. He told me that the Philharmonic had this policy that, as a minority, I could, if I wanted, audition for the finals. I don't know, given my background, that seems wrong. I would hate to win a position because of that, you know.

Author: Okay let me give you the history on that deal. In 1969, a year before you were born, two Black string players sued the New York Philharmonic for racial discrimination. It's actually mentioned briefly in the very beginning of that *New York Times* article about the screens coming down. The two players lost the suit, but the Philharmonic began a mad search for Black instrumentalists, because during the trial they were accused of not knowing or having contact with any Black players. They also compiled a "List of Negro Musicians." So they made this agreement with the New York Human Rights Commission that any person of color after auditioning has a free pass to the finals. I recall running into this when I auditioned for the Philharmonic. It was quite shocking and almost humorous, the way the personnel manager, after telling me I had not advanced to the finals, went into this kind of proclamation: "According to the New York Human Rights Society you can, as a minority, if you so please, advance to the finals and be heard by the music director . . . etc." I thought he was nuts talking like that.

So, that's the story behind the minority advance to the finals deal. But all that madness was part of a big rebound from a time when no matter how well you played, as a Black musician, you were absolutely prohibited from even getting an audition, because no orchestra wanted you in their ranks.

Trumpet: And now, the thing I thought about most recently and that is affinity bias. This affects everybody, it doesn't matter who you are. If you have a certain look, there's an affinity, but if you don't, it's not good, it breeds bias. For example, I'm one African American in my orchestra, okay? And I think there's a tolerance level for that, okay? However, if there's more than one, if the numbers tend to creep up . . . if there's three or four. It's my feeling that the audience, the board of directors, to your point, will start to think the product is inferior, not as good. Do you ever think about that sometimes?

Like if you're on a gig and if you're the only African American it's chill. But when there are more, I feel this bias. I don't know! It's something I feel, it's not justified, but I feel it!

Author: Interesting . . . tell me more.

Trumpet: I can't help but feel that the average concertgoer, coming to a concert in a beautiful concert hall, when they see more than a few African Americans in the orchestra they're gonna think that the product is not as good, just because they're not used to seeing an orchestra that way, it's suddenly out of the norm for them. If they see a Black conductor, it's not going to be as good, yet it could be twice as good, still via their affinity bias, they'd perceive it as inferior.

Author: Wow, what an interesting picture you paint of affinity bias. Of course, you know, what you just described, a lot of people would be afraid to verbalize it quite that way.

Trumpet: Yes of course, but I think it's worth saying.

Author: Yes, absolutely!

Trumpet: And you know, women go through this all the time. Take that famous woman conductor, who we we're considering as our next music director. A brilliant conductor, every time she conducted us it was amazing. I was talking to a colleague of mine about her as a possible music director and he actually said, "We wouldn't hire a woman, would we?" And I thought, *are we really still there?* And this was a young guy in his thirties and I thought, *you son of a gun, this woman was what we really needed* . . . and then I had to admit, this is where we are.

Author: Yup, we're still there too. That affinity bias really emerges between men and women. I remember meeting an Austrian French horn soloist at an International French Horn Symposium in Germany. We were having a drink and he said, "You know, there are a lot of females at this symposium." My response was, "Yeah, that's great!" He corrected me and said, "No this should be a man's thing. I mean, these women, they can't play." I thought to myself, *I'm not going to be hanging out with him anymore.*

Then if you look at Austrian orchestras, they are or used to be all men. In fact, the Vienna Philharmonic got picketed while on tour in the United States for their lack of females.

On a related topic, I was invited to attend the Gateways Music Festival last August. They wanted me to be a keynote speaker at one of their events. They also wanted to know if I wanted to play in the orchestra as well.

At first, I said no, then I changed my mind, knowing I could never live down not bringing my horn and playing in the orchestra. Those East Coast horn players would kill me if I did that. So, I enjoyed the entire festival. I noticed in the string section, which was mostly women, that the tone of the high strings, especially when they were in the harmonic range, was a little rounder and slightly darker in sound. When I asked the maestro about it, he said, "It's colored, it's just colored, that's all."

Trumpet: Okay, that's the essence of the issue. What is the quality of the music? We talk about diversity, and we talk about inclusion . . . but what about the artform itself? I don't know about you, but I see the artform becoming so much more visual, we're playing movies scores, we're playing pop concerts. It's becoming visual media. It's not about the quality of the artform itself anymore. We've lost the concept of being a group of musicians playing classical music at the highest artistic level possible. It's good to be diverse but not at the expense of the artform.

Author: Okay, let me back up for a moment, for the sake of clarity and to your point about quality. When I mentioned that the Gateway's string section had a slightly different over all darker string sound, I didn't mean to imply it was less than. In fact, it was a great improvement and for sure an enhancement of the artform. I don't think anyone would argue against the purely artistic sound of that string section. It was just something that stood out, especially to a guy who sat in an all-white orchestra for over three decades. It stood out as an added quality. And if it was, as the maestro said, a Black thing, well, all the better.

Trumpet: So yes, the quality of the artform is paramount. And if we don't keep the level of classical music ensembles, regardless of diversity, on the level of say a Vienna Philharmonic, Berlin Philharmonic, or the Cleveland Orchestra, we're not doing the artform justice for anyone.

Let me ask you, are you teaching now, and do you see the small numbers of minority students in music schools? What's your perception of this?

Author: Well now we're talking relativity, compared to when I was at conservatory, there are more Black students at conservatories now, on every instrument, besides voice, than ever before.

However, that doesn't mean large numbers. It's just a general reality change.

Trumpet: Are there really? I don't see them. I taught at two major music schools, one for five years and another for twelve years and I had one Black student in all that time. So where are all the Black candidates?

I mean, who's gonna show up for these orchestra jobs to create diversity if the Black kids are not there. They're not in high school programs, they're not in middle school programs, not even in the college programs. I don't see them."

Author: So how were you received when you first joined your orchestra? You're like a history maker there unless I'm missing something. Is there another Black player in your orchestra?

Trumpet: No, no, I'm the only one. But like I said before, to me it wasn't an issue at all, until the music director mentioned race at the audition finals, it never even crossed my mind. And it really hasn't been an issue since. I mean there were a couple of things here and there.

When I auditioned for another orchestra and won, management came to me asking why I wanted to leave, and I told them it was because the guys in the section were just basically assholes. Of course, what I said got back to the trumpet section. So, one of the guys in my section said to me, "Well they wouldn't have made such an effort to keep one of the other trumpet players." He was intimating because he was white and the only reason they wanted to keep me was because I was Black and represented diversity. I mean the guy was a knucklehead.

Author: So that trumpet section is a problem?

Trumpet: Oh yeah, man it's a dive, yeah, it's a dive situation. It's more of an ego thing . . . like this is how trumpet playing should be and this is the only way it can be. In fact, there were a couple of really great trumpet players that ran out of here because of this rigid, over-the-top, knucklehead attitude about trumpet playing.

On a more positive note, I wanted to ask you if you're familiar with a trumpet player, (Pat) William Fielder, who passed away a few years ago. He was in the Civic orchestra here; I believe in the 1960s. He was a student at Northwestern.

Author: No, I didn't know him . . . a Black trumpet player?

Trumpet: Yeah, he taught in New Jersey at Rutgers University for several years. I think he became professor emeritus there. He was a fantastic player. In fact, Wynton Marsalis would go to him all the time for help. He's in a video with Kathline Battle and Wynton Marsalis. There's a section in the video where they're getting ready to record something and Wynton is having some trouble with the piccolo trumpet. There's a short segment where he and Wynton are backstage and Proff (we called him) is there talking to him about using his air and attacks. It was really cool to see that interaction. So, as you know, there's this thing called the Chickowitz book. And the first few pages of that book are exercises by a W. Fielder. His name is at the bottom of the page. I don't think people realize that it's him, William Fielder. I think most trumpet players would be really surprised to learn about who he is and his history. The contributions he made and that he's part of this very celebrated book of trumpet exercises.

Author: So Proff was like a Black version of Arnold Jacobs who helped brass players with their playing problems?

Trumpet: Exactly.

Principal Tuba of Two Major Southern Symphony Orchestras

Author: So, I must admit that I don't recall your talking much about your early years as a brass player. When I first met you during our brass quintet days, I guess we were too busy rehearsing and negotiating the narcissistic machinations of our fearless quintet leader. There never seemed to be time for socializing.

Tuba: Compared to many of my musical friends and colleagues, my musical background started late. As far as instrumental stuff, I didn't really start until high school.

Author: Oh, really, okay. I didn't know that.

Tuba: Yeah, literally, I didn't know anything about the fact that people took private instrumental lessons. I didn't know anything about that, or that scene. I grew up in an urban background. Strictly urban . . . kind of an inner city environment, that I was dealing with and everything around me at the time, along with all my friends who were all kind of headed into Historically Black Colleges and Universities and football marching bands. That's what we knew about the music world. That and gospel. Yeah, you know, I'm a preacher's kid so.

Author: So gospel music?

Tuba: Yeah, that's what I knew. Gospel music and whatever was current with the marching band kind of thing. And, you know in high school we all tried to be like Florida A&M Marching band. Yeah, that was the base and extent of my musical knowledge in those days. And of course, with all my friends the thing was to get into Florida A&M or Bethune-Cookman, because of their football marching bands.

Author: Did you march in the football bands when you were in college?

Tuba: No, I was marching and dancing and doing all those amazing antics on the field, in high school, not in college.

Author: With the tuba . . . sorry, I mean with the sousaphone?

Tuba: Yeah, yeah, that was the musical culture and that was what I was good at, spinning around with the sousaphone, yup!

Author: And playing those loud, gigantic basslines?

Tuba: Yeah, exactly . . .

Author: Just like that Junkanoo in the Bahamas. Man, they blow the hell out of those baselines with those sousaphones. You can hear those guys coming from four blocks away.

Tuba: Yeah, that's right Junkanoo, they used to do several Junkanoo parades in Miami. That's exactly where my musical head was in those days.

Author: I actually went down to the Bahamas one year and marched in the Junkanoo parade. I played a conch shell with my French horn mouthpiece stuck in it. I marched with a kind of Do- Da band that had no uniforms just all kinds of crazy instruments. Compared to all the costumed bands we looked like hell, but it was so much fun. They told me I had to be up at 4:30 in the morning to cue up for the parade.

It was pretty chilly that time of morning, even in the Bahamas. They kept us warm serving pork souse, a warm soup that they were passing around.

Tuba: Oh, souse, yeah! I could never quite get into that stuff. My dad was big on pork souse though, ya know. Yeah, yeah, you're bringing back some good memories though.

Author: I still have my Junkanoo suit that someone gave me, when I was down in the Bahamas, as a gift. I love wearing it here. It's black and yellow with Junkanoo down the side of the pants and the West African symbol on the back. Then no one has a clue about Junkanoo here in my town.

Tuba: I would die to have something like that.

Author: Well, I'll see if I can get you one. I'll check with Duke, the high school band director and the guy I stayed with on my visit. I could use a new one anyway.

Tuba: That would be great.

So, on another note, growing up in Miami in those days, early 1970s, it was quite diverse despite being still racially segregated, in an urban segregated kind of way. So that was the backdrop of my young musical life in those days. Then a dean from the University of Miami heard me play at an all-state audition, I don't know, or an all-state ensemble. She approached me about taking private lessons on tuba.

And that was the first time anybody, outside my football marching band/gospel music world, had shown any interest in me as a serious tuba player. So, this dean, who thought I had some potential as a serious music major, encouraged me to apply to the music school at the University of Miami.

Author: So you had been playing regular tuba all along?

Tuba: Yeah, I was also playing regular tuba in concert band and all that kind of stuff. But as far taking lessons, me and my friends had never had formal lessons, even though we had made all state band and stuff. Actually, Miami had a small pocket of talent for a handful kids like me. So those kids of color who did make all-state band tended to be from some of the inner city schools from the Miami area. So, when we arrived at those all-state band rehearsals and events, we all knew each other, but we didn't know anyone else there. So, it was like you stepped out into a kind of whole Mars vibe. But it was relatively positive, because they were talking about stuff that we didn't get into very much, like phrasing and dynamics. You know that kind of thing, which we didn't get into much when on the football field, doing fancy band maneuvers and dance steps.

So in our brass quintet days, there's an inspiration that you played a major part in, but I don't think you realized it back then. But hearing that French horn, ring tone on your I-Fone, brought back some of those memories, you know what I mean?

Author: Not sure, tell me more.

Tuba: Well, when I played in our brass quintet, and I'm being 100 percent candid with you, listening to you play, was the first time that I heard the kind of quality, like really, really, what I know now as, first rate, quality brass playing. A quality of playing I hadn't heard before and it happened to be coming from an African American French horn player.

Author: In our brass quintet?

Tuba: Yeah, in our quintet, but it wasn't the whole quintet, it was just you. That's what I'm telling you.

Author: Me?? Thanks, you're very kind.

Tuba: So I'm telling you, playing with you at that time, was the first time, in my professional career, period, that I heard, what I immediately recognized as, yeah, that's . . . man, I'd never heard anybody making that kind of sound before. The kind of sound you were consistently making. And I'll be honest with you, I was very new to the business and the LA Philharmonic didn't resonate with me, at that time, the way it does now.

Author: So how old were you then when our quintet first rehearsed in Dallas?

Tuba: So . . . at that time, I would have been about early twenties.

Author: Oh really, you were that young, okay. Glad you enjoyed the quintet.

Tuba: So when I did the University of Miami thing, there weren't very many people of color, especially on the classical side of things. I had one or two friends, one who turned out to be a fairly successful conductor. He got to conduct a few major orchestras. So, what happened is, I won the tuba position for my first real orchestra job before I finished my undergrad studies at University of Miami. I had to learn how to get into the classical music world and orient myself, without losing my early musical roots, that I so valued, when I was growing up. Those early roots, I could see, would not necessarily be valued in my new world of music. So, I had to orient myself for that first real orchestra job and the new symphonic world at large.

So, for my first orchestra job, in the new symphony orchestra world, in the deep South, I was the first and only Black person in the history of that orchestra. That was a very social-political hotbed of unknowns for me, especially since I wasn't totally aware of all the social-racial issues I would face walking in and being so young. I soon found out that the orchestra never had any African Americans or people of color on their stage.

Author: I can believe that.

Tuba: So suddenly, I was put right in the spotlight. The media spotlight and especially with the Black community.

Author: What was your experience like with the orchestra players?

Tuba: Yeah, it's funny man, for me, the people I would've expected to be the roughest racially actually ended up being the people that helped me through that anticipated racial hurdle. They were the ones that actually ended up helping me through that process and kind of protected me. And I think, to be honest with you, I think they were concerned and knew that there was so much heat coming from the outside media about racial equality. So much heat coming on me, because that symphony was the only state orchestra and we toured all over Alabama, playing in a lot of the smallest little towns.

Author: Whoo!!

Tuba: Right, so we'd go into those small towns that were the home of the KKK. In those tiny Southern towns to play concerts. That was in like, 1983, which was only about what, fourteen of fifteen years after Martin Luther King was assassinated? And that Bull Conor stuff . . . and all of those people were still around.

Author: Yes!

Tuba: Still, the truth of the matter is, I was only twenty years old when I hit my first orchestra job, and I was not totally, culturally, and/or politically aware of the magnitude of the whole Black-white dynamic.

So, when I was on tour with the orchestra, there was a lot of social-political heat from the locals. When I got off the bus with the orchestra, people driving by, would yell, "Hey Nigger, hey nigger!"

Author: Oh boy . . .

Tuba: Yeah man, so my colleagues were, of course, experiencing all of this with me. And honestly, like I said, my colleagues in that southern orchestra that I thought would be the most problematic and indifferent ended up being the most protective and helpful. They actually embraced me and showed me the ropes of the deep South. They would say things like, "Hey man you need to stay out of this situation or don't go out anywhere in this town without one of us."

Author: I see, I see . . .

Tuba: That kind of thing, yeah! That's really what happened and I'm glad I had the support of the brass players, who by then realized that I was going to be a good fit and that I could play, even though I had a lot to learn, as a twenty-year-old, they took me under their wing. Otherwise, I would've gotten myself into all kinds of trouble traveling through the deep South.

Author: Indeed, so did you get any kind of racial push-back from other members in the orchestra?

Tuba: Yeah, in most orchestras that I'd played in, there were always a few people that I had issues with, but in that orchestra, it was from administrators more than the musicians in the orchestra.

Author: Administrators, really?

Tuba: That had been my experience mainly because I worked with a lot of administrators over the years. So that's where I experienced the most class A racism, but I was a little bit too young to effectively deal with at the time. I'll give you one example: I was chairman of the symphony orchestra committee for my first eight years during my first orchestra job. I went as an orchestra representative with the general manager to a cultural council type meeting where he was going to make a pitch for funding as always. I'm just there . . . so this general manager stands up and tells how the symphony had openly developed a program to recruit Black players into the orchestra.

Author: Oh really?

Tuba: No, the fact of the matter was, we didn't have anything like that. It was totally 110 percent fabricated. Literally nothing anywhere close to that had even been discussed.

Author: So . . . that just came from out of the blue?

Tuba: Yeah, he was up there, kind of winging it, literally. So, for me, this was the first time I had actually seen someone stand up and tell an absolutely bold face lie. And the people on that cultural council were probably 70 percent African American.

Author: Is that right? I didn't catch that at first. So that's why he was pitching that lie.

Tuba: Yeah, he was saying that we actually had such a program, not that we were going to develop one, but that we actually had one already in place. And that the orchestra was going to Historically Black Colleges and Universities looking for candidates and all . . . and not one word of it was true. So honestly, that was the kind of thing I was too young to know how to deal with for sure.

So right after the meeting, like five minutes after the meeting, I confronted him. I said to him that we both know that we didn't have such a program, so why would he say that? And he said, "Ah well, you know the most important point is to keep our funding going. In fact, why don't you speak instead of me, at the next meeting and tell them all about the audition process."

So, at the next meeting of this cultural council I stood up and spoke about the audition process and how we had everybody play the same repertoire and how we used screens to avoid discrimination, etc. However, after I spoke no one asked any questions, no feedback at all. So after that meeting can you guess what happened?

Author: I can only imagine . . . tell me.

Tuba: What happened was, I became a favorite topic of much discussion on talk radio. So for my first two or three years in the orchestra I was quite often the topic on talk radio.

Author: Ah! Fun!

Tuba: Yeah, on the Black radio station. I would say that 20 to 30 percent of the time I tuned in to that station, I was the topic of discussion. So, after my talk to the cultural council with its "70 percent of Blacks folks," for some reason I was labeled an Uncle Tom.

Author: Really, after that little talk?

Tuba: Yeah man, at that cultural council meeting my little three- to five-minute talk was interpreted as defending the racial practices of my orchestra and I was therefore made out to be an Uncle Tom.

Author: But you didn't speak about a recruiting program that didn't exist.

Tuba: No, I did not do that. Ha! No! But I'd be driving in for a concert and I'd hear on the radio a program about the orchestra. People would be calling in joining a heated discussion about me in the orchestra as a token. I mean it was crazy!

People would be saying things like, "Well they finally got one of us, but they put him in the back row of the orchestra. We got through all that in Montgomery, back of the bus stuff with Rosa Parks. We won't be in the back no more. You think they would at least have the gumption to put him up front."

Author: Ah What? But the tuba is always in the back row of the orchestra! What do they think you should be up next to the concert master? Really? Such, ignorance . . .

Tuba: I swear, in my first two years, it must have been fifteen/twenty times that I heard that conversation about my position in the orchestra as token. Thankfully, there was another opinion about me, in that I was a very nice man, very talented and not an Uncle Tom or a token, and that there should actually be more like me in the orchestra. Also, the way the local whites reacted to my being in the orchestra was very different from the way the local Blacks reacted, very different than the way it would be in Miami. For example, my speaking at a cultural council meeting and the way in which I spoke is very normal to me, but a Black person, just speaking coherently, with normal articulation was considered very outspoken, almost brash and uppity, at that time in Alabama.

Author: So, you mean to tell me that just because a Black person could talk coherently would be considered militant at that time in Alabama?

Tuba: Yes! Yes! Exactly!

Author: Amazing!

Tuba: Well, that was the general state of affairs in Alabama, the way Black people related to whites was very different than what I was used to in Miami. For example, in Alabama, Black people greeted and addressed all white people like, hello sir and yes sir, no ma'am and yes ma'am, damn near shuffling and cooning. We didn't have quite that situation in Miami, so I was quite uncomfortable and surprised by that when I witnessed it. But I must say the players in the brass section of my orchestra were very protective of me and understood the volatility of my situation in the racial sense, even more than I did at that time in my life, but I didn't have to address them in any overly respectful manner. However, I did get into trouble because I had to stretch [punch] a guy in the orchestra for insulting me.

Author: Stretch? Is that what you said? I've never heard that term. So, you took somebody out?

Tuba: Yes! So, where I grew up in Miami, stretching somebody for assaulting you would not have been the ideal way to settle a dispute, but it made a certain kind of statement for sure. But the two times I went on to stretch this one guy; I was being publicly and verbally attacked by him in an indirect racial way regarding my intelligence.

So briefly, what happened was, as the orchestra committee chairman, in a position of leadership, I probably shouldn't have reacted in such a manner, but I confronted this guy in the orchestra who was always mouthing off using super big words, so that nobody ever understood what in hell he was talking about. So, one day, in front of a large group of orchestra players, I told him that people didn't know what he was talking about most of the time. For example, he would rattle off a phrase like: "So folks, shall we inveigle this mundane situation into a phantasmagorical display?" I told him that using such big vocabulary did nothing to communicate to others. That he was, in effect, not communicating at all. I then gave him an example: "Okay, do you know what I'm saying here? 'Yo, some of my homies are meeting at my crib to barbecue some hams.'" [Hey, some of my friends are meeting at my place to hang out with some women.] I told him that my friends would understand, but he wouldn't. He got very offended and told me that someone with my lack of intelligence wouldn't understand anyway, even though the words he was using were of ordinary common everyday English. So, I stretched [punched] him right then and there, knocking him out in front of everyone.

He called the police, and they pulled me off stage to talk to me. I was told that I had to apologize in front of the entire orchestra, or I would be arrested for assault. So I apologized. But I must say that most of the orchestra was behind me on that, because that guy was a real annoying, pain in the behind, to most of the players.

Author: Amazing stuff, I've got to remember that phrase, "I stretched him." I love it.

On another note, I was talking to another player in one of the major orchestras and he related something to me that I can't say I ever experienced. He said that having one Black player performing in a symphony orchestra caused no social eddies at all, but when it gets to be, four, five, or six he said he got a vibe on some sensitivity level that the audience perceived or believed that the quality of the product was diminishing. Now he didn't say that he had any actual conversation about it with anyone, it was just something that he sensed. So, I'm asking you, have you ever experienced such a phenomenon?

Tuba: To be perfectly candid with you, I have. But I've actually had people express it in conversation, as a compliment of sorts. For example, "Hey the orchestra is still sounding pretty good." Or "Wow! The playing level is hanging in there still, that's great, sounds great." That was my experience with this, in that kind of subtextual expression.

Principal Percussion of a Major Southern California Symphony Orchestra

Author: So, I'm sure people would like to know how you got started, because I didn't know you until you started to substitute in the percussion section.

Percussionist: You didn't know me until I approached you at a rehearsal of the Rite of Spring, at the Hollywood Bowl, when I was a senior in high school, brother. I was trying to ask you if it was difficult playing those complex meters, but you seemed more focused on the woman who was with me, brother.

Author: Oh, really? I don't recall . . . ah, sorry.

Percussionist: Yes, brother, you were quite curious and a bit nosey too. I knew who you were though . . . I didn't know your name, but I saw you playing in the orchestra when I was in high school. You know, I first heard the Rite of Spring on the radio. I was already semi-interested in classical music, so when I heard that recording on the radio, I went out and bought it: a recording with the Boston Symphony led by Michael Tilson Thomas. I think it was that same year the Philharmonic played at my high school . . . and Zubin Mehta conducted, which was kind of a big deal. The music director conducting an in-school concert was special.

Author: So, before that, were you into or playing classical music?

Percussionist: Yeah, I was in the high school band and orchestra. But before junior high school, I went to the Boy's Club and took my first drum lessons around sixth grade.

Author: The Boy's Club taught music?

Percussionist: Oh yeah, they had a band too, but I started lessons there because a friend of mine was playing drums in the band. So, that's why I started taking drumming lessons and got in the band. I also took beginning band in junior high school, seventh grade.

So, like I said, at some point in high school, freshman or sophomore year, I heard the Rite of Spring, and that was really the drawing point to classical music for me. Also, my family was into music. My dad would play a variety of music on the record player: Tchaikovsky, Ravel, Duke Ellington, Count Basie. He played all styles around the house.

Author: Around the house?

Percussionist: Yeah, yeah, so my family was always well rounded with all types of music. I was the youngest of five and my oldest brother was really into R&B, so I heard a lot of that at the time . . . you know, the 1960s music and the Motown sound. Then my middle brother, whom you know, really got more into Jimi Hendrix and jazz. So there was always a variety of music going on around me.

Author: Speaking of music in the house, I remember my father coming home late at night, kind of plastered, he would lie down on the floor and play his trumpet with the mute in and then he would actually scat a little before passing out. I used to get out of bed to peek at him from the top of the stairs. In fact, there was an amazing thing that happened when I was home with my family last year. I asked a friend of my father's, who played with my father's band, who is still alive believe it or not, what kind of musician my father really was. Could he read better or was he a better improvisor? So, the guy said, his name is Mr. Cliff, that my father was the best reader in the group but was by no means the best improvisor. It was quite amazing to find out something about your father that was true so long after he had passed on. My mother played piano by ear and most people who do that play on the black keys only.

So, when I sang something in C major for my mother to play, she said she couldn't play it, she couldn't hear it. Then on the other hand I don't ever recall my mother and father playing music together, strange.

Percussionist: My Mom played piano at church in Jamaica. She could read music very well, my dad couldn't read music, but he sang in the Morgan State choir. In those days Morgan State was one of the top Historically Black Colleges and Universities. I remember him telling me a story that, if you got accepted, for example, to the University of Maryland as a Black student, the university would pay to send you to a Historically Black College. Just to keep your Black ass out of their university, brother.

Author: Really? They would pay just to keep you out of their white university? That is unbelievable!

Percussionist: So that's what my father did; he went to Morgan State. In fact, in connection with you, when my family moved here from Baltimore in 1961–1962, the choir director at Morgan State, his name was J.O. B. Mosley, lived a couple of streets away from where you live now.

Author: Is that right? And this was in the early 1960s?

Percussionist: Yeah! I don't recall the address, but I remember that my family would drive from Pasadena on Sundays and visit him near where you live now.

Yes, my dad's old choir director, J.O.B. Mosley, lived in your neighborhood until he passed away.

Author: Was my neighborhood all Black in those days?

Percussionist: Oh yeah, it was pretty much all Black. He had a North-facing house with a fantastic view. So that was my introduction to your neighborhood with all those "Don" Street names. Don Jose, Don Juan, Don Carlos . . . so many Dons, brother. I was there way before you.

When I was in high school, I took music theory (which was amazing that they offered it at the time). So my dad recognized my interest in classical music, called Mr. Mosley, and set up lessons with him. Once a month I'd go to your neighborhood and study theory, piano, and orchestration with Mr. Mosley. This was the early 1970s. Yeah, I was very much into composition then.

Author: So, I imagine you didn't get much resistance for playing the drums in classical music. The drums . . . well, which was not considered unusual for a Black person.

Percussionist: No, of course not.

Author: But you know a lot of instrumentalists start on the drums. I once hired a woodwind quintet from the philharmonic for my chamber series and when they spoke about themselves and how they chose their respective instruments they all had first started on the drums. So, you said you first heard the Rite of Spring in high school?

Percussionist: Yeah, I think maybe when I was a sophomore?

Author: I know you said Stravinsky ended up being one of your favorite composers.

Percussionist: Oh yeah, once I heard the Rite of Spring, I started researching all of his works: Firebird, Petruska, the symphonies, Soldier's Tale, etc. As a lot of drummers will tell you, once they heard the Rite of Spring, that was it for them. They were hooked; they were drawn to symphonic percussion.

Author: I remember my percussion player roommate at conservatory told me that when Leinsdorf was conducting the Boston Symphony in the Rite of Spring, that he was having a hard time with the rhythms. So tympanist Vic Firth said that he was really conducting the piece.

You know, what I always found amusing and curious in our orchestra was during the Danse Sacre movement of the Rite, all the feet tapping trying to count and get the rhythm precise. However, to my amazement all the foot tapping was slightly different.

I always thought, *how can we all be playing the same piece, with all these different interpretations of the meter*. Amazing!

So, when would you say you became really serious about a career in music?

Percussionist: So that fall after meeting you, I started at Cal State LA and that was, I would say, when I really started taking serious lessons. The lessons I took at the Boy's Club were just basic, rudimental stuff, like how to hold the sticks, etc. But I didn't take lessons all through high school. So I would say I got kind of a late start. I didn't start until college with the percussion instruments. And that's when I started studying with the Philharmonic's principal timpanist/percussionist Mitchell Peters. We clicked, no friction, just a smooth connection. I started studying on snare drum and mallets. Eventually we included timpani. Mitch and I hooked up; we immediately connected. He was low key; I'm low key.

You know, looking back through all the years I worked with students, certain ones just didn't click with me. And then there were those that meshed fine with me. It can make a huge difference, as it did for me. I was so fortunate to have the relationship I had with Mitch!

So sometime around 1975 the Philharmonic started a Minority Training Program and Mitch suggested I audition for it. This program allowed me to get additional inexpensive lessons outside of my school lessons with Mitch.

Author: Yes, I remember that program well. All those lessons prompted you to be quite the percussionist and timpanist. However, I felt that because of the level of player you were, even at that early time in your career, that your level of musicianship actually helped to validate that program more than it helped you as a player by just helping you pay for your lessons.

Not long after that, you started playing extra with the Philharmonic. I remember when you first showed up. I was very pleased and impressed to see you there, brother.

And not so long after that, there was a co-principal timpani opening and you auditioned. I remember we talked about it. You felt that it was quite a lot of material to prepare. I remember fussing at you a bit and the next time I saw you, you had made the finals. Then you won the damn audition flat out and got the job, brother. I was thrilled! In fact, there were like four new players, and you all came into the orchestra at the same time. I remember the day they announced it at a rehearsal, playing one of your favorite composers, Stravinsky's Petruska. I do recall one of the trumpet players making a nasty remark because two of you were Black.

He said something like, "The standards are going down!" And it was so grossly ironic that I was sitting next to one of the principal horns, who was having trouble with the simple rhythms in Petruska. I remember saying to the trumpet player, "The standards are looking pretty low over here in the horn section too."

So, the way it all turned out, about you not getting tenure on co-principal timpani was the work of the unfortunate wicked political climate in the orchestra at that time.

A kind of unholy combination of a few king-shit principals in the brass section and a management that just couldn't see you in that position. And the way it dragged on for some years, passing from one music director to another. It was a travesty.

However, it was wise for them to have made you principal percussion, because, even though I thought you were the best timpani player I'd ever heard in my life, brother, you could also handle, just as well, running the percussion section better than anyone else. So, would you mind sharing some of your experiences as principal percussion?

Percussionist: You know when I joined the Philharmonic in 1983, the administration had a string player doubling on percussion when an extra player was needed in the section. To me, that was very disrespectful to the percussion section. It would have been different had the string player been a decent percussionist. It was obvious that the administration was saving money at the artistic expense of the percussion section! Eventually I was able to hire extra players from outside of the orchestra, thank God!

Author: Yes, yes, I do remember that. In fact, I remember there was more than one string player doubling on percussion. I agree, not a good idea.

Percussionist: You know one incident I do remember. We were rehearsing a Shostakovich Symphony under a German conductor, and I was playing crash cymbals. The conductor stopped the orchestra and said to me, "What are you doing? This is not jazz!!"

Author: Ah yes, I remember watching that unfold.

Percussionist: And I'm just standing there listening, as in, well what do you want? I wasn't giving him any attitude, and I finally realized he wanted it louder. So, I used a bigger pair of cymbals and played louder, fine. At the rehearsal break . . . a bunch of colleagues came up to me and said, "You really handled that well." And I'm like, what? Handled what? For him to make that reference to jazz . . . threw me off at first.

Author: It must have been a bit puzzling because what he said didn't communicate anything except the racial image he had in his head and that's what popped out.

Percussionist: Yes, he was attaching a racial thing to it and that clouded his communication. He was saying, hey, don't be playing jazz here. Because I was playing softer than he wanted, I guess he thought I was playing a too laid back, "jazz style." All he had to say was play it louder and not, "This is not jazz!" At first, I wasn't connecting that he was looking at a Black guy and saying that.

Author: I understand, but that was also a very oblique and noncommunicative way of expressing it, using a racial reference.

Percussionist: But a lot of the orchestra picked up on that racial overtone for sure. At the break of that rehearsal, some of the players complimented me on how I handled it, as a racial micro-aggression, then it dawned on me. I connected the dots, that it had a racial reference.

You know, ideally on the job, as in life, I think we all want to be respected for who we are, for what we do, and how we carry ourselves, not judged based on appearances. Clearly this conductor had other thoughts in his head.

There was another incident when I was playing timpani that had the opposite tone. Another conductor (Herbert Blomstedt) at a rehearsal break passed by me backstage and said, "Really nice job" but his tone and the subtext suggested that he wasn't expecting it to be as good as it was. [Laughing] In fact, it was obvious that he had a much lower expectation seeing a Black guy back there playing timpani. Somehow, I just couldn't shake the feeling that he was surprised that a Black timpanist could play that well. And you know, if I had been anything but Black, he might not have said anything. Everything would have seemed status quo.

Author: Then you know, it's quite possible that he had never seen a Black timpanist before, especially in such a racially cloistered world as classical music.

Percussionist: Quite possible and at the time, probable, brother. So those were two opposites, that occurred.

Author: But it was definitely something you felt, which is usually quite correct in these situations. You felt the tone and subtext of it.

Percussionist: Yeah, yeah, the subtext . . . hard to shake that gut feeling, brother.

Author: And they have no control over that subtext, when you think about it. So, this conductor was kind of a fish out of water, experiencing something he probably never expected, how could he not be awkward? But I must say, despite all those awkward cultural surprises, there were always those situations when musical things went fantastically well, and such moments were indescribable. That magic that got us all into music in the first place, seeking an endless amount of such moments. Like the time I got to play that nice slow movement in the Star Wars suite at the Hollywood Bowl with film composer John Williams.

On the other hand, I remember your telling me about certain players in your section that didn't enjoy the music for music's sake anymore. They only look at the orchestra schedule for the first opportunity to take off from playing.

Percussionist: Well, let's take the players in the string section, excluding the basses, but the rest of the string instruments. My understanding is that most of them, when they were at a conservatory, were looking to be soloists.

Author: Oh, absolutely . . .

Percussionist: They're not thrilled to be sitting in the middle of a sixteen-piece string section. Which brings to mind one of the players in my section who didn't have aspirations to be a soloist. He had aspirations, because he knew the Philharmonic would be a good job, but not for the love of music.

Author: And also, it was something that he could do.

Percussionist: Well yeah! He was very good on the technical side of playing. He played an amazing audition. I'll admit to that. He did everything he needed to do while on probation. But once he got tenure, he changed and took every opportunity he could to get off work. This is an extremely different mindset from my own.

Author: So finally, after a long, successful career, I hope you enjoyed the music. You know it's still hard for me to get my head around the fact that some players, who went to top conservatories and won major orchestra positions, where they got to play some of the greatest music in their field, became so detached from the joy of playing music.

Percussionist: Well, brother, we are all different. We come from different environments and have different experiences and influences in our lives that shape us into who we are as musicians and who we are as people. In my experiences, yes, I enjoyed then and continue to enjoy the music in my life.

In fact, brother, I recently started a nonprofit, Alliance of Black Orchestral Percussionists (ABOP; www.abop.us), whose mission is to increase the diversity of percussionists in symphony orchestras.

Author: Oh really? How'd that come about?

Percussionist: In 2021, I arranged a Zoom session with a few of my Black colleagues across the country: Tim Adams, former timpanist with the Pittsburgh Symphony; Douglas Cardwell, former timpanist with the New Mexico Symphony; Michael Crusoe, former timpanist with the Seattle Symphony; Jauvon Gilliam, timpanist with the National Symphony; Joshua Jones, principal percussion with the Kansas City Philharmonic; and Johnny Lee Lane, former director of percussion studies at Eastern Illinois University.

Individually, we had all reached the top of our fields performing and teaching. So collectively, we thought we could join together in an alliance and make a difference for future generations of Black orchestral percussionists. That's how ABOP was born.

Author: Well alright, what a fabulous idea. This kind of organizing and collaboration is so vital to initiating change in the symphonic field, especially for young African American percussionists.

Percussionist: So ABOP's goal is to change the paradigm of representation in orchestras by guiding, supporting, and empowering future generations of Black orchestral percussionists.

Specifically, in order to reach this goal, we've implemented the Mentorship Program, a training program—the first of its kind—to guide and motivate Black orchestral percussionists to realize their full potential. As you and I know, having a support system for guidance and direction can make a difference in reaching your goal. And, to have the folks in that system look like you! Very powerful.

Author: I like this, I like this . . .

Percussionist: Simply put, we must want to increase the number, as well as raise the performance level of Black percussionists preparing to audition for universities, conservatories, and eventually orchestra positions.

Principal Trumpet of a Major East Coast Opera Orchestra

Author: My father was a trumpet player and didn't want me to play French horn. Did you get any push-back or resistance for choosing the trumpet?

Principal Trumpet: No, not really, and since Texas had such good music programs, I had the opportunity to be introduced to classical music in sixth grade. There was this special school day when they laid out various instruments for us to choose, a trumpet, a viola, a saxophone, etc. For me it was either the viola or the trumpet. So, I thought, ah . . . maybe I'll go with the trumpet. It was smaller and would probably be cheaper.

Lucky for me, my music education from grade school through junior high had teachers who were very positive and introduced me to lots of things musically that exploded my curiosity. Then of course, my mom said, "Play whatever you want, just practice in the garage." The garage was of course, blazing hot and when I practiced, I created buckets of sweat.

Author: So, you started in the sixth grade?

Principal Trumpet: Yeah, sixth grade, but I didn't really start practicing until grade eight, when my teacher played a recording of Maynard Ferguson for me. Man! I wanted to play high notes like that!

Author: I bet, and where did you go to school?

Principal Trumpet: I did my undergrad at University of Texas at Austin and my master's at Julliard.

Author: Who'd you study with at Julliard?

Principal Trumpet: I studied with Ray Mase and Mark Gould. Ray Mase was a member of the American Brass Quintet and principal trumpet of New York City Ballet and Mark Gould was principal at the Met orchestra. My undergrad teacher was Ray Crisara, a New Yorker, who played in the NBC Symphony and the Met orchestra back when he was younger. He was an Army band guy and my most influential teacher. I really, really matured my trumpet music making and etiquette with him. It was a magical time for me. A time when I learned the absolute most.

Author: Wow! Impressive. I love hearing about great teacher-student connections. So, did you audition for Tanglewood or Aspen?

Principal Trumpet: I did . . . after my undergrad and working with Ray Crisara, I went to National Repertory Orchestra, Colorado from University of Texas at Austin and then Tanglewood the following two years. The reason I was so intent on going to Tanglewood was because I had listened to Wynton Marsalis. I felt that if Wynton went to Tanglewood, it just had to be a goal of mine, if I wanted to be a soloist like him. Yeah, so at some point I wanted to be a soloist. I studied solo repertoire; in fact, during my undergrad I did a solo every semester just to learn the repertoire and try to figure out everything. Entering Julliard, that's what I wanted to do, be a trumpet soloist.

Author: So how are the Tanglewood auditions done these days?

Principal Trumpet: I did a live audition. Tanglewood people showed up at Julliard. So I did one audition in Boston and one at Julliard. The one I did at Julliard, one of the judges recognized me from the Kingsville Competition. An international solo competition in Texas. Rodger Voisin was one of the judges, and I won that division. So I was thrown in the pool to win the grand prize, but Rodger said, "Kid, you play the hell out of the trumpet, but you're not gonna win!" He said that because the competition was against pianists, violinists, vocalists . . . and my repertoire was like, the Gregson Trumpet concerto and I was going up against works like Prokofiev piano concerto, Mendelsohn violin concerto, nothing against Gregson, but you know, I'm sure the judges wanted to hear those big romantic concerti on violin and piano.

Author: So, I guess the Gregson was a bit too twentieth century for them? And so, how old were you then? Because Rodger Voisin goes back to my days.

Principal Trumpet: I was like in my second or third year of college at University of Texas at Austin. I'm guessing I was about twenty-two.

Author: Oh, I forgot to ask, did they have a screen for any of these auditions and competitions? Did Tanglewood use a screen?

Principal Trumpet: They did not have a screen for Tanglewood, but none of the college auditions I took for my undergrad had screens. Julliard, Cleveland Institute of Music, San Francisco Conservatory, none of them had screens. So, I just went in and played without any screen.

Ya know, for me, in those days, my work ethic was pretty nuts. As an undergrad, I practiced hours and hours, day in and day out. I wanted to be a soloist, so I did a full recital every semester. Just to learn repertoire and get used to playing that stuff. And when I won a couple of those solo competitions, I was like, I'm going to be the next Wynton Marsalis.

Author: Why not, love it. [Laughing]

Principal Trumpet: So, my teacher at the time, Ray Crisara, was super influential on me and I remember in my freshmen year, I never had like a top-of-the-line instrument, because I couldn't afford it. So, during a lesson I missed a note and cursed the horn, "Ah stupid trumpet. Gotta get a better instrument."

So, my teacher looked at me and said, "Now, son I don't care what instrument you're playing . . . even if it's from Sears and Roebuck. You should be able to pick the trumpet up and play Twinkle-Twinkle Little Star and sound beautiful on it." Then he picked up my trumpet, played that tune and sounded like a million bucks. So, I thought, aw shit, right . . . God!

Author: So, it wasn't the horn! [Laughing]

Principal Trumpet: Eventually I did get a better instrument, but that kind of inspiration . . . you know, lit a fire under me. So, my goal . . . I really, I mean really, went after those competitions, my goal was to get at least third place in order to pay for my flight there and back.

Author: It was so important strategically to hear the right things from your teacher in those days, because it was quite a difficult road at times.

Principal Trumpet: Definitely . . .

Author: So, Tanglewood still didn't have a screen for auditions?

Principal Trumpet: No, Tanglewood did not have a screen.

Author: Really? Tanglewood didn't use a screen for me either. When I auditioned for Armando Ghitalla, it was just the two of us in the Boston Symphony orchestra lounge. When I finished, he said, "Yeah, Harry said you could blow the hell out of that thing. Welcome to Tanglewood." That was it, no screen, no committee.

Principal Trumpet: Harry Shapiro? Now I knew him from Tanglewood as well.

Author: Yes, that's who we're talking about. He was my teacher.

Principal Trumpet: Oh, he was your teacher?

Author: Yes, he was my French horn teacher. How interesting that he knew both of us . . .

Principal Trumpet: I considered him as one of my teachers as well. He was a very good friend, and I have mini discs from lessons with him. He would say, "This is what ya have to do, ya see . . . "

Author: Yup, that sounds like him.

Principal Trumpet: So I played something for him, and he said, "No, ya gotta play it softer."

And at first, I was like, "whadda you talking about old man?" But he was right and so very, very helpful and always available, anytime I wanted to play for him.

Author: And he was very honest about things, he would tell you straight out, "Ya can't read well enough . . . but we'll work on it, that's all." He would not bite his tongue.

Principal Trumpet: One of my favorite Harry quotes was at Tanglewood. There was this very brash, hot shot horn player who was playing a solo and Harry walked up to him and said, "Hey, you're good, but you're not that good. Ya gotta lot further to go!" [Laughing]

Author: [Laughing] Oh yeah, he had quite a natural honesty about him, but it was a perfectly correct and exact honesty, that we needed so much as players in those crucial moments early in our careers. I'll always remember how positive and supportive he was. When my conservatory ran out of money, and I was on scholarship and wouldn't be returning the following year. He was the one who told me it was time to go looking for a job. I was a bit surprised to hear that, being caught up in school and all, I asked, doing what? He looked at me sternly and said, "Playing your horn, dummy." He then mentioned the two vacancies at the time that I should consider, it was the Los Angeles Philharmonic and the Chicago Symphony.

Harry Shapiro was one of those people who truly believed that change could happen. He was like one of the people on the front lines of the Civil Rights marches. There were not only Black people, but white priests, Jews, Native Americans, Muslims, everyone! So, when I was finally ready to take those auditions, I asked him point blank if he believed if I won one of these positions that they would actually hire a Black person. He looked at me sternly and said, "Look, ya go to these damn auditions, ya play your ass off and ya cross that bridge when ya come to it." That was the level of belief he had in change. He said, "Listen Bob, the most powerful thing you have is your playing in this music world. Not your looks, your race or your politics. Because when they want to hear the notes none of those non-musical attributes will be of any value."

So, I made the finals in both of those auditions. Los Angeles said they'd get back to me. So I went on to Chicago, made the finals there on a Monday and they wanted me to stay until Friday to play the finals. Well, I was out of money and headed back to Boston when the secretary stopped me from leaving. I told her I didn't have the money to stay until Friday. She said, "Is that all?" She picked up the phone and the next thing I knew a guy came down on the elevator, in a three-piece suit and started putting hundred dollar bills in my hand.

I lost count after twelve and he said, "Now, go practice."

I'm so glad you met and studied with Harry Shapiro. He was one of the giants. So, what year did you get your major orchestra job?

Principal Trumpet: So, after I left Julliard, I thought I'd do the orchestral thing, because those jobs sounded pretty good. After I started auditioning, I got to play a little bit with the Dallas Symphony, because they needed someone to step in immediately. The principal in Dallas called my teacher and asked if he had anyone who could step in and play second trumpet. So, he called me in, and I played second trumpet for a little bit. Then they had an audition for that position, and I came in second, so I didn't get that job. Then my only option was to go down to Florida and play the New World Symphony and that's exactly what I did. However, during that time I took many, many auditions. Like . . . I would say, I took around twenty-eight auditions.

Author: Wow! Really? Twenty-eight?

Principal Trumpet: Yes, and at some of those auditions I would make the finals and others, nothing. And it was always with the big name orchestras that I advanced to the finals, like San Francisco and Boston. But with the smaller orchestras I had the least amount of success and never advanced.

Author: That's so interesting.

Principal Trumpet: Yeah, isn't it? So, after New World Symphony, that was like two or three years after 9/11. I went back to New York City to try and freelance, and the entire scene had changed. It was very difficult to find work. So I used that time to just practice. I would often go back to Miami to visit my girlfriend, who was still there. We went to yoga classes together, and I remember one specific class where there was a special guest, an ex-Thai Buddhist monk who was sitting in the corner. So I went down to shake his hand and his energy was so strong I started sweating. He looked at me and said, in a very soft-spoken voice, "You should take my meditation class." I was like, alright! So, to make a long story short, I took that guy's meditation class, and it changed my life . . . to the extent that I won the next three auditions I took. So, third trumpet in Grant Park, second in Baltimore, and principal in my present position. All of my Grant Park stories were insane. I always stayed at a friend's house while auditioning there and one time I was almost late to the audition because his toilet got clogged.

Author: How's that? Really? [Laughing wildly]

Principal Trumpet: Yeah, we had eaten at his favorite Mexican restaurant the night before and pigged out on chimichangas. So the day of the audition I woke up with a horrible stomachache.

My friend's house was just down the street from the audition, and he told me to make myself at home. I went into the bathroom to poop and when I tried to flush the toilet, it was broken and started flooding. So I found some towels which turned out to be their wedding towels with their wedding initials printed in big letters.

Of course, I was starting to worry about getting to the audition on time. Just then I got a phone call from the Grant Park Symphony. They wanted to know if I was coming to the audition.

So I did my meditation, went to the audition, played, and was successful. But the Baltimore audition was the real crazy one. I took a plane from Miami to

Baltimore and then took a train to a local stop in the city to meet a friend. While I was waiting, I decided to check my phone messages. To my surprise I had all these phone messages from my bank. Of course, I'm wondering what was wrong. The bank had called to tell me my account was overdrawn by about sixteen hundred dollars and possibly hacked. My flight was delayed and when I finally arrived in Baltimore, I had no money. It was very late, and all the trains had stopped. So, I went to the hotel shuttle phones and found a ride to the Red Roof Inn. When I arrived, with no money, mind you, I asked if they had a room. They did, for seventy-five dollars a night, so I took it.

They asked, "How would you like to pay for that?" So, I looked in my wallet and all my credit cards were red hot [maxed out]. [Laughing]

It was like, don't touch 'em, you'll burn your hand! So, I closed my eyes, did my breathing, picked one, and handed it to the guy. We looked at each other, and he looked underneath the desk and pulls out one of the old school credit card swipe machines and swipes my card. So, I thought, oh my goodness, how lucky, if my card was hot, it wouldn't show for a few days. So, I took a deep breath, because then I had a place to stay for the night, I had some change in my pocket, and I looked to see how much the bus cost. There was a bus that went from that hotel straight to the hall. I was all set. I woke up the next morning, did my little warm up, went to the hall, and realized that I still had absolutely no money. Yet I was so relaxed and peaceful because of that meditation and the techniques that teacher had taught me. So, I ended up getting through to the semi-finals and had to come back for the finals on a different day. My next hurdle was I had to get back to New York City, because that's where I was staying. So how am I going to get back to New York City? I had no money! I called a few relatives and none of them had any money. [Laughing]

Author: My God! What did you do?

Principal Trumpet: So the personnel manager of the Baltimore Symphony picked up on my state of mind and asked, "What's wrong sweetie?" So, I explained to her that I didn't have any money and was it possible that the symphony could pay for me to get back to New York? When I return, I'll pay them back. She looked at me, with a tear in her eye and said, "Here. . . . " She actually booked an Amtrak ticket for me. I thanked her and said I'd pay her back, but she said, "Don't worry about it. You just get on that train and come back here for the finals." So, about a week or so later I was back in Baltimore.

I played the finals and won the job. Many of my trumpet friends swore I would never win that audition, because the other guy in the finals was friends with the principal and they played Monet trumpets, and I played something else. So I blocked all that stuff out. In fact, one of the people I played for before that audition was Harry Shapiro. I played all of my audition material for him.

So, we did a section round, where each applicant played with the orchestra, and I remember the conductor looking at me like I was crazy or something. So, the principal trumpet said, "We had another guy in mind, but I don't even know you and when we did the section round, you matched me perfectly, so we had no choice but to give you the job."

So, after that the opera orchestra auditions in New York were coming up, and at that time, I played my audition list for my girlfriend, and I figured I'd take the opera orchestra audition and see what would happen. I thought, *well, I do need some money.* So the night before my flight, I played the Bach B-minor Mass. Next day I took the flight back to New York and stayed at my buddy Kenny's house in Harlem. I went to the opera orchestra audition and played the first couple of rounds and when I got to the finals, I remember thinking that my B-flat trumpet wasn't working right so I had to borrow my friend's.

I played the final round and won the job. And I remember I was kind of shell-shocked. I also recall that I couldn't even celebrate because I didn't have any money. [Laughing]

Author: Wow! Great to hear! And you are still playing that position?

Principal Trumpet: Yes, that's been my current position for the last sixteen years.

Author: My God! I can't tell you how great this makes me feel. To see this kind of success with young Black brass players. It's so impressive. Makes me wanna say, I'm glad I practiced . . . to get to see all these amazing young Black brass players come after me and win these top positions.

So, after winning the job, did you get any resistance? Any push-back?

Principal Trumpet: Oh yeah! I wasn't necessarily welcomed. To make a long story short, I basically had to do a private audition with the music director to be granted my tenure. He was getting negative feedback about me from players in the orchestra, who felt that I shouldn't have that position.

Author: Because?

Principal Trumpet: For whatever reason, you know, but I have my own theories. It started with people saying there are people who have problems with your playing, without describing anything specific or what I needed to fix. So, for me, that was a big red flag. After that, every player or management person I met, I made a personal record. Those vague objections about my playing were coming from management and unknown other players. So, for me, the job became, very much, a challenging work environment, which I got through by doing my meditation. I did have a few people who were very supportive during that time. Because the work environment was very hectic and fast moving at times, it was good to have some support. So, my first two years of probation were quite the learning experience for me and a very challenging period in general.

Author: I bet . . .

Principal Trumpet: However, the music director went against the nay-sayers and because of his shoulder injury, and long absence, he wanted more time to hear me play for himself.

So that extended my tenure period into a third year and another audition, which entailed going into a rehearsal room with the music director. I brought in all my excerpt books and all my trumpets. I was in assassin mode!

Author: Whoa, what kind of mode?

Principal Trumpet: Assassin mode!

Author: Oh, really? I see, so you were ready to carve ass. I love it! [Laughing wildly]

Principal Trumpet: So, I asked the music director what he wanted to hear. I played almost all the famous trumpet excerpts, from Petruska, Pines of Rome, Mahler Post horn, which he conducted me, to see how I followed. Then I played opera excerpts, piccolo trumpet, you name it. We were in that room for three hours, talking, and then I played, talking, and then I played some more. Then he said, "You know what man? You have such a natural singing quality to your sound, which is so difficult to teach." Then he asked me, "Why there is so little involvement with classical music in the Black community?"

Author: Okay, now that's an honest, insightful question. Hmmm?

Principal Trumpet: So I explained how most Black kids don't grow up listening to classical music and then there's Black culture in general that doesn't include it. He seemed to be genuinely interested in understanding. He asked how I got interested. So I explained how growing up, I saw the Nutcracker Ballet on television and I liked the music, so I kept the television channel on PBS. I told him how when I was in high school, my Latin teacher introduced me to opera and many other artistic things. Then I played some more for him. This was probably the most I'd ever talked to him since I joined the orchestra. We were, like I said, in that room for three hours. Then he finally said, "I can't see any reason why you can't be our principal trumpet." So, he gave me tenure right after that. And regardless of the push-back from those orchestra members who didn't think I should have my principal trumpet position, in the final analysis, the music director was in my corner.

Author: Three hours? God! You know, not many players, even the top players in the country, could've gotten through that much playing, without collapsing. Brother, you must have an amazing amount of endurance as a brass player!

Principal Trumpet: Well no, like I said, I used to practice and play for hours. I was also a fierce listener of music, intent on learning my craft. My mother always told me that I'd have to be three times better to be considered on the same level as them [the white people].

So that stuck with me, but I didn't see the reality of it, until I got older and started climbing up that classical music ladder toward classical music's glass ceiling, so to speak. Then . . . if you were not Black, you would never think about such things.

Author: No, of course not.

Violinist of a Major Southern California Symphony Orchestra

Violinist: My experience being an orchestral player . . . ah, I am a great sight reader. I'm great at listening and playing at the same time. I'm not the greatest solo player and when I think about it . . . oh, what some forty years later. I should've stayed at university and studied the art of violin playing more. I should've gotten a master's and/or a certificate degree, where you just play recitals. But I was thrilled to start working and supporting myself. And only now, having this break because of the pandemic, do I realize that I've worked continuously since I was nineteen.

And now, since I've been off from work for over eight months, I've discovered so much I didn't know about the violin, just from teaching my students and intense practice.

Author: So, you've been playing steadily, since you left University of Southern California (USC) and auditioned for the concertmaster, at the time, and put on the substitute list, you haven't stopped since then?

Violinist: Yes, I've been playing steadily . . . which is great.

Author: Yeah! I was gonna say, not a problem. [Laughing]

Violinist: I have been playing steadily, but not in the sense that you'd put a microscope on your violin playing for solo tone production and things like that. I think if I was in another culture or something, I probably would've gotten my masters, but no one was encouraging me to do that at the time. Then how would I have done that and paid for it? I probably would've had to have a sponsor or something like that.

Author: Were you on scholarship at USC?

Violinist: Yeah, I was on that California academic scholarship that Ronald Reagan got rid of. It was a special scholarship, that if you had a B plus average in California you would qualify. It paid a major portion of your tuition. That's how so many of my friends went to college and suddenly, Reagan just got rid of it. So, after getting into USC academically, I then took the audition for the music school and thought I'd just minor in violin. That's when Eudice Shapiro, renowned violin pedagogue at USC, said, "You can study with me." So, I think my first year was actually violin performance, but eventually, I took everything at USC. That's what you did, it wasn't just music courses, it was sociology, Spanish, math, history, logic, etc.

Author: Math too? You could've taken math if you wanted? Great!

Violinist: Yeah, I think I took statistics . . . yeah.

Author: Oh, I was thinking more along the lines of a conservatory curriculum, but math, wow.

Violinist: You know, I took a lot of courses at USC, besides the violin, music theory, and orchestra. The music courses were in the afternoon, and you took your other courses in the morning. It's not like that now though. Also, now so many of the musicians, especially string players, are coming into the orchestra highly trained as soloists, but they can't sight read, they can't blend in with the other players and they don't know how to play while listening. Then most soloists don't believe they need those skills, because they are all such super fine, highly trained individual players.

Then I remember our music director made a comment once, during rehearsal. "You know you all played so beautiful in your auditions, you phrased, you did everything with such high musical quality. Then you come here into this orchestra, and you play like this?"

Author: Hmmm! Interesting observation, on his part. Then he's heard many of them audition, I'm sure. He was referring to the strings mostly, right?

Violinist: Yes, he's heard most of them play for sure, and there was quite a turnover since you left. But you know when I auditioned, I wasn't the finest solo player, but my excerpts and everything else were right up there. I'm really comfortable doing what I do, in this job, playing in a tutti string section with a major orchestra.

I remember once, at USC, playing for the student conductors, when we didn't know what music they were going to conduct—they would just give us music. So, the professor, who was overseeing the class, said to me, "You know, you're really good at this." Because I got so sick of hearing from other students saying to me that I had to catch up with this or catch up with that musically and I finally said, "I know!" The professor was really taken aback that I snapped at him.

Author: You know I often wondered why they always want to hear solo material in these orchestra auditions, when they know you're not going to be doing that at all.

Violinist: Hmmm? Well, you're right . . . why the emphasis is on solo playing rather than sightreading, for example.

Author: Well, I think it's an older concept, asking for solo material. However, most violinists playing in orchestra string sections at one time wanted to be soloists. You see it in the facial expressions of the violin section during the cadenza of a famous soloist. That look of, "I should be up there playing as a soloist." Rather resentful expressions, I might add. I remember one of our concertmasters rudely finishing a phrase for the soloist after the conductor had stopped the orchestra. That was so petty and obviously envious.

Violinist: Yeah, yeah, and some of them have a real hatred for the orchestra repertoire.

Author: Hatred, really, that bad?

Violinist: Oh yeah, they never listen to orchestral works with a large string section. But I always enjoyed listening to music that had big string section parts. I would always choose that over just listening to a violin soloist.

I remember when I started taking my daughter, at age six, to violin lessons, it was so interesting, in a sense, to be sitting there, vicariously learning violin again through my daughter's lessons.

Author: That is so interesting to hear. It was also very wise not to try and teach her yourself.

Violinist: So, like I said, it was like learning to play again, watching her lessons and accompanying her on piano. I think everybody would benefit from having a refresher course on their instrument.

But you know, on another matter, playing in the orchestra . . . I didn't feel I had a power base in there. A woman, a business consultant, was telling me that I needed to have a power base, musically, like people in the orchestra who really knew the quality of my playing or friends on the board of directors, like anyone in business would have. Because at university, I didn't have that kind of support from any of the students in the music school.

Most of them would be of the opinion, "Well, she'll never get a job anywhere" . . . or when they actually see me in the orchestra, they're of the opinion that I'm only there because they needed African Americans. But most of those students never bothered to notice what qualities I had or ever really witnessed my playing for themselves. But unfortunately, that's human nature.

Author: Oh absolutely, especially at conservatories. As I recall, there was so much jealousy and competitiveness. After returning from auditioning for my job, I ran into one of the student conductors at the conservatory. He said, "So how'd it go with your auditions?" I said, "I'm still waiting to hear from one orchestra." And he chuckled and said, "You didn't expect to get one of those big jobs on your first time out, did you? Oh, and don't get your hopes up." And once I got the job, people at the conservatory would walk by me quickly and say, "Mr. Philharmonic, Ha!"

Even when I got hired as a substitute horn with the Boston Symphony and that got around school, students at the conservatory would make snide comments during rehearsals of conservatory ensembles, if I happened to miss a note."'Mr. BSO, yeah, right!!'"

Violinist: Yeah, fellow students were not at all encouraging.

Author: Not at all! But just imagine what it was like, back in the 1920s, 1930s, and 1940s, for someone like African American composer Florence Price, the envy, hate, and abject racism, at a major conservatory, not to mention her trying to get her music performed.

Violinist: Yeah, now, some of the students who remember me from USC music school, some of the snotty ones, telling me that . . . I was one of the nice music students and thank you.

But they wouldn't have said that back when we were students together and now, forty years have passed since then. Wow, forty years.

Author: Really, they said you were one of the nice ones? One of the nice music students, Interesting.

They meant, just a nice thoughtful music student. So that was forty years ago, but it was the perfect time for you to start a career in music. Because in music, one has to strike when the iron is hot. There's a window of time that only comes once and if you don't seize it in that window of time, it won't happen. It's not the type of career one can put off and then pick up some years later. When I first met you, I could see that you were ready then.

That's why I believe it worked out so well for you. I'm glad I got in when I was young, because it would've been a lot more difficult had I started at age forty.

Violinist: Age affects you completely different when playing in a large violin section.

Author: How so?

Violinist: Well, for example, if your fingers slow down you have a lot of other people picking up the slack. [Laughing]

Author: Oh, you mean you can coast somewhat?

Violinist: Yeah . . . [chuckling]

Author: I mean that's gotta be a whole other dynamic, playing in a sixteen-player string section, especially playing with a lot of players who originally wanted to be famous soloists.

Violinist: Oh yeah . . .

Author: Then I imagine it can be rather difficult doing it on a regular basis. Bet you could write a book about it.

Violinist: Yeah, yeah, people really don't appreciate that there's an art to it.

Author: Also, a lot of people don't really believe that we get paid for what we do as musicians. I recall our former concertmaster telling me about the chairman of the board of directors of a major symphony orchestra, where he played, actually asked him what most of the orchestra players did for a living. Amazing!

Violinist: Yeah, you're right. A lot of people don't realize that we're actually working.

Author: Sometimes I think the idea that we play music might cause people to think that we're not working, but are in fact, playing and why would one get paid for playing.

How wrong they are, especially when you think of all the work involved for the second violins in a Richard Wagner overture like Tannhäuser. I often listen to the violins in his music. It was almost insane the way he wrote for them. No way he was thinking about the players.

Violinist: Oh, my God, yes!

Author: So, your daughter has gone into music as well?

Violinist: Yeah, she teaches full time at an elementary school. She doesn't know how long she will continue teaching, but I think she'll like it better when she's back in school and actually working with her students again.

Author: Oh, so she's a music teacher?

Violinist: Yes, but she also fiddles in the freelance music world.

Author: So she plays gigs?

Violinist: Yes, she does.

Author: So how did you get started playing violin?

Violinist: Well, all of my siblings started on piano in the first grade, and my father's family all played music; also my mother played viola in middle school. I remember there was a flute and a clarinet lying around our house. Also, my father played music; his family was musical. So, my mother decided that we would all start playing music.

They gave the clarinet to my brother and the flute to my sister and at that time we all went to Mount Saint Mary's School of Music, the Doheny campus. There was a violin teacher, and I started playing the violin and I think I told you last time, that I don't remember learning violin, I just remember knowing how to play violin.

Author: I see, so you started quite young.

Violinist: Well, like I said, we all started out on piano once we got to first grade, because there was a nun at our private school, Saint Paul's Catholic School, who taught piano. Sister Marie Esperie, who was just fun and kind, so she taught us all piano. Then each of us were looking forward to playing our respective orchestral instrument. That's when my instrument became violin.

Author: And where did you get the instruments?

Violinist: Hmmm, you know, that's another story. My dad knew this man, ah what was his name? He had a music store downtown on 8th Street, and my dad was painting his building. My dad was a painter in those days. So, my dad would paint his building in exchange for instruments for us.

Author: Ah, really?

Violinist: Yeah, he was a house painter and he hung wallpaper. So that music shop had (Roth?) violins and my dad got me a violin from that shop. There used to be a lot of music shops in LA and that guy sold string and band instruments. But eventually, my dad did get sick from all that painting work. And at the time, he was also a calibration technician for the space program at Borg-Warner, Byron Jackson. He still managed to pick us up for lessons and drove us just about everywhere we needed to go.

Author: So, he did both jobs at the same time? My God!

Violinist: Yeah, but he would end up in the hospital from exhaustion. He was in that veterans hospital during the San Fernando earthquake that collapsed.

Author: So, he was a mathematician too?

Violinist: Well, he was a calibration technician, and he was always very interested in mathematics. He used to tutor us at home with the slide rule. My brother and sister picked up math easily, but for me it was a lot harder. He tutored us in math, he tutored us in Latin, and I wasn't a straight A student, but my brother and sister were. I always got a B or two and I always thought that was . . . just horrible.

Of course, we were expected to excel in academics and music. My brother and sister were always playing concerti and recitals on their instruments, and I was just plugging away on violin. However, I must say that I did learn perseverance. Yes, perseverance . . . so that's how I got into classical music.

Then there was the Santa Monica Youth Orchestra, where my brother was principal clarinet and my sister was principal flute. I also started playing in that orchestra and my dad would drive us every Saturday morning out to Santa Monica. But we all had perfect pitch, and my sister had some kind of weird pitch ability where she could easily hear four-part harmony and a talent for taking four-part dictation. We all had great musical ears, it was just in our family genes and perhaps because of our dad always taking us to those music lessons over the years.

Author: So you must have had an easy time when you got to the university level.

Violinist: No, no . . .

Author: You didn't, really?

Violinist: No, I didn't . . . ah, I actually flunked freshman theory.

Author: Well so did I, but ah . . .

Violinist: [Laughing] . . . No, it didn't stick with me.

Author: Oh really? Even with all that early exposure?

Violinist: No, my brother and sister, yes it stuck with them, but not me. Perhaps because I wasn't really interested in it. And perhaps because of my being the third child, I started learning everything by ear. I learned a lot just using my ears. So, university was still difficult for me.

Author: You know there's a kind of false belief that if you learn something as a very young child that it will be cumulative if you stick with it, but that's not true. Most kids who learn at a very young age forget most everything by the time they are adults. So, the child prodigy myth of starting at age five and continuing right on through to become superhuman by age twenty-five is not true.

Violinist: But still, I don't believe I would've become a classical musician if it were not for my father taking us to all those music lessons and orchestra rehearsals at such a formative age. But I don't really think my brother and sister really wanted to be classical musicians as a career. I just liked that structure. The challenge of trying to make everything fit into that classical box. I know some people hate it, but I enjoyed it, in and of itself.

Author: So being the youngest of three, you in a sense absorbed each of your sibling's journeys as they went through their lessons. So, by the time you started your own lessons you were already inundated, giving you extra musical skills.

Violinist: Yes, because they were always ahead of me, and I would listen to their concerts as a youngster.

Flutist of a Major Southern Symphony Orchestra

Author: So where are you from originally?

Flutist: I'm from Washington, D.C.

Author: So, how did you get started on flute, and are you the principal flute or piccolo in your orchestra?

Flutist: I am neither. [Chuckling] I'm the second flute player. I got started in the DC Youth Orchestra, and I started playing flute because my dad was a lifelong lover of classical music and he wanted all of his kids to play a musical instrument.

I have two sisters and a brother who all learned to play an instrument. My first choice was the flute. My dad kind of had one just laying around the house.

Author: Really? Sounds like my family. All of us played an instrument except my oldest sister. My mother played piano by ear and my father played trumpet. So, it was really quite interesting growing up. In fact, I got curious one night about my father's trumpet, which was on a shelf above the fireplace. I couldn't reach it, so I put my little brother on my shoulders. Just as he grabbed the trumpet, I lost my balance and we both fell, denting the trumpet.

So, believe it or not, I tried to take the dents out with a hammer. Big mistake!

Flutist: [Laughing]

Author: So much for instruments hanging around the house.

You know I saw a wonderful video online where you were demonstrating all of your different flutes. How many do you have?

Flutist: I have my one regular flute, my everyday flute, I have a back-up flute to that one. I have a wooden flute that I like to play.

Author: A wooden flute?

Flutist: Yeah, it's nice, it's very nice. It's my most modern instrument, oddly enough.

Author: Modern?

Flutist: Yes, it was made in 1997, I think.

Author: I would've thought it would be ancient.

Flutist: Not at all, it was made by a company called Powell. That flute was made special for their anniversary year, celebrating seventy-five years in business for them.

Author: So, did Miles Zentner make head joints or just piccolos?

Flutist: Piccolos, yeah . . . I have a Zentner, actually. It's one of my piccolos.

Author: Oh, you have one. That's great to hear.

Sorry to hear that he passed on. He was quite a big presence in the orchestra, especially during contract negotiations. He and others were largely responsible for the contract the Philharmonic has today.

You know, he actually kept me from quitting in my early years. I told him I was leaving the orchestra for some crazy thing that went down and he dragged me into a room and yelled, "Now, sit down, pal! You're not going to leave! This is a job! Do you have another job like this lined up? Do you?" Oh, he was furious with me. He was such a special human being.

So, then you must have a few piccolos?

Flutist: Yeah, I actually have two, I have at least five flutes, maybe six and I have an alto flute as well.

Author: Hmmm? Ya know I played on one of the Spiderman film scores and it included a bass saxophone. I had only seen one of those in photos. They had it on a platform and played it standing, amazing. The sound was so deep and vibrating that the entire riser shook. On the other extreme, the piccolo always fascinated me by how powerful it was, being so small. But with its timbre it could always tower over the orchestra and always be heard. Players in the orchestra used to make fun of the way Miles played the piccolo by imitating him scornfully, because he was such a powerful player.

Flutist: Actually I love playing the piccolo . . . in fact I wish I was the piccolo player in my orchestra. Of course, I play a little bit of piccolo, as part of my job description. So, if the music calls for two piccolos, I always play second piccolo. But if there's a big piccolo part, the piccolo player plays it, because she's a wonderful player.

Author: So how long have you been in the orchestra now?

Flutist: Long time, I started in 1992, so it's been nearly thirty years.

Author: Okay, so what has the experience been like?

Flutist: I won the audition when I was twenty-two, super young and all of a sudden, I found myself with a job, a good job. [Chuckling] I didn't have a job before that, I mean I was in school and I managed to win a job before I graduated, so.

Author: Did you play behind a screen at your audition?

Flutist: Yes, except for the finals.

Author: In my day, at my first audition there was no screen for anything. The music director was at the preliminaries as well as the finals. At my second audition they had a screen dropped down on a fly, but it only came to my waist. Someone on the committee was very upset, saying they could see that I was colored. It was all quite amusing. Also, while I was playing my audition, I noticed that the personnel manager, who was seeing people on and off stage, came out on stage to listen to me play. And he had this real look of awe and incredulity, but he didn't do that with anyone else.

Flutist: No, I had a proper screen. [Laughing] Nobody could see me. They had a screen for the preliminaries and a screen for the semi-finals, but they took the screen down for the finals.

Author: Oh, so there are semi-finals now? And now I heard there's something called super finals?

Flutist: Yeah, they have that now, but they didn't have super finals when I auditioned thirty years ago. Now days they have preliminaries, semi-finals, finals, and super finals. [Laughing]

Author: God! They make people so crazy with all the levels and stages.

Flutist: Exactly, no, mine was just regular finals, but it had five people in it, which is actually pretty full for finals.

Author: So, when you first started out on your orchestra job, how was it? You got the job in the early 1990s, hmmmm?

Flutist: Early 1990s, yeah, but actually, it was okay. What happened with me was, I was pretty nervous, at my first rehearsal anyway. I had talked to the principal flute, and she said that it was a nice orchestra and there would be no problems. I also knew that one of the other players in the finals had been playing in the second flute chair as a substitute. And I knew that people were generally happy with her playing and were shocked when she didn't come away with the job. She ended up getting another job, which I was happy to hear, which was actually pretty nice. Still, I was pretty nervous coming into the first rehearsal because of that, you know.

Author: Of course, of course . . .

Flutist: So my first rehearsal with the orchestra they played the Moldau. Okay?

Author: Oh really?

Flutist: The Moldau starts out with a second flute solo. If you didn't know that, now you do.

Author: Ahhh! I don't recall. [Laughing]

Flutist: So, it starts out with a second flute solo, so everybody could basically hear me, you know? It starts out with the second flute then the first flute joins in, and we end up playing together, then others join in. But, while I was playing that Moldau solo, it went really great and people were like, "She plays really well." I felt content, because I was able to establish early on that I could really play and yes, I could really sound good and that I was the right person for the job. But I heard that I didn't have as much of a terrible time as some of my other colleagues when they first started out in the orchestra.

Author: And you were the only person of color at the time?

Flutist: Yes . . . I'm the only Black person now. That is, the only Black person who has a permanent contract.

Author: So, then you must have some Black substitute musicians?

Flutist: Yes, we do.

Author: My God! All of these large cities in America, with large amounts of Black folks, but with only one Black player in their symphony orchestras. It's hard to believe.

So, you got your first job at age twenty-two? That's so impressive! I also got my first job at age twenty-two. You know, I think it's better to get in at an early age, because there's so much pressure to do well in these jobs, it wears better on you when you're younger.

I had some difficult playing situations that occurred in my early years in the orchestra. The horn section was always a nightmare of intrigue, with the principal horns not showing up and my having to step in to play principal horn at a moment's notice. I never had a problem pulling off those crazy situations, because of my age and ability on the horn. In fact, I think the principals knew I could handle it, when they would call in sick and take a studio job instead of coming to a Philharmonic rehearsal.

During my first years in the orchestra, the personnel manager was in cahoots with the horn players, that is, he knew what they were doing and let them get away with it.

So, on many occasions I'd show up to a morning rehearsal to find out that the principal horn was not coming to work due to illness, as the trumpets would always joke, "Yeah, he's at Dr. Fox or Dr. MGM" suffering with acute studioitis. So, I had to play principal horn at the last minute. There was one morning, as I got out of my car, I saw the principal horn and the third horn. I spoke to them, as they walked quickly ahead of me. When I arrived inside the personnel manager told me I had to play third horn for the rehearsal. I quickly informed him that

I just passed the third horn in the parking lot, that he was indeed present. He argued with me yelling, "Just do what I said and go on stage!" When I arrived on stage the second horn spilled the beans saying the third horn was on the same job as the principal horn. I noticed that the other principal was covering for his co-principal. As it turned out, the principal horn and the third horn were on the fourth floor in the same building, playing with another orchestra, when they should've been at the Philharmonic rehearsal.

So, have you ever been questioned, after playing a concert, where friends and others attended and afterwards, while having drinks, you were asked what you did for a living?

Flutist: Sure, but not as much as I used to, when I was young and first started in the orchestra. Now it's "What else do you do?"

Author: I know, it's kind of sad that most people don't believe one can make a living playing music.

I remember our former concertmaster telling me when he was with the Chicago Symphony during a reception for the orchestra that the chairman of the board of directors asked him what most of the guys did for a living. (Of course, in those days, most orchestras were indeed just guys). He tried to explain that the symphony was their living, but the guy wasn't hearing him. He went on to say, "Yeah, I know the guys come here to play a few times a week, but what do most of them do for a living?" Or . . . as you mentioned, "What else do you do?"

Flutist: Unbelievable . . .

Author: It is, but I think that the orchestras kind of want to keep the board members a little naïve, in regards to the actual business aspect of an orchestra. I think they would rather have board members believing that they are financially supporting a high-level artistic, altruistic organization that is far above the fray of unions, profits, and pure business.

So, when you auditioned behind the screen did they tell you not to wear high heels, not to sigh or do anything to reveal your gender?

Flutist: I mean, I wasn't really told not to do any of that stuff. However, I didn't do anything to reveal my gender, and I certainly understood that that the purpose of the screen was to make everyone anonymous. I think I just wore my flat shoes because I typically wore them anyway.

Author: Got it, so on another note, what was your experience with the Black community in your city? How were you received as the lone Black member in your orchestra?

Flutist: Well, I would say the Black people that I met, some went out of their way to meet me and that was great. But I wouldn't say that they were very much into the orchestra at all. Maybe because there was never any history of Black people in the orchestra before me. However, the Black people that I did meet were very welcoming, very nice, and very happy to know that I was there. Even now when I talk to some Black people, they tell me that they are so happy that I'm there. And you know, it's a pretty diverse city. Some say it's the most diverse city in the state, which is probably true. It's the fourth largest city in America.

Author: Oh, it's more diverse and larger than Dallas?

Flutist: Oh yes, it's larger and way more diverse than Dallas.

Author: I'll never forget that enormous Intercontinental Hotel in Dallas . . . let's see, ah, Anatol! The Philharmonic stayed there while on a tour of the United States. One of my Black colleagues in the orchestra, a bass player, wanted to leave the hotel and have breakfast in the city at large.

He said he wanted a real Southern breakfast. So, we found a small breakfast place on a side street behind the hotel. We walked in and the place was empty.

Then, it was late morning about 11:30. When the waitress came over, I had a feeling we were in trouble, because I looked back in the kitchen and the Black cook was staring at us with a look on his face that said, please be careful what you say to her. The lone waitress walked up to our table, stares at us and literally throws two menus on the table. "Ah suppose y'all want breakfast, Huh! Comin in here this late. [Mumbling under her breath] Don't know why colored got ta always eat breakfast so late."

My friend ordered grits and poached eggs, and she looked at him like he had two tails and said, "Ain't no grits after 11:00 and I ain't never heard a no peached, parched, eggs." Then I ordered bacon and scrambled eggs with a side of toast. "Ain't t no toast after 11:00. We busy making cornbread for lunch so y'all outta luck for no toast. That's what y'all git for comin' in here this time a day for some goddam breakfast, shit!" We walked out.

So, you're from Washington, DC, and I've always wondered if DC is considered "the South." Did it have that Southern feel when you were growing up there?

Flutist: You know, it technically is, but I don't really consider it the South. I didn't feel that when I was growing up . . . and it's also a majority Black city. It was great growing up there. I loved it and I still do.

Author: But it's different than Texas though?

Flutist: Definitely! I never thought I'd be in Texas, you know? I never thought I'd step foot in Texas. Yet I've been here for thirty years now.

Author: But your orchestra, being in such a large city, wouldn't have that small town feel, with racial push-back and provincialism?

I imagine the players came from all over the world, am I right?

Flutist: Yeah . . . no I didn't get any racial push-back, at least I didn't feel like I did.

Author: You didn't feel it . . . good.

Flutist: Yeah, you know, everybody was always really nice. Honestly, it's a pretty nice orchestra. There are definitely orchestras out there that are considered really mean orchestras, you know, that have an attitude, like some of the old established east coast orchestras.

Author: Yes, yes, of course, I've heard.

Flutist: But this has always been like a very friendly orchestra. Players are always hanging out for drinks after concerts, and I was always doing that kind of socializing with the players, especially when I first got in the orchestra.

Author: You know, I saw an interview with your executive director, and he seemed to have a real understanding for what's needed in the diversity department. He mentioned that your orchestra has a council for African American, Asians, and Latinx communities. That's quite encouraging. I also got the feeling that your orchestra is much younger, player to player, than most major orchestras. This younger generation aspect is somewhat responsible for the absence of that old school racial push-back atmosphere that I experienced.

And if you looked at say, the New York Philharmonic seventy years ago it was all white men. Now because of the screens and women's rights issues that orchestra is almost half women. Things have changed, because seventy years ago players had to go to some hotel room of a conductor to audition and that situation was open to any and all types of discrimination. Also, certain other laws have come into play to improve the symphony orchestra world, like harassment statutes. In the old days if a conductor didn't like a player he could, for example, ask that player to play their part alone, over and over again. To the point of reducing that player to a puddle of nerves and embarrassment and still turn around and fire that person. And of course, now the sexual harassment issue is out the window, because of the new statutes. I remember in my first year, the orchestra was going through a metamorphosis from a metropolitan, twenty-eight-week orchestra to a fifty-two-week major orchestra. Many of the principals had been terminated and were playing out their contracts. There was a lot of friction from those who had been fired, especially if you were young and seemingly representing the "New Guard," so to speak. I had one of the principals ask me, "Did you have time to go to conservatory and train? My God, you're so young." I was quite mouthy in those days, so I fired back, "If you had time to go to conservatory, so did I." The worst part was after a performance when the music director gave one of the principals a bow, the principal in my section would yell out, "It doesn't mean a thing! You're still toast! You're going out the door with the rest of us!" It was a difficult period for the orchestra.

There were a lot of elderly people still playing in the orchestra. When my teacher saw the orchestra on tour, he said that our orchestra had a lot more elderly people than the Boston Symphony. Some of the older men actually thought it was just fine to greet me like, "Morning, Bob, boy." And then have the nerve to try and pat me on my ass with their greeting.

I do remember grabbing and twisting a few wrists. Many of them would actually be offended by my rejection of their demeaning behavior. They would actually say, "What, I can't touch you?" And I always had to say, "No, unless you want me to 'touch you up' street style."

Then, we have to remember, that was 1970, when white privilege was still deeply imbued in our society, left over from Jim Crow, even slavery.

Flutist: Yeah, so when I joined the orchestra in 1992, sounds like I sort of came in just past that difficult era. Like you mentioned earlier, there were a lot of young people in my orchestra compared to your day.

Also, our music director at the time had hired a lot of the new people, almost 50 percent of the orchestra. A lot of new young people, that were thinking differently, I might add. [Laughing] So I think that was why it was different when I came along, because I wasn't interacting with the sort of Old Guard kind of people.

Author: Well, I'm so glad you missed those types of experiences, because no one deserves that kind of grief while trying to play music.

But you know, someone had to show up on the scene first. Someone had to shake things up, in order for things to change, I guess. A pioneer doesn't know they are a pioneer; they just want something, and they go for it.

So, it looks like you were the first Black flute player hired by a major symphony orchestra, am I right?

Flutist: No, I can't believe that's right. That's not something my brain was aware of . . . oh, I don't think that's true.

Author: Really? Hmmm? Okay.

So, in talking to you, I'm glad to hear things have indeed changed in the symphony orchestra world, regarding Black symphony players. In fact, you're giving me the sense that things are a lot better since I came along twenty-two years earlier than you.

Flutist: But you know, I think it's also situational and specific to each individual orchestra. When I think about some of the awful things I'm hearing from Black friends in other orchestras in this same state, that just happened this year, it's gotta be completely situational. I also suspect that it makes a difference that I'm a Black woman. I think it's harder for the men.

Author: Yes, yes . . . I think you're right.

Flutist: I also think, you know, nobody's looking at me, a Black woman, thinking scary thoughts, like they're inclined do with Black men.

Author: Thinking what kind of thoughts? [Laughing]

Flutist: Scary thoughts! Like, [Laughing] "Oh, what's this Black man going to do to me?"

Author: Oh sure . . . all the insanely bogus, negative, narratives about Black men through films and literature, that they've created.

Flutist: Exactly, exactly, but you know, it wasn't like that for me, being a Black woman. I think women have it easier.

Author: And I'm so glad to hear that you did.

A sick example of, not scary thoughts, but one of the many negative narratives about Black men and a mentality most would never imagine existed in the artistically lofty, high-profile, intellectual environment of a major symphony orchestra and that is, the preoccupation with the Black male phallus: We were about to play an aria with a famous Asian soprano and as she entered the stage, I applauded her along with everyone else and the male horn player next to me said, "Yea, Bob, you'd kill her with that thing." Then, only a white male, deeply steeped in that particular negative narrative about Black males, could entertain or express such a competitive penis envy statement to another male, in my case a Black male.

So, who did you study flute with as a youngster?

Flutist: Ah, when I was growing up, I didn't have a real flute teacher until I was sixteen. . . . Actually, the youth orchestra taught me how to play the flute. So first you'd have your private lesson with the youth orchestra teacher and then you'd play in one of three levels of orchestras. So, I did that. I actually started when I was six years old. So, when I turned sixteen, my parents decided I should have private flute lessons. At that time the National Symphony had a fellowship program where they gave free lessons to high school kids, so that's where I got my first private flute teacher. In college I studied with two different teachers from the Philadelphia Orchestra, when I was at Temple University. In my first two years I studied with the principal flute, who actually died at the end of two years studying with him. Then I studied with the piccolo player from the Philadelphia Orchestra. That's when I got my Zentner piccolo, because I asked him to help me find a piccolo and he came up with the Zentner.

Author: Is that right . . . he called it a Zentner? Okay.

Flutist: Then I studied a year at Peabody in a graduate program with a flutist who played with the Cleveland Orchestra. After that I didn't have any more teachers, because I had a job. [Laughing]

Author: Wow, so you had a lot of good training and good teachers.

You and I both got our major orchestra jobs right out of conservatory, but you know, I recall that there was a false idea circulating around my orchestra about how players who had played in a lesser orchestra first were somehow better prepared as players when they got into a major orchestra.

However, there was one principal player in my section that did just that. He was one of the most poorly trained and uneducated musicians I'd ever worked with in my life. He had serious problems as a horn player.

He never truly accepted the technique for making an initial attack on the horn, he guessed at rhythms, couldn't properly read the bass clef, which French horns use all the time. He rushed all the time, claiming the horn was always behind the beat, making it impossible to play with him.

Anyway, I hope you didn't have to deal with anything that crazy and I'm glad to hear that you had a better experience than I did in my early days.

Principal Bass of a Major East Coast Symphony Orchestra

Author: So, where are you from originally?

Principal Bass: I'm from Savannah, Georgia.

Author: Whoooo! Okay.

Principal Bass: Yes, yes!

Author: And how did you start with music?

Principal Bass: So the very beginnings, I do have to attribute to my mother. She's a native of Savannah and . . . ah . . . she did not come from the affluent side of the city. [Laughing] She definitely had her challenges; well both my parents had their challenges growing up.

The strange thing is . . . she heard classical music on the radio and thought it was beautiful.

Author: Is that right?

Principal Bass: Yes, two things came from that: one, she wanted all her kids to be involved in classical music, and two, she wanted to become an opera singer herself.

Author: Wow! Love it!

Principal Bass: So it was really that connection with the radio that connected our family with classical music. My mother never went on to sing profession-ally, but she did study at Savannah State College at that time, where she met my dad. She sang at the Savannah State College and went on to do amateur singing across the city, ultimately, including the Savannah Symphony Chorus.

Author: What was her voice?

Principal Bass: Soprano.

Author: Okay. I see . . .

Principal Bass: So she . . . brought her own energy and determination to the love of classical music and to the world of music itself. Honestly, that's how we all got started playing musical instruments. My oldest brother started violin when he was nine, my twin sister and I . . . well I started on piano, and she was on cello at age five. All the kids started playing at the same time basically. So, my mom reached out to many of the Black music teachers in town. My brother started with a Black violin teacher, Miss. Capers, my goodness, this is going way back. [Laughing] Then I started piano with a woman named Rose Smith in Savannah, who still teaches a lot of young Black kids in Savannah today.

Author: Really? Great to hear.

Principal Bass: Yeah! And then my sister's first teacher was white, Irish, Adel O'Dwyer. So that's how we all got started playing music.

Honestly, so the rest of the picture is, we all grew up in the Black Baptist church. We were there six days out of the week. I grew up with a lot of gospel music as well. I feel like my early upbringing was equal parts gospel as well as classical. I probably heard gospel the most, to be honest with you. So that's how we all got started in music and playing musical instruments.

The story can take many different directions, but if you wanna know how we got started, it was basically that. My mom hearing classical music on the radio and wanting all her kids to play it.

Author: That is amazing, because that doesn't usually happen in Black families.

Principal Bass: You're right.

Author: My father played trumpet, he wasn't around that much, but when I came up with the idea of playing the French horn, he had definite ideas about it. Negative ones like, "Your lips are too thick to play that thin-lipped white boy mouthpiece."

Principal Bass: Right, right . . .

Author: My mother played piano by ear and couldn't read a note, but like it or not, however it might have happened, our parents are the ones who endowed us with our talents. So, you started on piano and how did you end up playing the bass?

Principal Bass: So, my brother and sister were always playing music with their friends, and I always knew that I was probably going to be playing some kind of instrument when I went to middle school. We all started off at a Catholic school. The plan was we would all go to public when we hit middle school. At the same time my brother had actually gotten some attention, because he was becoming decent on the violin. [Laughing] He was starting to be seen in the community as someone folks were watching in the music education scene.

And there was a teacher who really wanted my brother to go to a school where she taught. It was one of the nicest schools in the region. She was able to get my brother there on scholarship and basically my sister and I followed suit.

Knowing that we were all in music, our family had gotten some notice in town, instead of going to public school, we went to that private school. Had we gone to public school, it's likely I would have ended up playing the trombone. [Laughing]

Author: Interesting . . .

Principal Bass: So we ended up going to this private school that had a serious string program, where the strings met every morning every day. But I still hadn't taken up a string instrument at that time. Heading into middle school, the teacher said I could read music and I was a pretty good pianist. Actually, for a long time, I thought I was going to be a pianist for my career. [Laughing] So what happened was that same teacher, Lynne Tobin, who had gotten my siblings into that private school, said I should play the bass, because she needed bass players and she thought I'd be good at it and the rest is history.

Author: That was it, really?

Principal Bass: Yes, I got a bass in my hands and progressed quickly. The thing is, I didn't know that I was progressing that quickly. I thought my progress was normal.

I was just trying to get good at it, because Savannah was a small city and I didn't have, like, all these kids from around the world to compare myself to or anything like that. But honestly, I did have these recordings of cello playing and so my bar was, how do I get to sound like those recording?

Author: Huh! Okay.

Principal Bass: Ha, so that coupled with a piano teacher, who got me into music theory early on. I mean, literally, she was teaching me music theory as a five-year-old.

Author: Ha! Really, as a five-year-old?

Principal Bass: Oh yeah! Right out the gate! She had me learning I-IV-V-I chords as early as I can remember.

Author: Wow! So great to hear . . .

Principal Bass: That coupled with the fact that my bass teacher, Mr. Warshauer . . . the sky was the limit with him. He let me play anything I wanted to, work on anything I wanted to, and he would just guide me. So, I was able to flourish, to be honest. I didn't know how much I was flourishing until I started playing things outside Savannah.

You know, doing all the local stuff, like getting first chair in All-State Orchestra, being the winner at concert competitions on the bass, in the eighth grade, playing the Mozart Bassoon concerto on the bass. That was actually my first concerto, the Mozart Bassoon concerto. [Laughing]

Author: Really? On the bass? [Laughing]

Principal Bass: Ha, ha . . . yes . . .

Author: And where did you get your first instrument?

Principal Bass: Ah, ha, that's a story, and this is great. My very first instrument was from the school. Then, something my parents did throughout our childhood. They would do anything for their kids.

Author: So nice to hear that.

Principal Bass: Yes! They would do anything for their kids. When I started playing the bass, we had to get a new family car so my bass would fit, and we could all fit in the car along with it.

Author: Ah, exactly!

Principal Bass: [Laughing] And they got the money to get my first bass, an Emanuel Wilfer bass! That's the type of bass it was.

Author: What type of bass?

Principal Bass: Emanuel Wilfer bass, a German factory-made bass. It was a big investment, but when it came to their kids, my parents were willing to make investments no matter what the financial cost.

These are the things you realize when you get older about your parents, because I had no idea how much my parents had sacrificed to make sure we could have the opportunities that we had.

Author: And that can be a big financial risk, investing in an expensive instrument, because there's no way to know if a kid will stick with it. I always tell parents to rent, not buy, an instrument for their young children in case they up and decide to quit. But your family sounds amazing.

Principal Bass: Well, very faithful . . . [Laughing]

Author: Right, right . . .

Principal Bass: My mom will tell you to this day about the stuff that she prayed for when she was a girl, while growing up with nothing, literally, both my parents grew up with nothing, she definitely believed that if she sowed the right seeds, she could nurture them to grow into fruitful trees. [Laughing] So that's what they did, they just invested in their children.

Author: I'm sure based on how your parents grew up, they were deeply inspired and determined to provide a better life for their children. Then this was the case for so many Black folks in this country.

Principal Bass: Oh absolutely! They just wanted to make sure that we didn't miss out on opportunities that they may not have had.

Author: Although I wonder about my father, he was a bit selfish and wasn't around that much, but my mother was in total support of us. I think the fact that he played trumpet, and I went my own way and took up the French horn and went into classical music, caused him to resent me somewhat. Later I found out that my father had actually auditioned for Julliard on trumpet. He was afraid for me going into classical music because of his Julliard audition experience. He played a few things that he knew for the audition committee. They were impressed until they asked him to play a Bach Cantata from the audition list which called for a D trumpet. He got flustered because he had never heard of a D trumpet or the Bach Cantata. So he bolted out of the audition, leaving him with a bitter taste of the classical music world.

He was quite upset from that experience, saying to me, "Ah, I auditioned for Julliard, and they wanted me to play that lily-white classical shit, a Canta-ta, ta, ta, ta, ah! So, I just ran out of the God damn room. I had never heard of a D trumpet! I only had one damn horn . . . lily-white crackers.

Principal Bass: Oh wow!

Author: Yeah, that was his trauma from the classical music world, and it affected him deeply. Just as your parents were deeply affected by their upbringing, another kind of trauma, but one that inspired.

Principal Bass: Yeah, I mean, the thing is . . . they got this land and had a house built and there was a piano in that house. They had a house built on land next to Savannah State University. Everything was always an investment. Oh, I'd have to ask my mom this, I don't even know if they bought the piano, but that piano was always in the house as long as I can remember. I started playing piano when I was five years old, and the piano was already there. But that was a big part of Black culture as well. To have family, a home . . . and it was almost a thing of pride to have a piano in the home.

Author: Is that right? Maybe that's why . . . we had one too and I have no idea where it came from.

Principal Bass: [Laughing]

Author: That's interesting, because the house we grew up in was a cold-water dump, a no-heat nightmare, but we had a piano.

Principal Bass: You had a piano.

Author: My mother would play at night before we went off to bed. I recall that most people who play by ear play exclusively on the black keys. So, if I sang something in C major (white keys) my mother couldn't hear it or play it. She would say, "I can't play that the way you sang it." But those were the things that always amazed me years later, while playing a concert in Vienna, with the Philharmonic utilizing my mother's talent and her musical ear.

Principal Bass: Yeah, that is amazing. [Laughing] Because they didn't know what it would take to do what we ended up doing musically.

I'll say this, for me, and this goes for a lot of stuff in my upbringing. We were very fortunate in my family. It was like the perfect storm. Literally, all the people that came into play that helped put me on the path that I took. My parents, my parent's friends, the church, the people my mom networked with . . . honestly my brother and the attention that he got brought our family more into the music community and the music education community of Savannah.

This woman who recognized my brother and brought us unto the musical conversation, that my brother was as a fine violinist . . . Miss Tobin. And she was a huge music educator, but I didn't realize how much of a hippie she was. She was this incredible hippie.

Author: A real hippie?

Principal Bass: Yes . . . and she did not have any issues with teaching students of color. I reflect on this now, because, as a young person growing up in the South, and now as an older man looking upon my youth, it probably would have taken a hippie—a progressive thinker—to do the marvelous things that Lynne Tobin did for young people of color in Savannah, Georgia. She made playing music with friends normal, she made us all a family. It was a beautiful thing.

Author: Indeed . . .

Principal Bass: I think she thought it was musically empowering for her to see our Black family, with all its musically talented children . . . and that she was able to provide all those musical resources for us. And as I said, I think it was like the perfect storm, because she helped our family, literally. She helped guide my older brother to do what he needed to do and when she moved on there were other people who came into our lives who guided us in a way that we needed.

I was doing the All-State Orchestra stuff, and I was going to music camp. My mother knew that putting us in music camp was important. We went to Brevard Music Center like three summers in a row . . . ah 1995, 1996, 1997. I learned more about the music world there. . . . I mean, there were all these little things that so timely materialized. . . . I didn't know I was being prepared to be a bassist in a major symphony orchestra! I was just expressing a passion and I had a talent and parents who were giving me the opportunity to build on all of that. And I won't pretend I knew what was going on and where I was headed, because I didn't. [Laughing]

Author: And the violinist in your family was your older brother?

Principal Bass: My older brother, yes who went on to Northwestern and majored in chemical engineering, but he played in the college orchestra all five years he was there.

Author: I see, I see . . .

Principal Bass: Yeah, he took the academic route, but music definitely played a big role in getting him into Northwestern. Because it was music that helped broaden his application along with his other qualifications.

Author: Exactly . . .

Principal Bass: Yeah, so like I said, there were all these people and series of events that walked into our musical lives at the perfect time. Like the Sphinx Organization, that started in 1997, I was part of the original twelve. The first twelve semi-finalists for the Sphinx competition.

Author: Oh, really?

Principal Bass: Yeah, I was sixteen years old, and I got wrapped into that family with other Black classical musicians. That was such a transformative experience, because here's the deal:

My life was so siloed [sheltered, isolated, cloistered], and I got used to it. I went to a Ritzy-hoity-toity private school, then we were in church six days out of the week, for bible studies, choir rehearsals, and church meetings. [Laughing]

Author: Right . . . impressive . . . busy.

Principal Bass: That church was literally located between two Black housing projects, the church my mom grew up in, so . . .

Author: So, then a Black church?

Principal Bass: Very much a Black church, oh yeah! I think . . . it's so interesting, I mean I never tried to analyze, my life, like how did all this stuff work out so well. I think it was because I was easily able to segment and silo my life. Does that make sense?

Author: Silo your life? Explain.

Principal Bass: Yeah, I was able to silo my life: So, there was my Black experience in the Black church, my Black friends, and the Black experience, I had my home experience and then I had a very white experience . . . [Laughing] at that hoity-toity private school I went to.

It wasn't that I was trying to mix these experiences in my head at the time, but that was life and that's what was normal for me. Does that make sense?

Author: Absolutely, that's just the way it happened. You were very fortunate that you had all that amazing structure and were able to balance it so well. That you didn't have to struggle in pursuit of something that no one in your environment understood. Instead, you had amazing support.

Principal Bass: Now, to your point about struggle. I am from the South, so when it came to, like, music. The general world in the South was not supporting me in classical music. In fact, I remember being at an event where I got this award in high school and someone asked me, "So what are you going to do after music school, because you obviously aren't going to have a career." [Laughing] That's essentially what he told me.

Author: He said you aren't going to have a career?

Principal Bass: Yeah! Literally . . . here's the deal . . . when it came to race. I knew I was a Black boy. It wasn't a defining thing for me, because my love of music was greater than that. Does that make sense?

Author: Oh, absolutely!

Principal Bass: People didn't really know about me. I wore my music skills like a badge of honor. I felt a little like Clark Kent, being Superman, but no one knew, because I looked like this nerdy guy who works at a newspaper, wearing a suit and glasses. [Laughing]

Author: Right, right . . . [Laughing]

Principal Bass: Because people actually underestimated me, they may have underestimated me my entire life, even when I was a kid. But in my head, I was saying to myself, "I'm gonna prove to you that I can do this!"

Author: Yes, yes . . .

Principal Bass: Because my parents were always saying to us, "Be proud of who you are, know where you came from and know that you are fulfilling the dream of folks who died, so that you can have this opportunity."

Author: Oh, I like that.

Principal Bass: That was always the narrative that was in the back of my head.

Author: Ah! I wish I had more of that when I was growing up! Wow!

Principal Bass: Those words from my parents gave me the agency to succeed and I didn't care what people thought. Because I was working on me to do something that was great. And racist stuff did happen, I mean, I grew up in Savannah and the Confederate flag was everywhere. In fact, two-thirds of the flags in Georgia were Confederate flags, up until I was in college. So, that stuff was normal to me. So, it's funny, people would always ask about all the stuff white people did against me. That was normal for me! Does that make sense?

Author: Of course, but it's still hard to hear.

Principal Bass: It's not like I accepted it in a way that I would say, well, that's the way it is, and I can't do anything about it. For me it was, this is what I'm dealing with and how do I make it better? Does that make sense?

Author: Absolutely! Yours was the opposite of a defeatist attitude. In fact, it was a very positive attitude of new possibilities. Sure, the problem was there, but how to get around it and proceed despite the situation. This is very uplifting to hear compared to some of the stories I've heard in this book. So, what are some of the things that happened, if you'd care to share, that you considered racist against your playing the bass in classical music?

Principal Bass: Whew! That's the thing . . . you know, I keep trying to think back, if someone were to put me into some sort of trance or something, I might be able to talk more specifically about racial experiences, but I let so many of them roll off my back.

Author: I understand . . .

Principal Bass: You know, it was always more of a surprise factor.

Author: Always, so true . . .

Principal Bass: I remember my first time auditioning for All-State Orchestra. They messed up the audition scores and they put me in the wrong orchestra. To remedy the situation, they put me in the back-last chair of the orchestra that I was supposed to be in and had actually won first chair. Now was that fair? No, but I didn't care, because I was just so excited to be accepted in All-State Orchestra and I was only in seventh grade. We played music like The Royal Fireworks, Mendelssohn Symphony No. 5, and Phantom of the Opera. And I will never forget, I was blown away by just being a part of that sound and that experience! I didn't care where I was sitting as long as I was part of that musical experience. Does that make sense?

Author: Of course! Seating was their problem, you just wanted to be there. I mean you were a kid who didn't care about the petty details. [Laughing]

Principal Bass: Right, right . . . but the next year, I was principal bass. That's when I got everyone's attention. They were like, "Who's this Black kid playing principal bass in the All-State Orchestra?"

Author: Whoa! So, was that a problem?

Principal Bass: No, it was not a problem, I wore it as a badge of honor. If someone had a problem with it, it was on them.

Author: God! I remember a similar situation when I won principal horn in all-shore concert band in New Jersey. Whenever I had a solo to play the entire horn section would peer down at me, almost in disbelief. As I mentioned in my first book, it wasn't their problem that they had never seen a Black French horn player. Nevertheless, we were all there and it was music that had brought us all together at such a tender age. And no one said anything racially, but I could certainly feel that my being there, playing principal horn, was a new experience for them.

To me, that's how it should be, like in your case, how would they have ever imagined that they would see a Black guy become principal bass. It was a thing that needed to happen, for everyone.

Principal Bass: [Laughing] I mean, you have me thinking about my church's Black History Month, Martin Luther King Day, it was like Christmas. [Laughing]

Author: Ha! Is that a fact?

Principal Bass: Yeah, because it was a celebration of Black culture and our contributions to this society. That stuff was so embedded in me, so I never went into those musical organizations with a defeatist attitude, because I was armed with this source of Black pride.

Author: Now that's great to hear, love it!

Principal Bass: I don't have the same stories that some Black folks have. I got over the other things that happened racially, because my career had blossomed and any racial stuff that came my way then, I just ignored. School was the same way, being Black at Curtis . . . people didn't know Curtis was always a very international school, I think it still is. Back then, 50 percent of the students were not from the United States.

Author: Right, I believe it.

Principal Bass: Culturally there was always this mass of internationals, which I thought was unique; however, we did have a little Black student alliance. At one point there were like five Black players in the Curtis Orchestra, so we felt like . . . we were like, like, taking over. [Laughing] Yeah, five Black people in that orchestra. Eric Compton, Melissa White, she's a soloist and plays in the Harlem String Quartet, Greg Thompson's a bass player, he's in Charlotte, Weston Sprott, trombone in a major orchestra now.

Author: Yeah, I heard about Weston, that is so impressive! And you guys were all at Curtis at the same time? I love it!

Principal Bass: Yeah . . . [Laughing] There was an oboist, who became associate principal of the Baltimore symphony, got his tenure, and resigned. He actually works at Curtis now on the administration staff. He's a bit younger than I am, maybe thirty-eight. He was a finalist, maybe even played a one year, as principal oboist with the San Francisco Opera Orchestra.

Author: Oh really?

Right, but remember you're standing on mighty shoulders, we all are, of our people who endured so much more, so it stands to reason, that things are easier for us and that we know how to cope with difficulties. By now, it should be in our DNA.

Principal Bass: I get the coping thing though. There was a time once when I was a student at Curtis. I was invited to play chamber music somewhere and had to play a solo or some exposed part in the music. There was apprehension as to whether I could play the part well, but I don't know really, see, but now it may have been conjecture, because I didn't know, know.

Does that make sense? I didn't know, know, what those people were thinking, but I do know that there may have been apprehension about whether I could play well. Because they know they're often doubtful and apprehensive about you. I've walked into many playing situations in my career where there may have been apprehension that is, I felt it. Then once I started playing, people were like, "Oh, okay. Never mind, we're fine." [Laughing]

Author: But it's their problem! It's their lack of knowledge and exposure to someone like you. They're like totally at wit's end, because they've never had to ascertain, instantly, as to whether a Black classical bass player could play. Also, when most of them my not even know any Black people and then you show up doing something that they think is so totally elitist themselves, it's a lot for them to process in a matter of seconds, like just before they shake hands with you, hence that awkwardness you sense in them.

So, you perceive from them this barrage of rapidly streaming questions in their white psyches which manifests itself as apprehension: "Oh? A Black person playing classical bass? Well, how did you? Where did you learn? How did you come to learn? Where did you study? Can you actually play???"

Principal Bass: There is one more thing that you made me think about particularly regarding the aspect of life's journey. With my upbringing, I learned a lot of Bible stories, between the Baptist Training Union, Sunday school, and all those different ways to learn stories.

Throughout the Bible, it's so interesting that there are so many stories of folks who had to overcome immense adversity.

Author: Yes indeed . . .

Principal Bass: Again, I think because that was so much a part of my upbringing, it helped with the discovery of my own purpose. Literally, as an individual, that understanding was it for me. It allowed me to take on things in the world with the perspective of yes, I know, everything is going to happen to try and prevent me from making [my success] be possible, but I'm going to put in all I can through faith and prayer, to get beyond it. I think that also played a major, major part in my not only being able to maneuver the bass, but to really almost deflect any of the negativity that may have been coming my way, to prevent me from reaching my dream. Does that make sense?

Author: Yes. . . . Of course and what these principals teach is that it's not about us. It's about the world at large and how to interface with those principals. There's a kind of universal theory and apparently you really internalized those principals.

Principal Bass: I really I did . . . [Laughing]

Author: Which is impressive that you absorbed that at such a young age. I grew up in the Black church as well and, well it was difficult to focus on those principals sometimes, because of the arm swinging from excited church members feeling the spirit, that resulted in me and my little brother getting hit in the face and being frightened by the swooning, foaming at the mouth, and screaming women. In fact, sometimes, my little brother and I felt we needed to escape by dropping down beneath the pews and crawling out, because we didn't understand what was happening. Also, in those days people didn't explain anything to children; we were expected to just do what we were told.

So, I guess, now that you mentioned it, I'm sure I did absorb some of those overcoming immense adversity concepts from Sunday school and Bible stories. I think they gave me the vision to imagine possibility instead of always defaulting to doubt.

I remember, whenever I auditioned or competed for anything, I always said to myself, "What if I won?" Just to do it out of youthful curiosity and imagining visions that I wanted to happen. I always thought that was fun to do. By the way, no one has talked about this like you have.

Principal Bass: How interesting . . .

Author: No, not quite the way you have. [Laughter] But that's the beauty of this project. That people get to see just how immensely different and diverse Black folks are in their respective personalities.

So, any final stories, anything "scary-racial" you'd like to share?

Principal Bass: Well, I think the other thing about me, and I should name them, I'm really busy, which makes me not the most social person. That said, I've had mostly, like literally 99 percent, wonderfully supportive colleagues while at work. As a Black musician, however, things have been said to me in passing—a micro-aggression, as they are called now—that may have made me pause. Things said . . . maybe by a board member or a colleague without their realization. I can't remember all the incidents, but I had a board member from one orchestra where I was playing say, "Oh, it's good you're helping your kind," regarding my community work. [Laughing]

Author: Ha!

Principal Bass: As if it's on me (there are so many layers to that) [Laughing] like it's on me, because I'm Black to then do the outreach (for them) to my community. No, I do the outreach, because we care about the whole of our community. Yes, I definitely had conversations like that. I've had other musicians say things like, "Oh, you're an affirmative action hire." There often seemed to be an active will to diminish my success, because there was no way I got this kind of success on my own merit.

Author: Yes, a classic rational on their part.

Principal Bass: So all these remarks I would put into a micro-aggression category.

Author: Of course . . .

Principal Bass: So nothing overtly racist for me, but when I moved to this town, probably the most direct thing that happened to me was when I was looking for an apartment. I was looking at a nice place near the concert hall. And I had an appointment to see the place, so I walked in, it was summertime, again I lift weights and I can get rather buff. I was wearing a short-sleeved T-shirt. So, I go into the rental office and the woman asked, "So, whadda do?" So, me being very modest, I said that I had just got a position with the orchestra in town. So, she said, "Oh! With our orchestra here? What do you do there? Because you obviously aren't a musician."

Author: "You're obviously not a musician?" Wow!

Principal Bass: Yes, she goes, you obviously aren't a musician.

Author: Gee, thanks . . .

Principal Bass: [Laughing] But again, I put that into a micro-aggression category and those things don't even phase me.

Author: But they're not even half-way conscience of such micro-aggressions. Imagine being that unconscious and unaware of how you see other people in the world? Wow!

I have a woman friend in a major southern symphony orchestra, and she believes it's a lot easier for Black women, in general, being in these orchestras, than for Black men. Mainly because Black men have different and far more severe, scary stereotypes than Black women, which I would surely have to agree.

So, in closing I must say to you that your story, your outlook, and the way you absorb the world, is very impressive. It was indeed a pleasure chatting with you.

Bass Trombone of a Major Southern California Symphony Orchestra

Author: So, you know, I always wanted to tell you, that I'd never heard anything or knew anything about you. Then, all of a sudden, there you were. None of the trombone players in the orchestra, who obviously knew of you, ever said anything to me about you. Then it always seemed odd to me that the musicians in the orchestra were never very forthcoming with their knowledge of another prominent Black classical instrumentalist to me, especially if said Black player, happened to be a great player.

Bass Trombone: Ya know, it's funny, I had a conversation with an African American trombonist who basically freelances in LA and also works in New York. We were talking about how you would think that all African American classical musicians would know each other, but we really don't.

Author: No, we don't, you're right.

Bass Trombone: And I think this book is a really good opportunity to at least hear each other's stories. Like there are African American players that I've at least heard of, for example there's this Black female tuba player who I think teaches in Baltimore. I'd heard about her for quite a long time, but never met her. Then I did this kind of compilation thing that was supposed to be on behalf of the Joe Biden presidency. It was potentially going to be part of his inaugural program. I don't know if they ever used it for that, but it's been on the internet and it got a lot of play, you know. And that was the first time I'd ever even played with this professor of tuba. It was amazing that I had never actually met her. And she's somebody that a lot of people knew about, but it seems really odd that Black classical musicians can have these parallel lives and parallel careers and never run into each other.

Author: Well, I had an interesting incident happen when we were playing Berlioz, Symphonie Fantastic. The tuba player had hired a young Black kid as the second tuba. I had never heard of the kid or seen him playing around town.

But this young tuba player behaved quite strangely when I noticed him walking right past the Black bass player in the orchestra and not wanting to even speak.

99

So, the bass player stopped him in his tracks with a very loud and reprimanding, "How ya doing BROTHER!!" Still, the young tuba player barley uttered a word and kept walking.

Later after the rehearsal I noticed him with the tuba player and few other brass players, talking his head off, gregariously, the only one talking. I was never introduced to the young tubist. I talked to the bass player about it, and he believed that the kid was told not to associate or speak with any of the Black players and that's just what he did.

Then I recall, in extreme contrast, to that strange, young tuba player, the celebrated trumpeter, Wynton Marsalis, walking through the entire Philharmonic to shake hands with all the Black players, before starting the rehearsal.

So, can you tell me a little about how you got started in music, how music came at you in life?

Bass Trombone: Well, I'm originally from Philadelphia and basically, I got started on trombone because in those days they had like, school groups. They actually had school bands and orchestras then. Then, there was a woman volunteer who came into one of the school groups who was looking for somebody to play the trombone and I was the tallest kid in the class, so I got chosen. I was kind of interested in music anyway; my parents weren't actually musicians, but they liked music, and I always heard it a lot of it growing up. Then my older sisters both played piano . . . and you know music seemed like a really good thing and I really, really enjoyed it. So, I started to learn trombone and I kind of got pretty lucky because . . . well this is kind of a surreal situation, me and two other people from my neighborhood . . . and I grew up in the ghetto. We went to a music magnet school in Philadelphia that was on the other side of town. That part of town was all blue-collar white people who really despised the fact that African Americans were coming to their school. And every day, and this is no exaggeration, we were beat up or on the verge of getting our butts kicked and hearing the N-word every day.

It was like, really unbelievable. I was a shy kid, not knowing anybody, I remember on the first day of class, taking my seat, the white students would get up and sit in another place in order not to be near the Black guy.

You know a lot of people don't think that kind of thing really exists, but it does. I mean, not only did I have to deal with regular school challenges, but I had to deal with that omnipresent racism all the time.

However, in the midst of all of that madness, there was this lady who was volunteering in the schools. She was like the opposite of my life experience, you know, she was old Philadelphia money. I don't know if you've ever heard of the Gimbels Department stores.

Author: Absolutely . . .

Bass Trombone: Well, her father and her uncles were the Gimbels Brothers.

Author: Oh, I see . . .

Bass Trombone: And her husband was from the family that owned Sears and Roebucks. So, they were like, well established in Philadelphia, you know, very old money.

Somehow, someway, they were really committed to donating to Historically Black Colleges and Universities. So she took her philanthropy one step further by involving herself in the magnet school I was attending. She would actually find the time to take the three of us Black kids around to all kinds of cultural stuff. We started going to museums, every possible type of museum we could possibly imagine. Then we would go to concerts, with the Philly orchestra, we would go to chamber music concerts, ballet, opera, you know it was the kind of stuff that I'd never really heard of . . . well, I'd heard of it, but I'd never had any real exposure to it.

It was one of those things that was really exciting for a kid that was in seventh grade. It was an unbelievable eye-opener for me.

Author: And there were three of you?

Bass Trombone: Yeah . . . three of us, who were all at this music magnet school for music, but we all ended up taking different paths.

One became an engineer; the other guy ended up being kind of an entrepreneur, and he started creating educational curriculums and became very successful. So, for the three of us, when you think of what might have been, growing up in the ghettos of Philadelphia, we really escaped the possible negative ghetto future, after our experiences with this philanthropic lady. The interesting thing about it was, even after that period of her exposing us to the world of art, she was still really interested in being a part of our lives. She actually kept in touch with us right up until she passed away. It was really kind of an influential thing, you know. I remember going to a Philly Orchestra concert and they were playing Also Sprach Zarathustra and Seiji Ozawa was conducting. And because she was such a big muckity-muck, her family gave money to the Philly Orchestra and all, she took me backstage and introduced me to Seiji Ozawa."

Author: Whoa! Good for her . . .

Bass Trombone: I was like, oh my God this guy is a famous conductor . . . and he was very nice. You know, and because of that exposure, I decided that the classical music thing was a real possibility for me. Then I started basically taking private trombone lessons at a school in Philadelphia, called the Settlement School. This school basically offered quite a lot, so not only did I have trombone lessons, I had ear training, music theory, and some chamber music. I was also able to do recitals and stuff like that. This was all from seventh grade through high school.

Author: Wow! Several years of great training.

Bass Trombone: Yeah, so when I got into college, I was able to skip first-year music theory, because I had already had that course at Settlement School. But I also got a chance to study trombone with some of the guys in the Philly Orchestra.

Author: Really?

Bass Trombone: However, I don't think they liked it, because I was like this ghetto kid coming in and for them it was just like another, you know, duty they had to perform. But they were really helpful to me. In fact, the bass trombonist I was studying with, I'll never forget, at the first lesson with him, he gave me some things to play, and I played them well I guess and the very first thing he said was, "It sounds like you're going after my job!"

Author: Ha! What . . . really?

Bass Trombone: I was like, oh my God! I was just this little high school kid, and I was a little intimidated, but I have to say, those lessons were great.

Author: So how did you manage to get lessons from this top professional in the Philly Orchestra? Did you just walk up to him and ask?

Bass Trombone: I got the lessons because of some kind of a grant. I don't remember the source of the grant, but it might have been because I was first trombone in All-City Orchestra, even though I was a bass trombonist. But I think it might have been because of that position. So, I did get to study with the two Philly orchestra guys at different times and for a kid my age, that was quite amazing. I felt very fortunate that I was able to do that.

Author: And all of this happened in high school?

Bass Trombone: Yeah, this was just before college. And then when I got to college, which was Oberlin College, you know, I only went there because my sister was already living in the City of Oberlin.

So, I thought it would be nice to go and audition for Oberlin College and spend a weekend with my sister while I was at it. But I had already gotten into Temple University, but Temple had a marching band. I had never played in a marching band, and I didn't want to start.

Author: No, no, you were wise, trust me, you didn't want to play in a marching band.

Bass Trombone: And they had a contingency, if I didn't play in their marching band, I wouldn't get a scholarship.

Author: Yup, that's always the deal.

Bass Trombone: So Oberlin offered me a scholarship and they didn't make me play in a marching band, well because they didn't have a marching band.

Author: Exactly, exactly . . . [Laughing]

Bass Trombone: So I went to Oberlin, and you know, at that point, I was thinking I would be a music education major and be a schoolteacher.

Author: Oh, not that!

Bass Trombone: But you know, as it turned out, my professor at Oberlin, he decided for me, as a freshman, that wasn't gonna be the case for me. I was gonna be a performer.

Author: Who did you study with at Oberlin?

Bass Trombone: Yeah, his name was Thomas Cramer. He was not a famous guy. He was a former graduate of Oberlin and after the Army, he taught there for the rest of his career. He was a great musician. One of the things I felt was good for me and that goes for the teachers from the Philly Orchestra is that none of them played for me at my lessons. I learned a great deal and from not having any of my trombone teachers play at my lesson, it forced me to develop and create my way, my own musical style as a musician without copying or imitating any of my teacher's playing or musical style.

Author: I see, it forced you to grow and develop into your imaginative own style. That's great.

Bass Trombone: Yeah, because we've all heard about, probably the most famous one, would be like Jacobs, who taught his student to imitate him exactly. What was great about my teacher at Oberlin was teaching me to be a musician first and not just a trombone player, but a musician, who plays the trombone.

Author: I like that, yeah . . .

Bass Trombone: So that was really drilled into me. And there was a point in time, I forget when he said this, but my teacher said to me that the biggest issue I was going to have in my career was that I was going to have to audition for other trombone players. Because they won't be able to recognize what you are as a musician, they will only be able to evaluate you as a trombonist. And you know, that really has turned out to be true.

Author: Absolutely . . .

Bass Trombone: You know what I'm talking about. You've been on these audition panels. You've heard these loud fast and high type players. Who can play the trombone and can punch in all the notes in all the right place but make no music to speak of when they play.

So that idea I was taught, of being a musician first, really did stick with me.

So basically, after school I went back to Philly for a few months. I hated my job; I had a little day job at a convenience store selling lottery tickets and cigarettes to people. So, I thought, *man I gotta get out of here*. So, I heard of an orchestra in Mexico that sounded interesting, so I sent them a letter telling them to let me know if they ever have an opening on trombone. I also sent out a few other letters to various orchestras.

Low and behold, I got a letter from the orchestra in Mexico, telling me that they did have an opening on trombone and that they would be auditioning in New York in four days. So, I literally quit my day job at that very moment and, you know, practiced for three and a half days and took the train to New York and ended up taking that audition. You know ironically the audition was held at the very same hotel that many famous players auditioned for various other orchestras.

Author: And which hotel was that?

Bass Trombone: Ah, the Hotel Wellington.

Author: Ah yes, I know it! Funny thing about auditioning in New York hotels. Back in the day most orchestra auditions, before audition screens and committees, players auditioned for conductors in their hotel rooms. Leaving them open for any kind of bias or discrimination. When I auditioned for the New England Conservatory it was in the same hotel that the famous American author F. Scott Fitzgerald and his wife had their honeymoon and held wild parties during the jazz age and Roaring Twenties. Yeah, so hotel auditions were a classic.

Bass Trombone: And when I think about it the audition for that Mexican orchestra was not for a large metropolitan symphony orchestra like Mexico City. It was for a much smaller city. Almost rural in size. In fact, they didn't really have any Black people in that city. I was literally, the only Black person in the town.

Author: I'm sure . . .

Bass Trombone: So when I got that job in Mexico, I was still twenty-one and dealing with what it was like to live in a foreign country and also you're dealing with the fact that you're the only African American in the entire area.

Author: So, did you learn Spanish?

Bass Trombone: Yeah, I did learn how to speak Spanish and I felt like I got pretty good at it too. At the end, I was dreaming in Spanish.

Author: Yes, that's the ultimate place to arrive in a language. Great.

Bass Trombone: You know I did what I could with that situation. I was still taking auditions in the States. I thought that was a thing I should keep going.

In fact, I took an audition in Nova Scotia and at the end of the audition, in my opinion, I was thinking that I had won the job and when I came out from behind the screen and they saw that I was African American, they said no.

Author: Whoa! Right then and there??

Bass Trombone: Well yeah, pretty much. When I came out from behind the screen, things kind of went silent. The committee adjourned for a bit and then came back to me and announced that they were going to hire the runner-up, the white guy.

Author: Amazing!

Bass Trombone: In fact the guy they gave the job to looked at me and said, "but you played better than me." So, I said, "Well okay, that's how it goes." So, when people ask me if there is really such a thing as discrimination, I tell them, yeah, there's more to overcome for African Americans than people readily want to admit.

But that was my destiny, as it were, but I kept trying and I ended up taking another audition, which I won and ended up playing in this orchestra in Hawaii. So, I was in Hawaii for about four years, which was a really great experience for me on so many levels, but probably the biggest feature was that the orchestra was mostly people of color, who lived there. There were lots of native Hawaiian islanders, Japanese, and Chinese. About only a third of the population was white.

So, because of the amazing number of different groups the first thing people ask you if they think you're a local is, "what race are you?" So, imagine how bizarre it was to me to have people come up to me and ask, "Hey, what race are you?"

Author: Ha! Crazy . . . [Laughing]

Bass Trombone: Because you know, in the states nobody ever asks you that. [Laughing] You're a Black man and that's it. But so many of the islanders have so many of the Black traits, some have nappy hair, dark skin, but because of so many of these like traits to Blackness, they can't always tell your race, so they just ask. As I said, I found that issue to be very interesting.

Author: What did the orchestra sound like? Was it a good group?

Bass Trombone: I thought it was a good group, you know, the conductor who hired me was really fantastic at identifying really talented young musicians. He wasn't a great conductor, but he did hire great talent and many of those players went on to get much bigger jobs. So, you can imagine what it was like, with all those really great players in one place, so yeah, I thought it was a really great orchestra and a great experience.

Author: And the whites were really in the minority?

Bass Trombone: Oh yeah, yeah, it was really, really . . . I don't know how to describe, it felt so validating. It was like yeah, there are really people of color here who look like me, who are happy to be people of color. It was amazing.

Author: I understand, you know I did Gateways [an all-Black symphony orchestra festival] a year ago and the playing level was so high, it sounded like a major orchestra. But you know, I could swear, when I listened to the string section, that the string sound in general was a bit darker and rounder than what I was used to hearing in an all-white string section like the Philharmonic. So, I asked the music director and he said, "Yes! It's colored, it's colored, that's why!" [Laughing]

Bass Trombone: [Laughing]

Author: But it was so interesting watching an all-Black string section play together, how they moved together and felt together. It was truly sublime for me.

Bass Trombone: Indeed! I think most people really don't understand what's that like.

Author: No, they don't.

Bass Trombone: I remember right after college when I started taking auditions and I went down to Florida to audition for an orchestra in Orlando. And because I didn't have much money in those days, I decided it might be cheaper to fly down and stay an entire week and stay with my cousin, who lived in this little town called Fellsmere, which was close to Orlando. So, another bass trombonist came down to Florida and we were both staying at my cousin's place. You know these small towns in the South were completely segregated. You know, basically in Fellsmere, there was the Black section of town and the white section of town.

So, my friend, the other trombone, was a white guy, staying in the Black section of Fellsmere, walks into a store, and he still talks about this to this day. That was the only time in his entire life that he ever walked into a place and he was the only white guy there. Describing how it felt to him to be the only white guy in that section of town. Not only in the town, but when he was with my family and the fact that there was nobody in that section of town that looked like him. I could see that it was a completely different experience for him. And I think many white people underestimate what that's like.

Author: Absolutely! Well, because it's hard to imagine as a white person, if you've never actually experienced the carnal reality of it.

Bass Trombone: Yeah, say for example, if a white person from the Philharmonic could do a sort of reverse optics on it and have them imagine what it would be like for them to be in an all-Black orchestra.

Author: You know, actually I experienced that feeling while on my way to Africa. I was flying out of Gatwick in London and before leaving for some reason I happened to notice the whiteness of London. Airplanes being serviced by white tech people and when I arrived in Ghana, West Africa, the entire world turned Black. Suddenly, Black tech people were servicing the airplanes and the entire populous was Black, jet Black.

I spent five weeks there traveling to neighboring countries like Ivory Coast and Nigeria. In fact one night I was out with my African friends and we entered a restaurant, and I noticed that the entire bar was filled with white men. To my great surprise, I said, "What are they doing here?" I couldn't believe that I actually said that. My African friends chuckled saying, "Getting comfortable being in the majority, brother?" The white men were all British who were actually born and raised in Accra, Ghana, which was at one time a British colony. Then a lot of African Americans will never really get a chance to experience such a thing, unless they travel to Africa.

Bass Trombone: Yeah, yeah, I ended up speaking a little bit about that with an African American woman who plays in the Cleveland orchestra. She said she had gone to Africa and had experienced the exact same phenomenon that you were talking about.

Author: Then one has to wonder, if being in the majority, surrounded by the false sense of security of it, even emboldened by it, if it makes it easier or even plausible for a person to venture or risk a micro-aggression on a minority, by making some kind of racist, off-colored joke?

Bass Trombone: Well in my orchestra, one of the brass players exhibited such behavior way too often. This guy was unbelievable, I remember we were on tour . . . I'll never forget this, we had one of the trombone players come on tour with us to support him because his orchestra was on strike. That trombone player was African American. So, a group of four or five orchestra members were sitting in a restaurant and this brass player that I mentioned was there and we were talking about famous movie lines.

So, this brass player started talking about a famous movie with Jeff Bridges, I don't recall the film title, but he talks quite a bit about the film and then he happened to glance over at me and my African American trombone friend and out of the blue, he asked the question, "What would you call the Flintstones if they were Black?" We all looked at him in disbelief and he said, "You'd call them The Niggers." I was like, you've gotta be kidding me!

Author: Yeah!

Bass Trombone: I thought, you've gotta be kidding me! I'm like halfway around the world and I've gotta hear somebody talking like that to me?

Author: You should've slapped him.

Bass Trombone: Yeah! I mean even at the time, one of the Asian string players overheard what that redneck said, and she was like, "What?" Then this guy had the nerve to say it again and that it was okay because we're talking about movies. So, I told him quite frankly, "No, no, you're talking about Black people plain and simple. Because no one else at the table said anything remotely close to that."

Author: And what did your trombone friend say?

Bass Trombone: Well he was offended for sure, but he didn't really say anything, of course, because he was a sub and just decided to stay out of it, but I was livid.

There was another incident on a different tour, when my wife was there and a friend of mine happened to ask my wife where she was from and this same brass player kind of joked and said, "Hey Mister, you wanna buy my sister?" I mean the guy was creepy racist like it was almost like he needed to wear a white sheet and burn a cross and that would be pretty much him.

Author: And you know he's a fundamentalist Christian and wouldn't you know it.

Bass Trombone: Yeah, well he's got the wrong fundamentals, if you ask me.

Author: Well, I had a problem with him during one of the rehearsals with the New Music Concerts. We were all just getting seated, and I turned around and asked if he could see, because I didn't want to sit in front of him. He responded with, "No, all I see is black!" So, the rehearsal started before I got a chance to respond to his comment. At the break though I went up to him and got in his space and said, "About your racist remark, you'd better watch your big mouth, or I will stomp you into the floor." I could see the guy next to him get a bit nervous. It's a bit like bullying, like you mentioned when you were dealing with that at your school. It's real effective to catch bullies off guard. I'm good at smashing bullies, because they are, in reality, the biggest cowards.

Bass Trombone: No doubt, because that guy was certainly in that category as far as I'm concerned. Yeah, I just found him hard to swallow.

Author: Really, sorry, I didn't know you had experienced that same problem with him as well.

Bass Trombone: Yeah, I think you had been out of the orchestra by then.

Author: Yeah, I think you're right.

Bass Trombone: I remember talking about it with another Black colleague in the orchestra, but I don't recall your being there. But yeah, that guy was overtly racist . . . I mean, you gotta be kidding me! That guy was a menace.

Author: Yeah, he thought he could actually get away with that racist bullshit. And to have the nerve to say that stuff in front of a group of people. I guess in his redneck mind, you were all supposed to have a big laugh along with him.

Bass Trombone: Well, that's who he is . . . he's got that arrogance about him. And the fact that it was all so hateful . . . and who knows why he does it? Maybe he's angry because of his size, who knows?

Author: Yeah, I recall that he was very sensitive about his height, but you would think someone like him would be cool and watch his big racist mouth to keep from getting stomped into the ground by someone.

Double Bass of a Major East Coast Symphony Orchestra

Author: So, you were the only one in your family that played a musical instrument?

Double Bass: Yes, but there was always like, recorded music playing in the house. And it was always great stuff. It was not necessarily classical music per se, but a lot of it was like, Motown, R&B, stuff like that playing constantly.

Author: Right, right . . . of course . . .

Double Bass: Music was a major part of my family's life, and I just happened to gravitate toward it. I went to public school and in those days, in was in the fourth grade that kids were allowed to start playing a musical instrument, if they wanted.

At that time, I was already learning to play the guitar, because I got a guitar for my birthday the summer before I started fourth grade. However, what I was learning on the guitar was the lower four strings and I was hearing basslines. I didn't know that I was actually learning to play the double bass at that time.

Author: Oh, right, interesting. [Laughing]

Double Bass: You know, I was playing stuff off of records I would hear and songs on the radio, things like that. When I got to public school, there were a few instruments to choose from and the closest instrument to what I wanted to play (the double bass) was the violin.

Author: Really?

Double Bass: Yeah, so that's what I first learned how to play. I played it from fourth grade until . . . the tenth grade. When I entered the tenth grade, my family had moved to a different school district and that district didn't have a string program, so I quit playing the violin pretty much for good.

So, you know, I just had to take percussion. I started playing snare drum in the marching band, and when the marching band season was over, I played the snare drum in the concert band and ended up being a percussionist. I have perfect pitch so I automatically became the timpanist, because I could tune the timpani without a pitch pipe.

Author: Well, you know a lot of percussionists don't have that kind of ear.

Double Bass: Right, right. . . . Then the school district started a string program in my senior year of high school. They had an orchestra, and by default, I was concertmaster of that orchestra.

Author: Really? So back to violin?

Double Bass: Yeah and I actually had to train the other string players, you know, the basic technique on how to play the violin, viola, and the double bass. I don't believe that school had any cellos at the time. So, by the time I graduated high school I was playing, percussion, violin, and bass guitar.

Author: Is that right? And you were teaching other students to play string instruments as well? Amazing!

Double Bass: Yeah, I was teaching the kids who played band instruments and who were interested in the newly formed string program. Many of them were trumpet players and clarinetists who volunteered to be in the orchestra. So, I had to show them some of the basic techniques of how to play a string instrument.

Author: Impressive. . . . I mean, learning and studying several instruments yourself and then teaching other students as well? Quite a lot to manage.

Double Bass: Yeah; however, I don't remember it being super challenging, because I think the kids really wanted to learn. Many of them were my friends, for the most part, so we were just basically having a good time.

Author: Amazing that you were able to do that.

Double Bass: So that public school district still has a string program to this day, and I think it's still pretty good.

Author: So, when did you start playing the double bass exclusively?

Double Bass: Yeah, so after high school, as I didn't really grow up in a classical music knowledgeable household, I ended up going to community college for two years and I was in the music program there. Plus, I was taking computer courses and all that kind of stuff. I was also playing three instruments at that time, you know. I was playing the violin in the college orchestra, and I was playing the bass guitar in the jazz ensemble and percussion in the college concert band.

Author: Wow! All that . . . impressive . . .

Double Bass: Yeah, at that school, the director of the jazz ensemble and the concertmaster of the college orchestra was the same person. He took me aside one day and told me, "If you want to be a professional musician, you will work so much more as a bass player than you would as a violinist and all those other instruments you play." His suggestion was that I drop the other instruments and concentrate on the double bass.

Author: Okay, interesting . . .

Double Bass: Another facet of this story about how I fell into becoming a double bass player exclusively is that I was playing in this orchestra at the community college, and we were preparing for a concert. At that time, I was playing in the second violin section but, in that orchestra, there were no bass players.

Author: Okay . . .

Double Bass: They actually played for weeks without a bass player so, eventually, I volunteered to play the bass and the rest is history from that point. I started to play bass exclusively and began to study with a really great player who was the associate principal bass of the Cleveland Orchestra, who brought me to a pretty good competent level, very quickly.

Author: Great . . . but you didn't go to a conservatory or a music school?

Double Bass: Well, at that point no, but then I ended up going to Youngstown State University, which had a fine music school called the Dana School of Music.

Author: I see, of course . . .

Double Bass: I went there for three years and then went for a master's degree at the Cleveland Institute of Music. After that I went to the University of Southern California for one year.

Author: University of Southern California, really?

Double Bass: Yep, studied with a very renown teacher who, at that time was teaching at Rice University as well. So, he alternated weeks teaching at both universities. I did some studying with Dennis Trembly at as well.

Author: Is that right? I think he just stepped down. The last time I saw my old orchestra he was in the back of the section.

Double Bass: Is he still playing in the orchestra?

Author: I'm not sure I'd have to check on that. Hmmm? I've been out of the orchestra over thirteen years now. When I see the orchestra these days, it looks like a different group.

Double Bass: You know, you and I did meet one time, I remember. It wasn't when I was at the University of Southern California, it was when my orchestra was on tour playing in your hall. That was in 2007.

Author: Oh, 2007? Did I behave when we met?

Double Bass: Yeah, of course . . . [Laughing] It was very brief, I think I was on my way out after the concert, and we briefly said hello. So, I do remember you from then.

Author: Okay so, 2007 . . . a year later I was out of there. Great so we did meet. I was joking with you, but you know that old adage, when one Black person is in an elevated position, said Black person would snub other Black folks in a lessor position. Well, I always sensed that sometimes, some Black folks assumed that I was like that because I was in the Philharmonic. So that's where my joking is coming from.

So, did you always have the idea in your mind to become a member of a major symphony orchestra?

Double Bass: Yeah, it was always a goal of mine because, at a pretty young age, maybe ten years old, I heard the Cleveland Orchestra for the first time on a field trip.

Author: Okay sweet . . .

Double Bass: Yeah, you know, that just . . . it just knocked me out and, in that moment, I just knew, that was what I wanted to do with my life. Oh, and there was one other particular inspiration I recall, and that was seeing an African American cellist in the Cleveland Orchestra named Donald White. He was one of the very first African Americans to play in a major symphony orchestra.

Author: Yes, exactly . . .

Double Bass: He was in that orchestra during the 1950s playing under Hungarian-born American conductor George Szell.

Author: The 1950s whew! Imagine what that was like for him as an African American in those days.

Double Bass: Yeah I mean, I heard stories about him going on tour with the orchestra in the South, but he had to opt out of touring with the orchestra because of threats from the Klu Klux Klan and stuff like that.

Author: I see, so they left him home?

Double Bass: No, but I heard that they had to somehow like . . . hide him.

Author: Yeah . . . I would've insisted on staying home for those southern tours.

Double Bass: Who knows, maybe that wasn't an option in those days.

Author: Perhaps you're right. Boy, but the 1950s was a hard time for black folks in any field. I got my job in 1970. I can't say that I had a lot of problems. It was post-1960s and racial things were a lot better, but I still had problems. But nothing like that Black cellist would have had in the 1950s. No one ever threw anything on stage at me or yelled, "Nigger get off the stage!" Something I always had in the back of my mind though. I've heard other horrible stories though, for example, a Black horn player who was hired to play substitute French horn for an opera orchestra and some of the players would walk by him, step on his feet, and kick him in the shins. His name was Robert Northern, a.k.a. Brother Ah. He played with Sun Ra's Arkestra and was a renowned jazz musician as well. I just missed meeting him before he passed away in 2020 when I was in Washington.

So, did you have anything approaching that kind of racial push-back? Hopefully not, but I was just curious.

Double Bass: Not so much, you know, when I came along like, the mid- to late 1980s I got my first professional job in 1989, with Atlanta through the Music Assistance Fund Fellowship.

Author: Ah! I see, I see, I remember that program.

Double Bass: However, there was only one other Black person in that orchestra at the time and I do recall some weird, kind of redneck dynamics back there in the brass section. I would hear some snide racist comments now and then. And you know, sometimes they were directed at me, because I sat basically right in front of them.

Author: Right, of course . . .

Double Bass: Other than that I didn't have any problems, people were basically fine.

Author: And how long did you play in that orchestra?

Double Bass: So the fellowship was two years long and then I got a job in the Florida Philharmonic, where I stayed for five years and then I won my present major orchestra position in 1996.

You know, perhaps I should tell you about the crazy audition experience I had for my present major orchestra job.

Author: I'm all ears.

Double Bass: So, I flew from Florida to the audition on Northwest Airlines. And I had my bass in a big fiberglass trunk under the plane. When I got to the audition, I had to rent a cargo van to transport my bass to the hotel. When I opened the transport trunk, my bass was damaged. The neck was broken completely off the bass.

Author: Wow! Insane!

Double Bass: It wasn't totally destroyed, but it was certainly unplayable.

Author: Of course . . .

Double Bass: You know, at that point I was pretty discouraged, so I called my wife and told her that my bass was broken, and I was coming home, and she said, "No, don't come home, you've worked too hard for this. Call somebody, there's gotta be somebody who has a bass that you can borrow."

Author: Sure, sure . . .

Double Bass: Right, actually I did know a violinist in the orchestra; he and I were roommates at Aspen. I called him and he gave me the phone number of a bass player in the orchestra. The bass player was very nice. He said, "Aw, no problem just come on over to the hall. The bass will be in the stall in the bass room." So, I met him at the hall, and I had about thirty minutes before my audition to warm up on a strange instrument that I'd never played.

Author: Oh boy, oh boy, crazy . . .

Double Bass: So I got on stage, passed through the first round and then the semi-finals as well.

You know I just . . . I think I kind of blanked out. I was so upset by that whole situation.

Author: Right, of course . . .

Double Bass: I barely remember what happened on stage while I was auditioning. I guess it was a blessing in a way because a lot of times I would get nervous at auditions, but in that case, I was just too flustered and upset, so nerves never even entered the picture.

Author: Interesting how that happens . . .

Double Bass: Yeah, yeah . . .

Author: But what a great show of support from your wife, to tell you to borrow a bass. That was so brilliant and timely.

Double Bass: Sure, for sure . . .

Author: So, then you went on to the finals?

Double Bass: I went on to the finals, but there were a few days between the first round of finals. I was still a little bit nervous because, remember, I was still playing on an instrument that wasn't my own.

Then the orchestra had a few performances during that time, and I had to return the bass to its owner in the orchestra. So, there were a few days when I had no bass at all and couldn't practice between the semi-final days and the finals.

Author: Ah! Boy . . . not good!

Double Bass: So that was tough, you know, but I ended up winning the job anyway. Actually, there were three vacancies at that time, and they only filled the one at that audition.

Author: Oh, really . . . how many basses did the orchestra normally carry?

Double Bass: Well, normally nine basses.

Author: Oh, nine I see . . .

Double Bass: Yeah, and the other two positions were filled like in the next concert season by two guys who were in the finals when I auditioned.

Author: So, when you got your job, the audition process was preliminaries, finals, and then super finals. Are you still behind the screen at that point? How does that work? It was quite different when I auditioned.

Double Bass: Yeah, there's a screen for the first two rounds and then the final round is without the screen.

Author: And you were the only finalist at your audition?

Double Bass: Ah, there were four finalists at that time. So, I guess they were very fair, not having a screen for the last four finalists.

Author: Oh, good to hear, because I've heard other stories, when a Black person came out from behind the screen there were audible gasps from the audition committee.

Double Bass: Yeah, I mean my journey has been a pretty fair and equitable one, you know.

Author: Yeah, I'm thinking that when you came along, circa 1996, things had slowly evolved into better overall. 1996, okay, so you've been there a while.

Double Bass: Yes, I have.

Author: And how is that working out for you. How's your section?

Double Bass: Yeah, it's a great orchestra, great bass section and when I arrived, I was one of four Black musicians on the roster. There was a violinist, a tympanist, and an orchestra keyboard player.

Author: Oh? Is that right?

Double Bass: That must have been some kind of a record in those days, I think. [Laughing]

Yeah, and when I talked to our orchestra keyboard player, who came along in the mid-1960s, she shared some real racial horror stories when she first joined the orchestra. She would tell those stories to me and the timpanist.

We are about the same age and got in the orchestra about the same time. She would always laugh at us, saying that we have it so easy now and have no idea what it was really like racially in her day.

Author: Indeed . . . so, anything else crazy to tell me?

Double Bass: No, I think that's all I've got, but I guess I could say the only other crazy thing is that I'm now juggling two careers as a full-time classical musician and a full-time jazz musician as well. And it's always been that way since I was in my early to mid-twenties, you know.

Author: So impressive. Thanks for sharing your journey. You are an amazingly talented and versatile giant of a musician.

Principal Percussionist of a Major Midwest Symphony Orchestra

Author: So where are you from originally?

Percussionist: Chicago, born and raised.

Author: And with whom did you study percussion?

Percussionist: I studied with Douglas Wadell and Patricia Dash, those were my first two teachers, and the list of teachers after that is way too long. I basically went to DePaul University, Chicago, studied with everybody there. Took a couple of lessons with Ian Dane and Keith Aleo, then the, the Detroit guys, the guys in Cleveland and Pittsburg guys, I took lessons with all of them and now I'm here. [Laughing]

Author: So go back a bit, how did you start playing? What got you into music to the degree that it took you to a major symphony orchestra?

Percussionist: Ah, lucky for me, I was always hitting and banging on stuff as a kid so my grandfather on my dad's side got me a drum set, a blue Micky Mouse drum set, when I was three years old. I was also hitting stuff at church, and I played a couple of times on the drum set there. And I was fortunate enough to receive a scholarship through the Chicago Symphony to receive free lessons from fourth grade until I graduated high school. So that's how I met Doug and Patsy, and they're still like my percussion mom and dad.

Author: Right, of course . . . so when you start out as a percussionist, is there one particular instrument that initially attracts you and later you find out that there are a lot more, how does that usually work?

Percussionist: Starting lessons on drum set, I thought that was what we would be doing, but we started lessons on a drum pad and so I was like, what is this? Where is the drum set?

Author: That's what I meant . . . [Laughing]

Percussionist: Yeah, so in the beginning my teachers basically took me through all the basic technique starting with drum pad and then an actual snare drum and then they added mallets instruments, which I was really horrible at starting out.

Author: I see . . .

Percussionist: Yeah, that's kind of how it grew from the drum pad. From there they added tympany and started adding accessories. They encouraged me to become a professional percussionist, because of how well I was progressing, up until I was about fifteen or sixteen.

Author: So, who encouraged you?

Percussionist: Ah, Doug and Patsy, they were the ones who said, "You should consider doing this for a living, because you're doing very well with us. We think you can make it if you really wanna do it."

Author: So mallets? I think would be the hardest part of playing percussion. I know I would have a hard time with mallets. It's an instrument one never considers about percussion.

Percussionist: [Laughing]

Author: So, tell me more crazy stuff. It seems you had a lot of support and all the instruction one could ever wish for coming up.

Percussionist: Yeah, I was very, very lucky. At that point in my playing, with the reach? I have now, everybody knows, my basic story, oh, yeah, that one guy who started on the Mickey Mouse drum set. Like if you say the Mickey Mouse drum set, everybody knows it's me. [Laughing]

Author: [Laughing] Is that really a thing?

Percussionist: It's really a thing.

Author: Well, okay, crazy, a Mickey Mouse drum set? And that's how people always knew it was you? But who knows, Vic Firth might've started out on a Mickey Mouse drum set. [Laughing]

Percussionist: Unfortunately, as far as I know, there have only been two principal percussionists who have been Black in any major orchestra in this country.

So, I have a story that I have never told publicly and it's about what happened on my very first orchestra job. Let me say first, the reason I want to share this story is for the sake of my mental health. I felt that keeping silent had caused me a lot of turmoil, unrest, and unnecessary stress.

So, I'm hoping that coming out publicly with this story, with this degree of anonymity will give me some sense of closure. So that's what I'm hoping for.

Author: Okay, so you're comfortable with having this story being published?

Percussionist: Oh yeah, this is definitely fine, with this amount of anonymity and the way the story will be told, I think this is comfortable for me and I don't foresee anything bad happening.

Author: So how old were you when this happened? Were you right out of school?

Percussionist: No, this happened after I had already done a couple of small gigs here and there. I had been able to play principal percussion in some areas and in some symphonies. I got to do the actual job of principal percussion, so I'd know at least what was expected and was useful and has worked in the past. I asked my mentors at that point, what they did when they played principal, what were their systems that they used and things like that. I made sure to ask all my mentors all the advice before I started.

Author: Okay.

Percussionist: As you know, as an untenured orchestra member, there are a list of unwritten rules of not rocking the boat. Not making too many changes, especially as a new principal. Kind of saying yes and staying under the radar until you get into the tenure position.

Author: Right . . . so it's a pretty stressful situation already, trying to do your job, with that fear and some other stressors. Let me ask you this. I've never heard of this particular line of thinking about tenure dos and don'ts. Who was it that laid out that line of thinking and behavior? I find that interesting.

Percussionist: Ah fortunately, for me some of my mentors, who either were principals or had similar experiences, they noticed that audition panels for certain orchestras might feel a little bit uneasy, if let's say, you're a new principal and instead of hiring the substitute players that had been playing there for say, the last fifteen years, you start only hiring your best friends

Author: Oh, okay. I see . . .

Percussionist: Yeah, things like that, things you would consider common sense, but it's still good to have some semblance of respecting the tradition of the orchestra, as well as having opportunities so that you can implement your own style. That's kind of the job of a principal anyway. You just have to find a way to do that in a graceful way that doesn't make you seem like you're dictating.

Author: And where did you go to school, did I miss that?

Percussionist: Oh, I went to DePaul School of Music for my undergrad and then I did half a semester at the Cleveland Institute and another half-semester at Carnegie Melon.

Author: Okay, so you auditioned for your first job right after school?

Percussionist: Yes, it was during my first semester at Carnegie Melon. I auditioned for principal percussion, which became my first major job.

Author: Great, so what happened there?

Percussionist: Okay, so, here begins the story: Upon arriving, I was introduced at my first orchestra job; I was introduced to all the local substitute percussionists. A great community of people, an amazing community of percussionists. One of the subs was, however, slightly different. While this sub seemed to get along with all the others, for some reason there was a lot of passive aggressive tones of actions from this person directed toward me. I was then told by many orchestra members that this was normal behavior for that particular sub and that it might take him a minute to get comfortable with me. Of course, being who I am [Laughing], a pretty easygoing guy, I believed them and just went on and did my thing and hoped for the best. Unfortunately, that discomfort from that sub would only escalate in my case.

So, the very first concert that I was in charge of as the new principal percussionist, I alerted the subs on a Friday that the parts would be available on the following Monday. So, I got a response from the disgruntled sub saying, "does it take three days to assign parts?" Of course, I responded to it saying, being in a new job and my first time doing this and that in the future, I would hope to improve and be more efficient, so that it won't take three days. When I did get the assignments out, I assigned a different sub, who was, I guess, technically second on the sub list or lower on the sub totem pole. I gave him a part that would be considered the number two part on a piece, alongside myself.

Author: Okay.

Percussionist: I was then contacted again by the same disgruntled sub with a message, basically stating that he was higher up on the sub list and that he should've gotten the second part instead of the other sub.

Author: Oh, okay. God!

Percussionist: Yeah, so I again responded with something like, as a new principal I'm trying to get a sense of everybody's skills. What they're good at what instruments they sound good on. So, you try to do that, within low stress situations like a pops concert. Like assign them triangle on a pops concert to see how well they do on triangle. I wouldn't risk that at a classical music concert.

Author: I see . . .

Percussionist: So I tried to explain that to them and that's the first episode of my existence there.

Then there was an opera thing that happened. So, the first opera that I was in charge of I had made a mistake with the instrumentation. The thing about percussion is, if you don't use the correct definition, for example, Glocken could mean chimes or an orchestra bell set.

So, the translation I ended up using said tubular bells and not orchestra bells. So, the first rehearsal comes around and one of the subs asked the conductor what the appropriate instrument was, and the conductor said, "orchestra bells." Now, if you know the conductor says for you to use a different instrument, you should probably just do it. But this one sub relayed the information to me that the conductor said it was orchestra bells. Then that sub said to me, "No, I'm going to play the instrument that you assigned me and if I get yelled at, I'm gonna blame you."

Author: Oh, thank you, chickenshit . . .

Percussionist: Yeah, so why do I venture these encounters? In any other orchestra behavior like this would be immediately dealt with or the sub would be removed completely. Every one of my mentors I asked about this, would ask me, "Why is he still there?"

Author: Indeed . . .

Percussionist: Well, this was a special case [Laughing] for a few reasons: At that point of the sub's employment with the orchestra, those subs had a reputation of that behavior and it had been tolerated, accepted, and normalized. So, whenever I approached either my liaison for the tenure committee or the personnel manager about any of those situations with the subs, they assured me that they would talk them down. My liaison stated that they wanted to keep that sub around, because he was a reliable percussionist and timpani substitute.

My liaison and the personnel manager assumed that at some point the sub would eventually get used to me (the new person) and it wouldn't be a problem.

Author: Really?

Percussionist: Now, that was the point that I began to question things, because that was like month two on the job. I mean for them to be protective of those subs for that kind of behavior against a full-time orchestra member, was a huge red flag immediately.

Author: Yeah . . .

Percussionist: I mean, it's hard enough for a new player, having the pressure of getting tenure, number one, coupled with a colleague who is disgruntled creating a very big stress for me. So, two big stressors already, after only two months on the job.

Month number three is where things got really bad. Unfortunately, I found out that I had a life-threatening medical condition that needed immediate attention.

Author: My God! What type of condition?

Percussionist: I was diagnosed with cancer.

Author: Ah, so sorry to hear that.

Percussionist: Yeah, I talked to Keith Aleo about this, and we just laughed. We just couldn't believe how domino effect this was after all the other stuff that had happened since I got hired on that job. I didn't really make it public that I had cancer until I had gone through the whole treatment process. I never even talked about it online. But fortunately for me, given the schedule, the end of the orchestra season wasn't that percussion heavy. So, I opted to take that time off to prepare for and start my treatment from the end of the concert season through that summer.

Author: May I ask what type of cancer?

Percussionist: It was a soft tissue cancer that grows out of blood vessels. It was actually a tumor. A seven by three-and-a-half inch tumor lodged in my lower left abdominal cavity. It was like I was having a baby. [Laughing]

Author: Yeah! [Laughing] Soft tissue, that's a new one on me, that sounds huge!

Percussionist: So picture like a small football lodged in your stomach.

Author: Yeah . . . wow! Amazing!

Percussionist: So I took treatments and basically had to take short-term disability, which I'll touch on later. I took off the rest of the season, took treatments from the end of the orchestra season through the summer. While I had the option to continue taking time off, the following season, I opted to continue my treatments and also work full time with the symphony.

Author: Unbelievable . . .

Percussionist: Some days I went to treatment in the morning and showed up for rehearsal immediately afterwards.

Author: So, there were no serious symptoms with this cancer?

Percussionist: Luckily for me the only symptom was fatigue. The medication they had me on, they were very surprised I didn't have that many adverse effects. But you are very tired after that chemotherapy which really takes it out of you.

Author: Yes, yes, I've heard.

Percussionist: But obviously I was able to do my job as far as playing goes, at a high level, so that no one could basically say anything. I was playing the best that I would ever play. But I did this because I wanted to show my dedication to the orchestra, despite my disease. Of course, I was thinking I would gain support of the orchestra and maybe even earn the respect of the sub. As you can imagine, dealing with a disease that will affect some productivity in some manner was expected, you kind of expect that.

Author: For sure . . .

Percussionist: In every instance, whether it was an assignment list coming out less than two weeks before a rehearsal or listing temple block as wood block for the piece Sleigh Ride.

The disgruntled sub was right there to correct me at every single turn. Of course, I ignored him basically, because . . . I didn't care at that point. I was doing my job; concerts were going just fine. No one was complaining about the musical integrity of the concerts, everyone was playing their parts well. I ignored the disgruntled sub, until I was made aware of a horrifying detail.

Author: Oh?

Percussionist: My tenure liaison of the orchestra was contacting all of the subs to ask how I was doing, as far as my work was going.

Author: What?? The subs??

Percussionist: The subs!

Author: And who was consulting the subs again?

Percussionist: The tenure liaison of the orchestra!

Author: Of the orchestra? No?

Percussionist: Yes, a tenured member of the orchestra's tenure liaison committee, was, in fact, asking the subs how the tenured track musician was doing.

Author: As if they had anything to say about it. I can't believe this! It sounds so . . . what's the R-word? Racist . . . did I say racist? [Laughing]

Percussionist: Oh, oh, just wait until we get there! [Laughing] So obviously you know how the orchestra process works. That tenure situation in that orchestra is very uncommon. However, it is done that way in some orchestras. However, with the knowledge that one of the subs had some sort of animosity (i.e., racist) toward me, you would think the liaison committee wouldn't ask the subs anything or take their word for anything, knowing that those subs had it out for me.

Author: Of course . . .

Percussionist: Unfortunately, the tenure liaison was constantly asking and consulting with the disgruntled sub about how I was doing my job. However, the tenure liaison assured me that they took everything they were told about me, with a grain of salt.

Author: Because?

Percussionist: [Laughing] They knew that person has been a problem for me in the past, will be a problem in the future, doesn't like me, and has threatened me.

Author: Threatened you?

Percussionist: Yeah, when he said he'd tell the conductor that I told him to use the wrong instrument, so I'd get blamed, kind of thing. The liaison knew about that whole situation too.

Author: I see . . . God!

Percussionist: Yeah! So, at this point, I really dig in my heels and think, something's wrong, let me ask my mentors for some advice. After telling my mentors the background stories and exactly what the tenure liaison was doing, like garnering information from subs, they all asked me the same question. "What does your contract say? Where is the tenure panel allowed to get info about you from regarding your tenure?"

Lo and behold, in black and white, my contract stated that the tenure panel cannot garner information about a tenure track member from non-full-time members of the orchestra. Also, they cannot garner information from anyone who has also auditioned for the same position won by the tenured track musician.

Author: Duh!

Percussionist: I didn't know this at the time, until I asked, but I learned that the disgruntled sub did take the very same audition that I won.

Author: Oh?

Percussionist: Not only did the disgruntled sub take the audition, but another one of the subs also took it, but lucky for me, that other sub loves me. [Laughing] But, contractually, they still shouldn't have been asked about me regarding my tenure either.

Author: Ah, no . . .

Percussionist: This is at the point, where again, I'm like, okay, if they're breaching the contract willingly and all that crazy stuff was going on. I thought, I've got to get back on the audition scene.

So, I was dealing with tenure stress, toxic work environment, sudden illness, pressure to work through sudden illness, and now pressure to get another job, even before being denied tenure or fired. What else could go wrong? [Laughing]

Author: So, then you were ready to get out of that orchestra and audition somewhere else?

Percussionist: Oh yeah! So, I was working through an illness, getting debilitating treatments for the illness, and preparing for an audition.

Author: Impressive, to say the least.

Percussionist: But unfortunately, the next thing was the treatment that I was going through was not working the way the doctors had hoped and the next solution was major surgery. To prepare for the surgery, I had to do radiation treatments. So, what did I do? I got radiation treatments in the morning and went to orchestra rehearsal in the afternoon.

Author: Gee . . .

Percussionist: I did that routine from the beginning of December to the end of the month.

Author: And how old were you then?

Percussionist: Ah, twenty-seven . . .

Author: Okay, that's why, you were a young man.

Percussionist: [Laughing] I was . . . yeah, call it, youthful ignorance. So basically, I worked all the way up until about a week before the surgery and yes, I took an audition three days before the surgery occurred.

Author: Insane . . .

Percussionist: Probably shouldn't have done that, but I did. Cause, I had to win another job.

Author: Of course . . .

Percussionist: Lucky for me, the surgery was a huge success and recovery looked to be super, super good.

Author: Great . . .

Percussionist: Again, I had the option to take more recovery leave from the orchestra, but did I? Nope, three months after surgery, I was back at work. Still recovering, but luckily for me, as principal I could choose to play as much as I wanted. So, I decided to come back and play as much as I could, but still take it easy like playing triangle on a piece or even smaller parts.

Author: Sure . . .

Percussionist: I had to rest and take it easy. So, during that time, while still recovering from surgery, but still trying to work, I was criticized by the disgruntled sub for taking small parts during movie score concerts. I was criticized for not having part assignments ready two weeks before I returned from surgery. I was criticized for assigning exposed parts to those considered to be the lower subs on pops concerts. All of that while still recovering from surgery, of course.

Author: Right . . .

Percussionist: Now, I'm still of the mind, get out, get a new job as soon as possible. So, I requested to take some time off for an audition that was not too far away. It just happened that the audition happened to be on the same day of my tenure vote. Of course, I had not been told anything about my tenure vote up to that point.

Author: How many years was your tenure probation?

Percussionist: I think it was two years but considering my time off for my surgery. I hadn't really been there exactly two years. You think they would've moved my tenure date. In any case, I still took my audition regardless of when they were voting.

So unfortunately, I didn't win the audition and when I returned to work, I found out that the committee wanted to extend my probation and tenure vote until the following season. Taken at face value, that made perfect sense. I had taken a good amount of time off during the season and well, one would think that would be the reason for the extension. [Laughing]

Author: Yeah, wasn't it?

Percussionist: The reason for the extension was to give me a chance to improve on my management skills.

Author: What? What? Management skills?

Percussionist: So the conversation with my tenure liaison went something like this: "The subs tell me that assignments and things have been late occasionally." Of course, I responded that yes, it was difficult juggling medical appointments at the same time. [Laughing] The liaison went on to say, "The subs say you don't make set-up charts." Normally for percussion there are a lot of equipment items we have to set up on stage. But, for concerts that call for, let's say, bass drum and cymbals, you probably don't need a map.

Author: Ha . . . of course . . .

Percussionist: That's basically what I said to my tenure liaison. As far as distributing assignments, I use a Google Drive folder. So that all the subs can get access to their respective assignments. You'd be surprised how many percussionists use Google. [Laughing]

Author: Right . . .

Percussionist: So my liaison told me that the subs say that the Google folder is not working for them. They say it's too confusing. Note that there was a folder for everything. [Laughing] There was a folder for assignments and all they had to do was look up the name of the concert cycle and they'd find what they needed. Then, of course, none of the subs told me that the Google folder was confusing for them. So that's what I told my liaison; I had no idea the folder was a problem.

Then, oh then, the final statement from my liaison. And I quote, "You know, we were really worried that we were going to lose you to the other orchestra last night. Had we voted last night, you likely would've gotten a majority vote. But we thought it would feel better knowing you got a unanimous vote instead. We also think this is a great learning experience to go through this entire process and improve as much as you can. When you get a handle on your management skills, that's when we'll be really worried."

Author: Worried?

Percussionist: Worried to lose me.

Author: I see . . . Hmmm?

Percussionist: I was then instructed to include a paper copy of part assignments instead of charts in all of the sub's individual folders on top of all the other requests that I got. Now, that is not uncommon, but if you're a sub, you'd never expect this kind of babying. [Laughing]

So of course, I take this as, okay, you want me to do this? I'm going to do this so well that you won't have anything to say. That was kind of the running theme of my career. I'm going to do the so well that no one can say anything about anything.

Author: Okay.

Percussionist: So that June, I proceeded to assign parts for the entire season.

Author: Oh!

Percussionist: Every part I had access to, everything I could get music for, and I sent it to all the subs via email and again through my Google folder, because I was adamant to keep that going, because that was the best way that I saw to get everything out. I opted to not only have the Google folder but also email the part assignments as they came around, so the subs had access via email and Google Drive, so two ways. And I had everything sent on the first day of July, three months in advance of the concert season. Pretty good, right?

Author: Really?

Percussionist: [Laughing] Oooooh boy! The first concert of the new season, I was asked by the same disgruntled sub why I didn't assign a specific percussion part, where at the time I was assigning parts, I believed would've been impossible to get to on stage, considering the stage situation we were in and we didn't have that many players to cover everything easily and I thought it would be too convoluted. The disgruntled sub complained to the personnel manager about the part assignments and one of the other subs told me that there was a problem.

So, I braced myself for the inevitable email, which was: "The conductor would like to meet with you."

Now given, number one, my distrust for the integrity of all parties involved, not only my liaison, but also the personnel manager and the disgruntled sub, all of them. At that point the conductor really didn't know what was going on. So, I chose to go and talk to the conductor first, before anyone else got to him. To give as much of my perspective as possible.

To avoid anyone else coming in with their many different tainted lies. I had the wherewithal to have a witness present, thank God! So, everything would remain kosher, and it wasn't just a two- person meeting.

Author: What was the complaint really?

Percussionist: That, again, assignments weren't coming in on time. I wasn't doing a good job assigning parts. Basically, the way the subs and the personnel manager put it to the conductor was, nothing was improving on my part. So, in my private meeting with the conductor he said, "They told me nothing was improving."

Author: What?

Percussionist: So, I gave them the entire assignment list that I did in July for the entire season. I told them about the subs and their issues with me. I told them basically everything, within five minutes before rehearsal. Fortunately, all of the issues that I presented the conductor took very seriously. Given the information I gave the conductor and my one witness, they concluded since everything seemed to be working that there was no need for another meeting. So, I thought okay, great. It got worse.

The conductor told the personnel manager that the meeting was off. The personnel manager said, "No, we're still having this meeting."

Author: Huh! Really?

Percussionist: Then I was approached by the personnel manager in a very aggressive tone saying,

"As far as I'm concerned, this meeting is still happening, I'll see you after rehearsal." Again, I wanted to have a witness there on my behalf. I didn't want to go into a meeting with the conductor, the personnel manager, and myself. I needed someone else to be present as a buffer. Unfortunately for me the only person available was my liaison.

Author: Oh, my God . . .

Percussionist: I figured, you know, how bad could it be? [Laughing]

Author: Exactly . . .

Percussionist: The meeting went as follows: The personnel manager was offended that I spoke to the conductor alone and saw it as an attempt to deflect my responsibility. The personnel manager stated that if another situation like my meeting alone with the conductor occurred, he would immediately resign. In addition, they also stated in that meeting that I had been deflecting ever since I'd gotten there. They said that if I didn't want to be uncomfortable, that my position was supposed to be uncomfortable.

That I could either be uncomfortable now or uncomfortable without a job. They repeatedly said that they were not my enemy and then mentioned how they helped get my short-term disability forms when I couldn't afford rent.

Author: What?

Percussionist: They said that the Google Doc method did not work and that all the subs were confused and complaining about things not being clear on the work assignments. They stated that assignments were late, but I immediately rebutted that. They also stated that they wanted me to succeed, because they didn't want to have another percussion audition because it was a nightmare for them.

They went on to say that the subs were not my enemy, they were just frustrated at seeing things that could be done better. Of course, I tried to go into specifics about that, but the personnel manager didn't want to get into it.

So, the conductor, obviously seeing my discomfort kept trying to bring it back to just trying to have assignment given as early as possible, you know, just trying to calm things down. The personnel manager went on to say that I should email the section about any detail that was going on. Like telling them to check their assignments as soon as they were available, constantly telling them what's going on.

Surprisingly to me, my liaison stepped in and said that this disgruntled sub has been difficult and that I had been under a lot of pressure given the behavior of the subs, with the process of the tenure thing and my illness. That they would be willing to supervise my work and duties so that they would be able to better defend me in case something comes up and there's another complaint and they can corroborate on statements made. Which I guess made sense, but of course at that point, I was ready to do anything. [Laughing]

Author: Ah, may I address the big greasy elephant in the room? [Laughing] What in hell did the subs have to do with deciding on your hiring, tenure, or anything about your situation? How could your liaison consult people who are not even members of your orchestra? Didn't you say a while back that type of thing was against the contract? Am I missing something here?

Percussionist: Those subs, especially the disgruntled one, had been playing with the orchestra a while, not even a while, about three years. [Laughing] Even the former principal percussionist had issues with that disgruntled sub. That problem had been going on for years.

Author: Again, my question is why would your orchestra consult outside players about you? Were there no other criteria to judge you?

Percussionist: Yeah, unfortunately with that orchestra there was only one percussion player hired and that player is the principal, and they hire subs when they need more players.

Author: Okay. Okay. I see . . . just one person?

Percussionist: Yeah, but to your point, with the same logic, there could be a situation with the principal piccolo; asking substitute piccolo players how the principal piccolo is doing as a player is completely off base. That would be like not asking the woodwind section of the orchestra, but asking the subs. [Laughing]

Author: That's what I'm saying.

Percussionist: The logic is stupid.

Author: And how come this one disgruntled sub in your section was allowed to stick around for so long? He must have been a crony of someone in management. I mean it's hard enough to get a job as a sub in one of these orchestras, and if you're gonna act a fool on top of it, such a person would or should be dismissed.

Percussionist: Yeah, but the next chapter of this story is the Musicians' Union. We're at the half-way point, luckily, thank God!

Author: Okay.

Percussionist: So, obviously everything was going wrong. After that meeting with the conductor and the personnel manager and my witness. This was where I thought, nothing was going right with the orchestra, I needed to go to the Musicians' Union.

After relaying all of the information to the union representative, the conclusion was that I should do everything the tenure panel requested of me as consistently and irrefutable as possible before the upcoming tenure vote, which was happening two months later. Also, I should consider filing a grievance against the disgruntled sub. [Laughing] Now at that point that conclusion didn't really do anything for me, because the entire process was tainted. And there was no way I was going to add to my stress with a grievance dispute, while still having to work with the disgruntled sub.

Of course, I opted again to just let the process run its course, do what I was supposed to do and just focus on auditioning and getting out of the situation. So, before the next process I talked to my liaison and basically poured my heart out and they assured me that they would take my words into account before the next tenure vote. But also, they asked me to ask myself if I had done everything I was supposed to do as perfectly as I could have.

So, the tenure came and went, and they decided to extend it again. They said there was more improvement needed from me. So at that point the liaisons meetings were about observing my work and stuff like that to check-in with them.

Things were going fine no issues were found with my work other than to let the subs know when I wasn't making a set up chart for a specific concert, which was the only issue.

Author: Ah hello! Another big greasy elephant in the room! Why were they only judging you on how you ran the section? All this about your leadership? Why was there nothing said so far about you as a player? Da! Who in hell has ever gotten tenue based solely on section leadership? What about you as a player plain and simple? God!

Percussionist: Oh, I'm so glad you said that. That's the next section I want to point out. There had never been a comment on the quality of my playing!

Author: Hello!!

Percussionist: "here had never been any comment on the sound of the section or its musical integrity, the quality of the concerts, nothing of that sort in the context of tenure meetings, or criticisms pertaining to the tenure vote had ever been made. Whenever any of those things were mentioned, it was in an informal setting and the responses were always positive.

Author: It seems up to that point all they had been focusing on were complaints from a bunch of disgruntled white substitute percussion players who were constantly sizing up the new Black guy. I'm sorry, but that's what it all sounds like.

Percussionist: [Laughing] So the next thing that happened, you'd think that would be the last straw. The next ordeal was the absolute last straw for me. It was like, I had to win another job, or I didn't know what I was going to do.

Author: I understand . . .

Percussionist: What happened next was a blatant attempt at sabotage. Again, at that point I was meeting regularly with the liaison committee. So, they saw all my work and how I managed the percussion section. They were basically able to corroborate any statements I made to my section.

So, any time the sub gave them a bullshit comment they could say, "No, he's been doing this. We don't see what you're talking about." So, there was nothing the sub or subs could fabricate about me on the management level. However, a concert cycle came up where there were three different concerts within one week. So, what I did was assign parts to the subs and then distribute the music to them.

I chose instead, for that particular week, to make one folder for each sub for the entire three weeks instead of making three separate folders, one for each of the different weeks.

Author: Okay.

Percussionist: Made sense . . . in my mind. A day before the first rehearsal, I received a message from the liaison that the disgruntled sub was missing music for that concert cycle. Of course, I panicked, so I checked the pick-up area, nothing. I checked the music library; they didn't have it. I emailed the other subs to check their folders; they didn't have it. I checked all of my music folders. Couldn't find it.

Author: I smell a big rat!

Percussionist: So [Laughing] again I emailed the other sub to ask if the music was in the folder that I gave each of them. Their response: "Yes, it's here. You can't expect me to know that all the music in one folder is for different concerts."

Author: That was the disgruntled sub?

Percussionist: Yep . . . [Laughing]

Author: Ah, I almost want to say, run that by me again, but really? He just pretended he didn't have the part, just to sabotage you?

Percussionist: Yeah, I guess the way that sub worked and thought, that one music folder was for one concert cycle. Instead of looking through all the music, like one should as a sub, to make sure all the parts were there. So, either the subs didn't look and didn't know the parts were there or they knew and played dumb?

Author: But I still don't like that those subs were allowed to have so much judgment of you, as a tenure track musician of an orchestra of which they were not even members. That just seemed like pure white racism and not orchestra or union policy.

Percussionist: Of course I told the liaison about the situation, and they said they would talk to the disgruntled sub again. Though I never heard anything further from them about that conversation or whether it even took place. Again, at that point I thought, I'm just going to win the next audition and be gone.

And that's what I did. [Laughing] Again, because the tenure review panel at that time was showing concern that I was actually auditioning, even though many of the members of that same orchestra were also on the audition circuit. Of course, I chose to hide any intentions of taking an audition.

Fortunately for me the next audition I took was on an off day from my orchestra job. I was so lucky to not have had to ask for permission to get off, which would've made everything worse.

Author: For sure . . .

Percussionist: So, I just said I was visiting family.

Author: Why would you have to tell the orchestra anything. It was a day off from the orchestra.

Percussionist: Yeah, and my colleagues were like, "Oh, so what are you doing on the day off?"

I think I told them I was going to take a lesson with my teacher, which I did, yeah.

So, I took the audition and got some text messages from several people asking, "Wait, did you just win an audition?" [Laughing] And I was like, yes!

Author: And that was for your present orchestra position?

Percussionist: Yup! Big time! [Laughing] Fortunately, I won the audition and returned back to my orchestra job with mixed reactions, of course.

That is where it should've ended! That's where everything should've been like, yay, he moved on, all the issues in the percussion section stopped, great. Here's what happened next. As you know, when an orchestra member wins a job in another orchestra there's an amount of leverage that player has. Especially for an untenured member. Then said member might ask for ask for an early tenure vote or perhaps a contract renegotiation if tenure was granted. So, my thought process was, I would ask for an early tenure vote and then ask for more money.

Author: So, the orchestra knew you had won an audition?

Percussionist: Oh yeah, oh yeah, I made it very clear. Honestly, I think even when I did win, I didn't announce it publicly. I just returned to work with the orchestra and word of mouth got around and I let social media handle it. So when I asked for early tenure, that was only after I think the personnel manager reached out to me and said, "We've been notified that you have won a new position, and we would like to know what your plans are." I wonder if I still have that email? I probably still have it.

Author: But you hadn't accepted the new job at that point? They just heard that you'd won. That didn't mean that you'd accepted it.

Percussionist: Yeah . . . [Laughing] that's exactly it. So, I asked for an early tenure vote, and it was granted, so I got tenure there, and I immediately requested a contract renegotiation. [Laughing] Now the industry standard salary for a principal percussion at that time, and will probably change soon, up until that point was 50 percent over scale. That's what all my mentors told me and friends with the same title all told me to ask for 50 percent. I also had knowledge, thanks to many friends in and outside the orchestra, that many if not all the other principals in the orchestra received 50 percent or more over scale. Upon my request for 50 percent, they returned with 30 percent going up to 35 percent within two years.

Author: Ha! Really?

Percussionist: Yeah . . . of course I didn't know at the time that was even less than the previous principal, who earned 40 percent over scale.

Author: Ah . . . you know that sounds like something that would take place in small town, South Carolina or Ludowici, Georgia.

Percussionist: Yeah, it was like everything that should not have been happening was happening on that job. Of course, I don't have to tell you, to be the only Black musician in the orchestra and being offered 15 percent less than all the other white principals was not only insulting to me, but the last straw.

So, I immediately sought legal guidance at that point, because obviously there just had to be a serious racial component. At that point there couldn't have been any other reason for that.

Author: Sure . . .

Percussionist: Needless to say, my attorney at the time helped me draft and argument explaining the concerns of racial bias and all that stuff. We demanded fair compensation to be negotiated and to be compensated for the contract violations that had been going on throughout the entire process of my tenure liaison consulting the nonorchestra member subs about my performance as principal percussion.

Now had I been a dick, I could've sued them up the wazoo for contract violations a long time ago.

Author: Oh absolutely!

Percussionist: Of course, you know, who knows how much money that would've cost. I didn't want to deal with that with a new job on the way and all. It was something I just didn't want to go through. And needless to say, I'm sure the orchestra didn't want that to happen either. So negotiations were fine after that and all that was left to document was the disgruntled sub's behavior while going through the union's grievance process. At that time all I wanted was documentation of the sub's harassment of me.

And now we're back to the union. I wanted to go through the union's grievance process, which I expressed and explained to the union representative, whom I also talk to previously, if you remember I mentioned earlier. The union representative stated that they wished they had known about this behavior of the subs before. Saying that's exactly what the union is here for. [Laughing] After that statement the union directed me to the human resources representative that the orchestra hired to begin the grievance process. Yeah, an external entity that was not in any way connected to or associated with the orchestra in house. A completely different firm that they hired to deal with the situation. So, at that point I wasn't thinking clearly, I was like, everything was going wrong, I just needed to get out of there.

Author: I bet . . .

Percussionist: So I was thinking the union was working with human resources. I was not thinking that the union's not involved. So, after presenting all my evidence to the human resources representative, as well as offering witnesses to all the events that I described.

All the events that I had documentation on, not just like, hearsay, he said, she said. Things that I felt I could prove was harassment, bullying, all that stuff, text messages, emails, witnesses, all that.

So, here's what transpired: My witnesses could not or would not come forward to corroborate my claims.

Author: Huh?

Percussionist: Of course, months later, I asked my witnesses if they had been approached by anyone or what happened. And all of them said, no one approached them or asked them anything. No one came to them about anything concerning my situation. They were even asking me how things were going and if the whole process was even occurring. So I'm not sure what happened with them; I just assumed that they talked to no one. Or they chose to ask people whom they knew were going to say certain things, I wasn't sure. So, months later, with the union and human resources, the findings were as follows: Now, this was after I had given my resignation. I was like, here's all my evidence, I'm out of here, goodbye. So at least I had an investigation on file, that was on going that I knew wasn't going end by the time the season started at my new job. So, I was just out of there.

Author: Right . . .

Percussionist: Some months later, this is what happened: Two things, number one, my whole process there was finished with the union and human resources and here's what they said: They first thanked me for having the courage to come forward, that it is never easy to make an accusation that may hurt another individual, but they understood that my goal was to make the workplace safer for everyone else there.

Author: And that was the union and the human resources committee?

Percussionist: That was the human resources representative after doing their investigation.

Author: I see . . .

Percussionist: So they said that based on the definition of workplace bullying, harassment,and discriminatory behavior based on race, the investigator did not find evidence for my claims in those areas.

They did, however, determine that there were acts of insubordination and that they would discuss those findings with the disgruntled subs and assure that they be made aware that their behavior was inappropriate. Any further action of that sort would result in suspension or immediate dismissal of the subs.

Author: Huh!

Percussionist: And they ended by wishing me luck at my new job.

Author: Duh! A sub? How in hell can subs get even that much consideration? I'll never understand that.

Percussionist: Now! That should've been the end, right?

Author: Ah yeah!

Percussionist: Of course not, there was one more juicy piece of information that happened right in between all of this. Right after I signed my resignation and sent it to everyone, something happened.

A musician from my orchestra was outed for using the N-word on social media.

Author: So, moving on from that first job. When did you start the new job that you won?

Percussionist: So I left, a year ago this very day. I went to my hometown for a short time, grabbed my partner, and she moved to the new city with me, where she's doing her thing there and I'm doing mine with the new job.

Author: So, I'm just dying to ask, how did the new job work out for you. Was it a totally different world?

Percussionist: Oh, it was, man, while I was trying to get my previous orchestra to give me a fair rate, the new job was like, "Yeah you know, we understand the pandemic is happening and we understand it might be difficult moving to a new place with nothing going on, if you want to wait a year, we'll hold your spot. We'll set it up so that you're here 2021, if you need a year to prepare and all."

Author: Hmm? Yeah?

Percussionist: [Laughing] I was like, thanks for the offer, but I think, I'll be ready to come and play in 2020.

Author: So did your new orchestra job have concerts in 2020?

Percussionist: Luckily for the new job, basically turned into a road orchestra. We played concerts outside; we had a mobile stage that we took around town.

Author: I see . . .

Percussionist: I was working with donor thank you videos, I did a bunch of social media videos for them, things like that. I was basically getting paid the same amount I did in my previously job along with free medical treatments, thank goodness.

Author: I know you don't have much history with your new orchestra job, but was it a better situation?

Percussionist: It's been just about a year, but what I will say is that everything is working the way it's supposed to be. I basically came in the orchestra asking them about trying new things for the percussion section, and they were very open minded to all of my suggestions and were willing to try them out. It was a completely opposite situation. The tenure process is extremely clear and up front. I'll let you know if something goes wrong. [Laughing] But I don't foresee anywhere near the same situation I had with my previous orchestra.

Author: Well at least you won't have a bunch of white people ganging up on you from both sides, like your previous situation.

Percussionist: Yeah! But so far everyone has been super supportive. I've even been able to play a concerto during the freaking pandemic. They were like, "Would you like to play the Vivaldi Piccolo concerto in two months?" I said "Yeah! I'll do it!" Even the conductor was saying he was so excited to explore music with me. So, I did the Vivaldi Piccolo concerto on marimba.

Author: Oh! Really, on marimba? I didn't know it was transcribed for marimba.

Percussionist: Yeah, percussionists like playing everything on mallets these days.

Author: Exactly . . .

Percussionist: I guess, looking back to my first job, I didn't think, up until the point of intervention of human resources and the union, that I could have been more disappointed in the orchestra situation. But I guess considering the amount of effort the orchestra put in to protect the white guy. When I didn't receive any such protection. I can easily give myself permission to have been grossly disappointed and appalled.

Trombone of a Major Symphony Orchestra

Author: Welcome, and please tell me where you're from.

Trombone: I grew up in Spring Texas, northern suburb of Houston.

Author: Okay.

Trombone: Yeah, that's where I had my early start in music. When I was in elementary school, like a lot of kids, I started playing the recorder. On most Friday and Saturday evenings, my parents and I would go to various high school football games. High school football was always a big Texas pastime, so we always went to the games. We sat in the crowd, often right next to the band, and my dad told me when he was in junior high school band, he played the trombone, and it was a really cool instrument. He would then point out all the different instruments to me in the band.

So, I got an understanding of what the different instruments were, and even as a young kid, I already knew the difference between a trombone, a French horn, a trumpet, the clarinet, etc., and how they sounded.

I was very intrigued by the band. So, during half-time, when most people would go to the concession stands, my family and I stayed in our seats and watched the half-time show, because we wanted to see the bands perform.

Author: Of course . . .

Trombone: We were big fans of the African American tradition of charismatic marching bands.

Author: Oh yeah!

Trombone: They played fun and exciting music and danced to great choreographies.

It gave me the impression that playing in a band was a really fun thing to do. Of course, you had those stereotypical images, from the movies, that playing in the band was the nerdy thing to do, but I didn't believe that.

Author: Yeah, I bet, after seeing those Southern bands with all those marching and dance routines, of course. [Laughing]

Trombone: Right, I didn't end up going to a Historically Black College and Univeristy, but the experience etched in my mind that when I got a little bit older and got an opportunity to play an instrument, I wanted to be in a band.

Author: Oh, okay, so you went to one of those high schools with the fancy bands, which one?

Trombone: I attended Kline High School, which is on the northern side of Houston and before that I went to a school called Doerre Intermediate. Doerre was my first time being in a band, junior high school, sixth grade.

Author: I see . . .

Trombone: When you're a fifth grader in Texas, the local junior high school teachers would come to your elementary school and tell you about all the different extracurricular activities you could potentially sign up for when you're in sixth grade. Some of the junior high school students came along with the band directors and different teachers and shared the options for extracurricular activities. You could be in the band, you could be in the orchestra, you could be in the chorus, you could do this, you could do that, etc. I wanted to try out for the band.

So, they took us to the band room and let us try out all the different instruments we wanted.

I tried out the trombone, trumpet and the saxophone, and the saxophone because my mom was a fan of Kenny G.

Author: Oh, really? [Laughing]

Trombone: And she said, "Oh, it would be really nice to have a little Kenny G walking around the house playing some beautiful tunes." [Laughing]

Author: I see, funny . . . [Laughing]

Trombone: As it turned out saxophone wasn't my favorite instrument.

Author: Right, okay.

Trombone: I also wanted to try out the drums, but my parents said there was no way we're letting you play drums in the house.

However, when I made my first sound on the trombone, one of the other band teachers from across the room, because there were about three band directors present, letting other kids try out instruments, turned and said, "Wow! Listen to that sound! That kid has to play the trombone!"

Author: Ah ha!

Trombone: Of course when you were ten years old that makes you feel really special. So that settled it. I was going to become a trombone player.

Author: Wow! Just like that . . . amazing!

Trombone: [Laughing] My young experiences as a musician were very much just the local junior high school band scene. My parents didn't know about the need to take private music lessons; they never pursued music professionally, no one in my family had ever pursued music or the arts as a career. So I was the kid who just went to band class and played in the school band concerts. I didn't take private trombone lessons, I wasn't in a local youth orchestra, I wasn't going to summer music camp regularly or any of those things, but I fell in love with the trombone.

Author: I see . . .

Trombone: I just loved the idea of producing that trombone sound. I would stay after school every day and just practice on my own. My parents never once told me to practice. I just enjoyed it.

My parents eventually started coming to find me at school, because the school day would end at 3:50 PM in junior high. I lived right around the corner from the school, and it would be 6:00 o'clock or so and I hadn't come home yet. My parents were thinking, "Where is this kid?" They would come over to the school and there I was in the band room practicing. And that was how I kind of spent junior high and high school. I also played basketball, which was my other extracurricular activity.

Author: Okay.

Trombone: So my parents would either find me in the band hall or on the basketball court.

Author: I see . . . and how tall are you?

Trombone: "I'm six foot two."

Author: Yeah well, there ya go . . . [Laughing]

Trombone: [Laughing] I was the shooting guard on the basketball team. I went to an enormous high school, and we had guys who were six-ten and six-eleven. I was actually the second shortest guy on the team, believe it or not. [Laughing]

That's what happens when you go to a Texas high school with almost four thousand students.

Author: Of course . . .

Trombone: When I finally got to high school, we lived in an area where arts education was really appreciated. Our public high school had five bands, four orchestras, and three choruses.

Author: Really? Four thousand students? That's amazing!

Trombone: Out of four thousand kids at that high school, about a fourth of them were involved in one of the music programs.

Author: My God! Now that's unusual for any high school.

Trombone: Being in music was super popular. On top of that, the music program was very competitive. In my freshman year, I was second chair trombone in the second band. In my sophomore year, I was first chair in the second band. And it wasn't until my junior year that I got to be in the top band at my own high school, which was not the traditional trajectory of someone who gets into a major orchestra at age twenty-two, but that's part of my story.

Author: And how many bands did they have again?

Trombone: They had five.

Author: Wow! Amazing!

Trombone: That was my high school. And it wasn't a special "performing arts" high school or anything like that. It was just a normal public high school.

Author: Boy, I tell you, Texas has the best and most comprehensive music programs in the country from grade school right on up through high school.

Trombone: It does. My junior year in high school was the first time I made the top band in my own high school. It was also the first time I made the All-State Band in Texas, which was a very pivotal moment for me.

Author: Really?

Trombone: That moment that provided an external recognition that I was really good at playing the trombone in a place that I knew was really competitive.

Author: I know the feeling . . .

Trombone: All-State Band was held in San Antonio each year and I placed first chair in the All-State Symphonic Band that year. It was interesting to me that the previous year I was able to make the All-Region Band and Orchestra but didn't make the top band in my own high school.

Author: What?

Trombone: It wasn't until my junior year that I was in the top band at my own high school. Like I said, I also made first chair in All-State Band. The difference between my high school and the All-State, Reginal, and Area Bands was that the auditions were all held behind a screen. The auditions that happened at my high school were not behind the screen. The band director was aware of which students played which audition.

Author: I see . . .

Trombone: I'm not suggesting that we had band teachers who were unfair or intending to be unfair. We did have a really good trombone section, and it's worth noting that the other two players in my section were also two of the best in the state. We basically had a monopoly on the top end of the whole state of trombone players. The guy who sat right next to me throughout most of high school is now principal trombone of the San Francisco Symphony.

The experience of having different results between blind auditions and nonblind auditions was my first time really giving a thought to what implicit bias was and what it meant to have a fair audition system. I realized that I would rather take an audition behind a screen.

I always felt like my chances were better. It was not that people were being intentionally unfair, but it made me feel more secure about the situation knowing, there was no possibility that bias was a factor.

Author: Right, of course . . .

Trombone: It even changed the way that I prepared for auditions. I was more motivated to prepare for blind auditions because I knew they would be fairer.

Author: Oh, I see, I see . . .

Trombone: Seeing the auditioner not only influences the judges, but it also influences the way the player perceives the audition and how they prepare and play.

Author: Of course . . .

Trombone: Back to the All-State experience . . . That was the first time I was surrounded by a bunch of other kids who were just as motivated as me and who loved music. We had a very inspirational band director named Gary Green. At the time, he was head of bands at the University of Miami. He was our guest conductor, and we played all those fun works like Tempered Steal, The Rolling Thunder March. It sounded great. Well, as a high school kid, I thought it did.

Author: Oh sure . . .

Trombone: [Laughing] It was the highest musical experience I'd had up to that point. And that was the moment where something clicked for me. I thought, this is something I think I'd like to do for ever. I should learn more about what this actually means.

Author: Okay, I get it . . .

Trombone: So I came home from that All-State experience completely enthusiastic about music. It was an over-the-moon feeling. When I talked to my parents about it, my dad agreed to take me to the symphony for the first time. Near the end of my junior year in high school was the first time that I ever got to see and hear a real professional symphony orchestra play. My friend Tim had gone to the symphony before, so I asked him about it. He said, "Well, they're doing a piece at the end of the season called Mahler 3rd Symphony."

Author: Ahhh! Now we're talking . . .

Trombone: He said it had a really good trombone solo in it, so that might be a cool one to check out.

Author: No shit . . .

Trombone: The dynamic of that conversation tells you something about where me and my friend were in our musical journey at that moment in time, right? [Laughing] So I told my dad, that my friend said the orchestra was playing a piece that has a really good trombone solo in it, so maybe we should go to that concert. My dad said, "Sure, let's go to that concert."

So, we went to the concert, and you know Mahler Three, probably better than I do. We heard Mahler Three with the Houston Symphony with Christoph Eschenbach conducting. That was his final concert as music director there and that was my first experience ever hearing a professional symphony orchestra.

And in that first moment—right from the beginning of the symphony—when the French horns come in with that really soaring opening melody. I was captivated from start to finish. Most kids don't have an attention span of an hour and fifteen minutes, but I was locked in.

Author: I believe it.

Trombone: I was hooked from the beginning. I thought, oh my goodness, this is the thing! My eyes were wide open and of course, the solo trombonist sounded amazing, and at that moment it became clear to me, and I thought, I could do that! [Laughing]

Author: Yes, yes! I remember that feeling! [Laughing]

Trombone: I didn't know exactly what it was going to take for me to get there or how I was going to do it but, I thought, I can do that, and I want to do that, and I loved it. If I could get up every day and do that for a living, I think I would be happy.

Author: Isn't that a great feeling and revelation? And we've all had that experience as musicians, that moment when, we just knew.

Trombone: Yeah, it was like what some people refer to as their A HA! moment.

Author: Oh yes!

Trombone: That was the moment for me. From the moment I went to that Mahler concert, my path was clear.

Author: Wow! I remember that feeling like it was yesterday!

Trombone: It wasn't clear which school I would go to or which teacher I would study with, but the idea that I was going to be a trombone player in an orchestra was internally decided.

Author: Indeed . . . I love it . . .

Trombone: Fast forward one year, and I was applying for colleges. As I previously mentioned, my parents didn't have knowledge of what it meant to be a music major at a conservatory or college, beyond the idea of the stereotypical struggling musician. They weren't exactly enamored with the idea that I wanted to become a music performance major.

Author: I see . . .

Trombone: They required that I double major in college, that I major in music and something else.

Author: Oh that, yeah . . .

Trombone: Basically to have a backup plan if the music thing doesn't pan out for me, as it doesn't pan out for so many people.

Author: Yup! My father said the same thing to me. "Major in music education so you'll have something to fall back on in case you don't make it as a professional musician." A classic fear.

Trombone: [Laughing] My parents told me I should major in music and business.

Author: Oh my God!

Trombone: My parents were very pragmatic people. They thought, maybe I could do business, law, or medicine.

Author: Oh boy!

Trombone: They told me, "Pick one of those. Something that would be a guaranteed return on our financial investment of your going to college." [Laughing]

Author: I know, most people don't see music as a serious career choice.

Trombone: And since I didn't have any guidance from the music perspective. I figured out where I was going to audition by looking in the *U.S. News & World Report* magazine. My family and I were standing in line at the local Kroger grocery store, when I picked up a copy of the *U.S. News & World Report*. There was a section that ranked different colleges. I flipped to one page, and they showed the top twenty music schools in the country. Then on the next page, they showed the top twenty business schools in the country. I did a real quick cross-reference, and I saw that the University of Michigan and Indiana University both had top ten schools in music and top ten schools in business. That was around 1999. That clarified things for me. I was going to audition for Indiana and Michigan.

Author: Okay.

Trombone: [Laughing] And those choices were not the result of my consulting with a private lesson teacher, because I didn't have one.

Author: What, you didn't have a private teacher all that time?

Trombone: Correct, I started taking private lessons on a weekly basis, for the first time, in the summer after I graduated high school.

Author: You taught yourself?

Trombone: Somewhat, Let's just say that I listened very closely in band class to what the band director told us to do in the practice room.

Author: Huh! Is that right?

Trombone: And then I took it from there on my own. Of course, I was consuming recordings and listening to music all the time, because I loved it. I was largely taught by going to the local Blockbuster music store and getting CDs. I would get one CD a week or whatever I could afford. And then coming home, putting on the headphones and playing along to a recording of the New York Philharmonic with Bernstein or the latest solo CD from Cristen Lindberg or Joseph Alessi and that's how I learned the repertoire.

Author: But you must have gotten the trombone method book to learn all the positions?

Trombone: Of course, that was part of the traditional pedagogy from my high school band directors. Because the level of band instruction in Texas was very high, we had good introductory education from our band directors.

Author: That's amazing.

Trombone: The idea of taking private lessons every week and having someone helping me lay out a routine of fundamentals and scales, helping me through etude books methodically and telling me what solos to play next . . . I didn't have any such guidance.

Author: Really, so you didn't have any of that? Wow! You absorbed all that from the band director's practice room directives. That is fascinating.

Trombone: Yep, I'll tell you, that junior year in high school when I made the All-State Band, one of the things that came from that was you got free admission to the Baylor University Band Camp during the summer. That was one of their recruiting tools, and the top kids got to go to band camp for free. But the highlight of that band camp, for me, was access to their music library.

Author: Oh?

Trombone: During my little free time there, I raided their music library and photocopied all the trombone solos. [Laughing]

Author: You did what? [Laughing]

Trombone: I must have copied every trombone solo and étude book that they had in that library. Of course, you're not supposed to do that, but I did it, because I was fifteen years old, and I wanted that music and suddenly I was sitting there with all of it at my disposal. I then went back and got the recordings of that same music and most days after school; I would just read through trombone solos. That's how I learned the trombone solo repertoire. I put all the solos in alphabetical order, and I would learn the Creston and then the Grondahl Concerto and then the Tomasi Concerto. I would put my headphones on to listen and play along and learn the orchestration. By the time I graduated high school, even though I had no private teacher, I basically knew all the standard trombone solo repertoire.

Author: My God! Your band directors must have had magical teaching skills to help you the way they did . . . and without giving you private lessons. It was like they were teaching by osmosis.

Trombone: We were in a very musically competitive environment, and I was a very competitive person. [Laughing] I didn't like to lose, so I wanted to make sure I was practicing as much as I could.

Author: Oh, so that's what it was!

Trombone: Yeah and I was really digging into it. That's how I did it. I auditioned for Indiana and Michigan as a double major, and I chose to go to Indiana University as a double major in trombone and business.

Author: Ah, so you actually did that? Impressive.

Trombone: Well, I didn't actually do it, but I started out that way. [Laughing] So as the story goes, the first day of school at Indiana University, they did blind auditions for ensemble placements.

All fifty plus trombone players—because Indiana University has an enormous music school—had to audition behind a screen and play four standard excerpts for the trombone faculty. I was a seventeen-year-old freshman on the first day of school at the time and had only taken private lessons for a couple of months leading up to that point. I remember in those months the teacher I was taking lessons from, Michael Warny, was playing second trombone in the Houston Ballet. He said to me, "You've never really taken private lessons before, you're a kid and you don't know anything. When you get to Indiana University, you're going to be surrounded by all of these other students, who have gone to different music camps, students with master's degrees, doctoral students, who are a lot older than you and more experienced. Make sure when you get there, you have your ears open. Stand next to the doctoral student's practice room to get a feel for what they're practicing and what their routines are like and why they're stronger players than you."

Author: What! Wow! Really?

Trombone: I thought to myself, okay, okay, cool, I get it. I'm gonna do my best at the audition, and because Indiana University is such a big place and a competitive environment, this will be a very good litmus test to determine if I'm cut out for this field. After being in a place with fifty trombone players, I will find out how I stack up and if I can rise through the ranks over time.

Author: Exactly . . .

Trombone: So when I got there, we had the audition the first day, and I won the audition! [Laughing] I was first out of something like fifty-five trombone players on my first day at Indiana University.

Author: Impressive . . .

Trombone: Of course, that didn't sit too well with the master's and doctoral students, who were twenty-eight and thirty years old, to have some kid, who had just started taking lessons a few months prior, win that audition. But it was fair and square from behind the screen.

Author: Right, of course, of course . . .

Trombone: [Laughing] And you know, I was just as surprised as they were to be honest with you. I remember it like it was yesterday. We were auditioning on the fourth floor of what they called the MA Building, an old vintage building at Indiana University. It was probably 10:00 at night when the audition finally ended, because it takes a long time for fifty-something trombones to play all those excerpts. The teachers finally came out from the audition room, and they were counting heads and saying all the different names of the players. When I heard them say first chair trombone of the Indiana University Philharmonic was me, I was shocked and I thought, *that can't be right.*

Author: Why not? But I bet that appealed to your competitive nature though. [Laughing]

Trombone: [Laughing] My former teacher told me that I'd probably start off like twentieth in the ranking of players, and I probably wouldn't advance past that until I was finished with my undergrad. It was my first day at school, I hadn't even gone to a class yet, and I was first chair trombone in the top orchestra.

Author: Amazing . . .

Trombone: That boosted my confidence immediately.

Author: I bet . . .

Trombone: The next day was my first lesson of the year with my teacher, Karl Lenthe, and he said, "Well, congratulations on your audition last night. You did a really good job. I'm looking here at your courses from the registrar's office, and I see that you're scheduled to take computers in business and introduction to business and music theory. I'm just curious, tell me a little bit about your interest in taking all these business courses." And I said [Laughing], "Well I don't really have any interest in taking those business courses, honestly. My parents told me I had to do it, otherwise I couldn't come to school."

Author: Very funny . . . [Laughing]

Trombone: And my teacher said, "Well that doesn't seem like a good reason." I said, if I didn't do it, I wouldn't be here at Indiana University. I told him that my parents had this concern that I needed to have a backup plan, because a career in music was not a reliable option in their opinion and that they wanted to make sure I'm able to eat when I'm an adult.

Author: Yeah, yeah, very common parent thinking.

Trombone: Then he said, "Well, I understand where your parents are coming from, but I can tell you this, I've been in the music business for a long time and I think the playing level does continue to get better as the years go by, but the top is always the top. The cream will always rise to the top.

"At every audition you go to with a hundred people, there will be five people who will be truly competitive for that position. There will be ninety people who aren't competitive, but are good players, and then there will be those five players who really have no business being there. And your goal is to be one of those top five people, who are truly competitive for the position on a regular basis. And the level of those top five people has not really changed that much over time. The top is the top." He went on to say, "Based on my experience, I feel like if this is something you really want to do, and you're going to commit to doing it, I don't think you have to worry about succeeding in it."

Author: I see . . . quite complimentary.

Trombone: And so, I left that lesson, walked across the campus to the registrar's office and I dropped all the business classes. [Laughing]

Author: All right, okay! [Laughing]

Trombone: And I didn't tell my parents about it until we were sitting at lunch during the Christmas break, and they asked me, "How did the business classes go this semester?" [Laughing] And I said, "Well, about that."

Author: Yeah, about that . . . [Laughing]

Trombone: I told them I dropped those classes. A silence fell over the table. They asked me, "Well, why'd you do that?" And I told them that it was not what I really wanted to do, and I think I can be successful in music. So, my mom said to me, "Okay, look, you're a grown man. You can do what you want, but we're paying the bills for your education. And if this is what you want to do, then do it. But understand this, we signed up to send you to school for four years. [Laughing] And our expectation was that after those four years, you'd be able get a job, make a living, and support yourself. When those four years are over, we will have done our part."

Author: Whooo!

Trombone: "We're going to pay for you to go to school, because we agreed to do that. But, when you graduate, you'd better be able to figure it out."

Author: Figure it out?

Trombone: Yep. They said, "You're choosing not to go to business school and do other things that would guarantee you a living, so when you graduate in four years and you can't make any money, don't come asking us for help, because we gave you the parental directives on how to do this, but you chose to do something different. As long as you know that decision was yours alone." So I said that's fine.

[Laughing] From that moment, I had this clock ticking on my shoulder and I thought, I need to get successful as soon as I can. I can't dilly-dally around; I need to get as good as I can, as fast as I can, and I need to take auditions and be successful. I took my schooling and my music seriously as a heart attack from day one. I was the first one in the building to practice and last one to leave at night.

I eventually transferred to the Curtis Institute of Music in Philadelphia, after my second year at Indiana. I went to Curtis for three years and my parents agreed to extend their four-year tuition offer to five years, because Curtis is tuition free, which actually saved them money. [Laughing]

Author: Great, I love it . . .

Trombone: As a student at Curtis, I got free tickets to the Philadelphia Orchestra concerts. I only missed three concerts by the Philadelphia Orchestra in three years. I was there every week like it was a religion. After those concerts I would go back to school and practice. I was about as serious a student as one could possibly be.

And I had the good fortune, while still a student, to have won a few auditions. I won principal trombone of the Delaware Symphony, which was a local regional orchestra, as well as principal trombone of the Pennsylvania Ballet, which was the Ballet Company of Philadelphia, and I won the official sub-list audition for the Philadelphia Orchestra. Those three happened while I was still at Curtis.

On my last day of school at Curtis, I won my present position. It was literally the last Friday of the semester.

Author: Sweet! Wow!

Trombone: I had the good fortune of going seamlessly from being in school at Curtis to being at my present major orchestra position.

Author: Yeah! [Laughing]

Trombone: I remember it like it was yesterday. My high school classmate was the next highest vote getter of the audition that I won. [Laughing]

Author: That is so crazy . . .

Trombone: [Laughing] That was such a crazy, hilarious coincident in a way.

Let me back up and share one other story: My present orchestra position was my fourth major orchestra audition.

Author: Okay.

Trombone: I auditioned once for Cincinnati and twice for Seattle and my present orchestra position came right after that. The first big major orchestra audition I took was the Cincinnati Symphony.

Author: Okay.

Trombone: For the Cincinnati audition I stayed with a clarinet friend of mine, who at that time was associate principal clarinet with the Cincinnati Symphony. We met while playing in the Sphinx Symphony Orchestra. I asked if I could stay with him during my audition and he said sure. I got into the finals at that Cincinnati audition, which was my first time ever auditioning for a major orchestra. I was twenty years old; I was excited to play, but I got really nervous in the last round, and I just tanked. I did a terrible job in that last round.

I called my mom, but she didn't pick up the phone. So, when I got back to my friend's house, we started playing video games. In the middle of playing, my mom called back. We put the game on pause, and I put my mom on speakerphone, and she said, "Well, what happened, how'd the audition go?" And I said I thought the audition went pretty well, that I played well in the first round and second round, but in the last round I got nervous, and just didn't play my best. But I got really far, and I was only 20 years old, so that was a good sign. But my mom said, "You said you didn't play your best in the final round?" And I said yeah that's right. So, she said, "Well that's when you're supposed to play your best, isn't it?" [Laughing]

Author: Yeah! [Laughing]

Trombone: I said to her, okay, fair point, Mom. You know how auditions are. They're very emotional and they take a lot out of you. I just wasn't ready to hear her comments. So, I told her that I'd call her back when I won something.

Author: Yeah, but that's your mother. Nobody can get to you like she can. She knows all your buttons, pressure points, and weak spots.

Trombone: So fast forward a couple of years. When I won the audition for my present position, I also called my parents. They were both on the line at the same time. So, I said, "Hey Mom, I just took this audition." At the time my orchestra was the highest paid orchestra in the country. That was seventeen years ago.

Author: Right . . .

Trombone: So my mom said, "Oh, so you won?" [Laughing] Even though my parents didn't know much about the music world, they knew in what orchestra I had just won a position. So, they said, "Wow! Okay." And at that time I told them that I think I'm going to be doing better than if I had graduated from business school. At that time my present orchestra paid over $155,000 per year as a starting salary. I was twenty-two years old.

Author: Outstanding!! Beats the hell out of minimum wage. (Laughing)

Trombone: So I laughed and joked about it with my parents, but it was really great to win that job.

Author: That is amazing, hats off to you! So how was your playing experience at your new orchestra job? How were you received as a young extremely talented Black man?

Trombone: To be completely honest, my first three years on the job were a real struggle. It was not a cakewalk.

Author: A struggle as a player or . . . ?

Trombone: As a player I think I did perfectly fine but navigating the interpersonal dynamics of an orchestra as a young Black person was very difficult.

I was blessed to have had a couple of other Black colleagues, because the year before I got into the orchestra two other Black players had already joined the orchestra. So, I had a couple of people I could bounce some thoughts off. But in the trombone section I was the youngest person probably by thirteen years or something like that. I think at the time I was twenty-two and the next youngest person was thirty-six, thirty-seven or something like that and the other players were in their fifties.

Author: I see, I see . . .

Trombone: I grew up with parents who taught me to be self-assured, stand up tall, don't mumble, shake people's hand firmly, and look them in the eye. If you believe something, feel free to say it, and express yourself clearly. So, I came into an environment, in my trombone section, where the expectation of me was: Do as you're told and just be happy that you're here.

Author: I remember that vibe.

Trombone: "Your job is to figure out how to be like us. Not so much about trying to find a way to work together." That was the vibe I felt.

Author: How to be like them? Really?

Trombone: Right! And that was a dynamic that I didn't fit into naturally.

Author: I can see how you wouldn't. You're too self-assured. But how did that dynamic manifest itself in your section. Were there conversations telling you how to be like them?

Trombone: No, there weren't any egregious, obvious, racist slights. They were much more subtle. I'll give you a couple of examples. I really tried my best to be a very diplomatic section member. I came into the section as a player who had looked at the trombone parts a thousand times and played every note with a tuner. I was extremely conscientious because I wanted to do a good job and get tenure.

Author: Of course . . .

Trombone: So I really tried to be on top of everything. You don't want to be the person who's not saying anything, then again, you don't want to be the person who's saying too much. You work to be a contributor to the section and manage the various personal dynamics.

Author: Of course . . .

Trombone: I remember one performance in particular. We were playing an opera and there was a section where the trombones had a loud Fortissimo passage.

It just wasn't very in tune. I didn't want my colleagues to think that I didn't know how to play in tune or that I wasn't aware of it. So, I very nicely said to one of my colleagues, at the rehearsal break, "Hey, do you mind if we go back to that one spot and play those couple of bars again? It didn't seem like we were lining up in tune. Maybe I was sharp. Can we try it?" So, we played it through a couple of times.

Author: Oh, you did? Okay.

Trombone: Yeah, we played it through a couple of times. Low and behold when we played it on the performance it sounded really good. It was in tune. I did the traditional thing that brass players often do. We played the passage, it sounded great, and I shuffled my foot to say, "Yeah that sounded good." It's a comradery building thing, which is very common in orchestras. When we got to the intermission of the performance, my colleague next to me said, "When you shuffled your foot were you trying to say that I was the person who was playing out of tune all the time?"

Author: Oh boy . . .

Trombone: Yeah, he was the one that we worked on the passage with, and I said to him, no. I thought we sounded really good. He got angry and red in the face. He was probably angry that I had said something in the first place, and he probably had his own degree of self-consciousness about his intonation.

Author: Wow! Just paranoid!

Trombone: If he wasn't playing in tune, he definitely didn't want to be hearing it from the twenty-two-year-old Black kid in the section who didn't have tenure.

Author: Of course not . . .

Trombone: Things like that would happen.

Author: I believe it.

Trombone: You know, a lot of the major orchestras come to Carnegie Hall every year.

Author: Of course . . .

Trombone: And because I'm a music nerd, I got tickets for every orchestra that I could on the nights that I was off from work. And having been a student at Curtis, I was a big fan of the Philadelphia Orchestra. So of course, when they came to town, I went to their Carnegie Hall concerts because that was the orchestra in which I came of musical age. When I came back to work, people in my orchestra would naturally ask, "So, what did you do yesterday?"

And I said, after rehearsal I went to hear the Philadelphia Orchestra at Carnegie and they sounded fantastic, what a great orchestra! Man, it was so awesome to hear those guys play! And people in my section would say, "Well, if you like the Philadelphia Orchestra so much why don't you go play there?"

Author: Oh, really? And these were your colleagues in your trombone section?

Trombone: Yeah!

Author: My God, how chickenshit! How revealing!

Trombone: Yeah, I wasn't making a comparison between our orchestra and the Philadelphia Orchestra or suggesting that I'd rather be in the Philadelphia Orchestra. I just went to a concert and said I really enjoyed it.

Author: Yeah, what's wrong with a little enthusiasm? Wow!

Trombone: It was almost like everything I would say or do, they would search for a way to hold it against me or paint it in a negative light. The result of that was, what that whole attitude boiled down to was, my tenure being extended. I did not get my tenure in the normal time frame.

Author: Because?

Trombone: I think they wanted to haze me and make sure I knew my place, and I think the music director was willing to go along with it. They wanted me to follow orders and show deference to people who didn't respect me. So, they extended my tenure another six weeks.

Author: So, who told the music director you weren't doing those things? Sounded like someone was talking about you.

Trombone: Yeah, I think some of my colleagues in my section were talking about me and told him. It's one of those things that's impossible to say, because things were never communicated to me directly.

Author: Right, I know that game.

Trombone: I was always in a state of wondering what's going on and why is this or that happening? No one ever explained things to me directly. I eventually had a meeting with the music director regarding my tenure. He said, "I would like to extend your tenure because I recently had an injury and missed a lot of performances and don't feel I had an opportunity to really observe your playing."

Author: I think your other Black brass player colleague had the same situation.

Trombone: Right, and the music director did the exact same thing with my other Black brass player colleague. But the difference between my Black colleague and I was that he had joined the orchestra a year before me, so his tenure revue went on a year longer than mine.

Then the music director told me that he wanted to make sure I could play louder. To me that was hilarious. And I actually told him, I said, "Honestly, I've never heard anyone say a trombone needs to play louder. Of course, I can do that."

Author: Of course, it's usually too loud, right?

Trombone: Exactly, so I told him I always thought since I was playing second trombone that my job was to blend in and make a beautiful sound and not disrupt the section. But if you want me to play louder, done! I can do that, no problem.

Honestly, I think all of that, making sure I could play louder stuff, was a distraction from the real reason they extended my tenure, which is because there is a power dynamic that allows colleagues to feel comfortable pushing down Black people.

Author: Ya think?

Trombone: They feel that they need to make your path more difficult and that "Can you play louder" request was the logic that was used to justify it, even though it didn't make any sense.

One other interesting point about that meeting with the music director was that my other Black brass colleague was going through the same thing with his tenure extension at the same time.

The music director said to me, "So we've talked about your situation and what I would like to see from your playing, is there anything else that's on your mind?"

I said, "Actually there is. I sit next to my other Black brass colleague almost every night here and he's a phenomenal musician and a great player, but he's surrounded by a lot of players who seem to be hoping for him to fail. Even though he's surrounded by all that negative energy, he still does a great job. In my opinion I think he deserves tenure, and if you don't grant him tenure then I don't want tenure either. I don't want to work in a place that would treat a player of his caliber that way."

Author: I like that . . .

Trombone: [Laughing] I was twenty-four years old at the time. I think that whole situation with my other Black colleague was just so infuriating to me that I felt I had to say something. On principal, I couldn't imagine coming back to the orchestra the next year and my colleague not being there.

That would've sat so poorly with me I don't think I could've delt with it. And of course, I had a lot of confidence in the way that I played, so I figured if this job didn't work out for me, fine. I could get some other job. There were plenty of other orchestras I could've gone to, where people would give me a hard time.

Author: All right, sir . . .

Trombone: [Laughing] And to his credit, the music director said that he agreed with me. Which I thought was interesting, because he had the power to give me tenure right at that moment, but he didn't. However, just a few weeks later he actually gave me and my other Black brass player colleague tenure on that same day.

Author: So, you both went through three years tenure as opposed to two?

Trombone: I went through two years with an extension of maybe six weeks, and my colleague went through three years, plus six weeks or so.

Author: When I talked to him, he said, "I was in assassin mode when I played for the music director for three hours." He said he took in all his horns and excerpt books, he had no nerves, he just played everything in the trumpet literature.

Trombone: Yeah, he's the man, he's got great chops and great musicianship. I mean, if you ever heard him play, the idea that he was someone who should not be considered for tenure would be laughable.

Author: Yeah!

Trombone: Can I tell you a story about my brass player colleague? We actually met each other for the first time in February 2001 at the Sphinx competition."

Author: Sphinx, oh right, the concerto competition. Sure . . .

Trombone: Yeah, we were both playing in the Sphinx Orchestra and at that time they put orchestra members together as roommates. So I checked into my room and there stood my future brass playing colleague. I introduced myself and asked him if he minded if I warmed up, since we both had an orchestra rehearsal in a few hours. He said, fine if you don't mind if I warm up as well. You know, twenty minutes go by with us warming up in the same room and my colleague turned to me and said, "Hey man you wanna play some excerpts or something? We can play together." Then he said, "You know Bruckner Symphony No. 4?" And I said, "Yeah, I know Bruckner 4."

So, we were just sitting on the edge of our beds playing excerpts from Bruckner 4 and then excerpts from Tchaikovsky, all from memory, just playing through stuff, you know, just having fun, saying, "Yeah man, sounds good."

Then of course, we had no idea that four years later we'd be playing together in the same orchestra

Author: Exactly, magical . . .

Trombone: [Laughing] But that's how our friendship started, playing in that Sphinx Orchestra together. So, my brass colleague got into our present orchestra a year before me. At the time he got in the orchestra, 2004, I was still a student at Curtis. And since I'd won that job in the Philadelphia Ballet, that meant I was stuck in Philadelphia for the entire Christmas break, playing all those Nutcracker Ballet performances and couldn't go home.

Author: Right, of course . . .

Trombone: And I remember my colleague telling me, "Hey man, you should just take the train up to New York for Christmas. We can have dinner or lunch, watch basketball, and hang out and . . . oh, there's an audition for second trombone in my orchestra coming up in May. They're probably going to announce it next month, but you should try and see if you can get the whole list of audition materials and start practicing man, because this thing is coming up soon, and you could win."

Author: Ah, so he was the first person to tell you about the opening?

Trombone: Yeah, he said, "This thing is coming up and the excerpts for this audition list, you're not going to know, because they are opera excerpts. Excerpts from Othello and lesser-known excerpts from the Wagner Ring Cycle, Lohengrin, and Wozzeck. Stuff that's not on a traditional symphonic audition list." He said, "Yeah man you might wanna see if you can find that list and start practicing, because it's gonna be a huge audition, but you can do it, man."

So, I started working on those excerpts and six months later I won the audition, and we were in the same orchestra. We've been in the same orchestra now for seventeen years, well he's been there eighteen and I've been there seventeen.

Author: Wow! I love hearing this stuff. So, any more crazy stories you wanna tell me?

Trombone: [Laughing] Yeah, relating to the orchestra, over time I got more involved with the orchestra politics. I joined the orchestra committee as an officer for seven years. I got to learn a lot about the orchestra and its inner workings, management, contract negotiations, and all those things. In the 2014 and 2018 contract negotiations, I played a meaningful role in those processes. I wound up on this path because in my first years in the orchestra, when we would have orchestra meetings and things didn't make sense to me, I would ask questions.

Author: I see . . .

Trombone: [Laughing] I remember the first year that I was in the orchestra, the orchestra committee had come to an agreement. The committee chair was standing in front of the group telling us about the new agreement, about the wages and healthcare. And we were looking at the schedule and I noticed that there were performances on Christmas Day. So, I said, "I don't know why we're required to play performances on Christmas Day. Can we get out of those performances if playing on that day is a religious issue for someone?" And they really gave me a hard time about that. They were like, "Well, it's the schedule and we're expected to play the schedule." So, I said, "So are we going to require that Jewish people come to play Wozzeck on Rosh Hashanah? I mean, really?" [Laughing] So anyway, I was that guy, you know. And believe me, I was not trying to be a smart ass. I always asked what I thought were informed and sensible questions. I just wanted to understand of how orchestra policies worked.

Author: Of course, but it was their problem that they had a certain place in their minds for you and that you didn't know that place. Because it seemed they had a certain idea of what you should be like, and you came along and just crushed it.

Trombone: Yeah, it always felt like, "Hey, you just got here, you should just be happy to have a job." I wasn't trying to be an agitator. I was just asking normal questions.

Author: And were you a tenured member at that time?

Trombone: No, I was not a tenured member yet.

Author: Oh well, so what . . . but it wasn't about tenure, they just didn't like your spirit. Your energy, your power. There's an old saying that goes: "Some people will never like you, because you spirit irritates their demons." This is so true when it comes to Blacks, especially Black males in white organizations.

Trombone: [Laughing] Right . . .

Author: And that's exactly what you were doing.

Trombone: And what I shared with our committee chair at that time, I was not just asking for myself. I was just trying to be supportive of the rights of the orchestra members at large. If the orchestra really wanted me to come play on Christmas, I'd do it.

Author: Yeah, but I don't think they wanted to hear that from you.

Trombone: Right, I did have a feel for organizational culture and development, and I'm generally a good communicator. That's likely why I ended up on the orchestra committee for a long time and that's why I'm a dean at an academic institution now, in addition to my work in the orchestra.

I remember a conversation I had with the orchestra committee chair after a new contract negotiation was ratified. After the contract was approved, it was time to elect a new orchestra committee. The chair of the committee came up to me and asked, "Are you going to run for the orchestra committee?" And I said, "No, I don't have time for that. I'm too busy playing shows and playing recitals, teaching here and teaching there." He said, "Well you know what? Fuck you then. Don't say anything else at the orchestra committee meetings." [Laughing]

Author: "Fuck you"? Really?

Trombone: Well, as if to say, "Hey look, I recognize that you're a smart guy and you have an opinion about everything and you think you know what's best. So, if you have an opportunity to serve on the committee, actually make some of the changes that you care about but are just too busy to serve on the committee, then stop commenting." Now he had a point, I must say. If I had so many comments and wanted to see change, then I should indeed serve on the orchestra committee to make said changes or be quiet. So, I thought about it, and I ran for the orchestra committee. I ended up being on the orchestra committee for the next seven years and two contract negotiations. I learned a ton about fundraising and starting a 501(c)(3), understanding interpersonal dynamics and negotiations. All those skills set me up really well for a position in administrative leadership.

Author: Yeah, how did that come about?

Trombone: I'd been doing a lot of teaching. I've taught at most of the major music schools in the New York City area. I amassed a lot of teaching experience, and I also started becoming a real advocate for social justice in the arts. I started using my performance and teaching platform as an opportunity to speak about other music industry issues that concerned me. I also started writing articles on the topics, and my name started getting out there as someone who, in addition to playing and teaching, has a larger vision for how things should be.

Over the course of those years, I wasn't gathering those skills with the intent of leveraging them into a job. It just so happened that I was inadvertently building them.

I was learning how to navigate people's interpersonal disputes on the orchestra committee. I was learning about organization and management. I was learning about fundraising and communication skills. I began to write more and speak in public more, in addition to teaching and playing the trombone. And it just so happened that each of those skills helped qualify me to

I was not a person who was actively seeking a job. But one day while I was backstage practicing some parts, an email came through on my phone.

It was a woman who worked at Julliard, and she told me to check out this job posting. She said, "I think you'd actually be great for it."

Author: And who was she?

Trombone: She was Juilliard's director of community engagement.

Author: Was she Black?

Trombone: Yes, she was a Black woman, who knew me from my time teaching in the Music Advancement Program at Julliard, which was a program for underrepresented youth in classical music. She said I should check out that job post. And I thought, really? I could be a dean? I had never considered such a thing. I never desired a job in academia, beyond being on the trombone faculty, but to run an entire program? Although, at that time, I had been having an internal conversation with myself about what would be required of me to have a greater impact in the classical music field, and then it occurred to me. That dean position would really align with that goal.

Author: More impact how, as a person or as a musician?

Trombone: Both, I was considering all the things I wanted to see change in the field of classical music. I wanted the field to be fairer to Black and brown people. I wanted to see the repertoire change. I wanted young people to have more role models in higher education. What could I do to impact all of that? Of course, I could talk about it all day, but what was I going to do?

Author: I see . . .

Trombone: And then I thought to myself, "You know what? That dean position actually makes a lot of sense. It would allow me to act on a lot of things that I care about. It's one thing to be on the sideline throwing rocks, but it's another thing to be the fold, grinding and trying to figure out how to make things better." So, I applied for the position. The provost of Julliard saw my résumé and called me. He said, "I just want to make sure you understand what you actually applied for."

Author: Humm?

Trombone: So I said, "What do you mean?" And he said, "Well, we really admire you and you're a great artist and all, but we really view this as a desk job. This is an administrator's job and not really a position for someone who is a full-time performing artist. Is this job something that you would leave your orchestra position to do?"

Author: Wow!

Trombone: I said, absolutely not. I think I could do my orchestra job and this job. I think my being a full-time performer as well as having a foot in the academia door would make me better at the job. I went on to say that I thought it would give me more common ground with the faculty and it would allow me to have a better understanding of what students are doing. And he said, "That's really interesting we've never really thought about it in quite that way. Perhaps that means we need to reconsider what we were really looking for. So let me get back to you."

Author: Indeed . . .

Trombone: As it turned out, that conversation was the phone-screening round of the interview process, and a couple of months later, I went to a larger panel interview with several people from the senior staff and leadership of the school. It was a long process altogether, probably six months. Later, I had an interview with the president of the school and another senior leader, and they offered me the position as a dean of the preparatory division of The Juilliard School.

A lot of my previous experiences happened to add up to the appropriate qualifications for that position. On paper, it would appear that I skipped some steps, because there are a lot of traditional steps that often lead to being a dean: assistant director, associate director, director, then assistant dean, associate dean, etc. However, I managed to leverage my previous work experiences in a way that allowed me to bypass that form of trajectory.

Author: So interesting, that you didn't have to go through any of those preliminary, move-up-the-ladder processes.

Trombone: I went through none of them, and it was interesting because, in the years leading up to that, I'd been having some conversations with Wynton Marsalis, who has been a real mentor to me. He has been someone who has really guided me in the right direction. I remember having a conversation with him and telling him that I had this internal feeling that I wanted to do something different. I wanted to have an impact that was more significant, but I wasn't sure how to do that. Considering the level I'd reached as a musician, I didn't know if I could stomach taking several steps backwards to go to business school and get an arts administration degree, start from the bottom, and take ten years to work my way up. I don't know if I can stomach that or if that's the right path. He said, "Just keep doing what you're doing and wait for the right opportunity. The most important thing is that you determine what it is that you really want to do."

Author: Absolutely . . .

Trombone: He said, "That's where the real power is. It's not so much about going through and checking all the ladder climbing boxes." So, the moment that I shifted to that mindset, was really the pivotal moment that gave me the presence of mind that I needed to jump from one ladder to the next.

Author: Exactly . . .

Trombone: He told me that I was going to have to struggle through a lot of things to get to where I want, but once I get there, nothing will be able to stop me. And that gave me some peace because, to be honest with you, the night before my first day as the dean at Julliard, I had two competing thoughts going back and forth in my mind, and one of them was: You've be working and training your whole life on how to deal with people. It's going to be fine. And then the other thought was, you've never worked a day in your life in full-time administration. You have no idea what you're doing, everyone's going to know right away, and it's going to be a disaster.

Author: Yeah, well of course . . . that's a normal reaction.

Trombone: So yes, I had those two thoughts racing in my mind, but I swear, within the first three hours of being on that job, all of those fears melted away.

Author: Yeah!

Trombone: And I felt like, you know what? I've got this. I already know what it means to interact with people. I know how to manage personalities; I know what good teaching is and what good management and organizational skills are . . . and this job is going to be fine. Once I got past that very initial feeling of fear, the job became almost immediately comfortable. It was like stepping into a pair of shoes that fit.

Author: It's amazing just how prepped and ready you really were for that position.

Trombone: It clarified something Wynton told me. He said, "Never stop playing your horn. The amount of work and effort it took you to get as good as you are on that instrument, nothing else you ever do in this life will be as difficult as that. Trust me."

Author: That is an amazing truth. [Laughing]

Trombone: [Laughing] And I think he's right. Because as you know, playing a brass instrument is unforgiving and it is not easy.

Author: Whooo! Indeed . . . I have to keep playing because one of my top students is auditioning for my orchestra and I have another one, a young lady, that I want to bring along. I had to stay in some kind of playing shape in order to work with them.

Now there is one Wynton story that I just love telling. First of all, he is one of the proudest Black men I've ever met. We were getting ready to rehearse his Jazz Oratorio at the Hollywood Bowl and the conductor introduced everyone to the orchestra and then asked Wynton if he was ready to start.

Wynton paused and said, "Give me a minute." He walked through the entire orchestra and shook hands with the four Black members, walked back to the front of the stage, and said, "We can start now."

So, I looked across the orchestra at the Black bass player and we nodded to each other with very nonverbal expressions of deep approval. And the most interesting part of that incident was that not one of the white orchestra players ever said a word about it.

He is fearless! He's the only musician that I know of to get a Grammy in both classical and jazz. I mean, who has ever done that? It's no wonder those American Powers that Be tried so hard to keep us down for all those centuries. They had to be frightened of this kind of potential.

Trombone: He's incredible. But the thing is, as great a trumpet player that he is, he's actually an even better personal motivator, speaker, and mentor.

Author: I'm not at all surprised.

Trombone: It's crazy, because I think he's the greatest brass player of our generation.

Author: I agree . . .

Trombone: He's given me advice and picked me up in moments of my life when no one else possibly could have. I wouldn't be where I am today if it wasn't for him.

Principal Clarinet of a Major East Coast Symphony Orchestra

Author: So, please tell me a little about your background.

Principal Clarinet: Yeah, so I grew up in Chicago on the Southside. My parents met at Teachers College. They were both visual artists who believed in a well-rounded education for my brother and I, you know.

Author: Of course . . .

Principal Clarinet: And they had a really strong philosophy about how they wanted to raise us. I started playing clarinet at age nine. I basically started to follow in my older brother's footsteps. Anything he did I wanted to copy and wanted to do. So they wanted to start a band at the school I attended, which is how I got started on clarinet. I think in those early years, what can I say, my first clarinet teacher was a jazz saxophone player who would come over to our house and I would just go through the band book with him, just like, reading the clarinet parts.

My parents were very concerned about making sure I had the best of teachers.

They didn't know very much about classical music, so I started getting clarinet lessons early on with different people in the city and eventually stumbled on the Merit School of Music in Chicago, where I studied clarinet with David Tuttle. That's where I got my first real taste of what it was like to exist in a music education community. I was there for the Saturday programs, where they had private and group lessons, orchestra, and we played recitals and studied music theory.

Author: Right . . .

Principal Clarinet: So that was my first chance to find out what it was like to take private lessons and be around all those other people playing music.

Author: But by then you were serious about clarinet though?

Principal Clarinet: Yeah, I had chosen clarinet at my first go, when I was choosing an instrument. I remember thinking that saxophone was too big, and the band teacher said I could pick the clarinet. I remember at that time the band at the school I went to was very small. It was a Catholic school on the Southside in Hyde Park.

The school started a band, but I don't think that there was more than a half dozen players. I don't have a clear memory of it, but it wasn't like a large ensemble.

Author: Right . . .

Principal Clarinet: So there were just like a few kids in a room learning how to play quarter notes on their instruments. I don't really remember who that first band teacher was, but it was really through those private lessons at the Merit School that I discovered I was talented on the clarinet and that I actually enjoyed playing music.

Author: I see . . .

Principal Clarinet: And I would hear older people play, like my older brother and people that were his age, who were really advanced. I got to watch them perform from the time I started learning clarinet. Then of course I heard my brother practicing for many years before I ever picked up an instrument. I started advancing really quickly on the clarinet and sometime around my second year playing, I got into Interlochen music camp. I was first chair in the orchestra there for all of the eight weeks, and then I think I joined the Chicago Youth Symphony as well during those early playing years. Actually, my first international tour was with the Chicago Youth Orchestra. And you know, I just fell in love with it, with music . . . and Michael Morgan was the conductor.

Author: Oh really? And where did you travel internationally?

Principal Clarinet: Yeah, we went to Japan. I was like . . . just twelve years old.

Author: Oh, great, what a great opportunity at such a young age.

Principal Clarinet: Yeah, so that trip just changed my perspective on so many different things.

And you know, because of that Merit School, I got scholarships to go to different summer music camps and I got to study with the principal clarinetist of the Chicago Symphony Orchestral, Larry Combs and also Julie DeRoche, who were both professors of clarinet at DePaul University.

So, after I got introduced to them, I started going up to DePaul University for lessons. Things went really quickly from there. I went from doing concerto competitions, working really hard on those to just learning how to play the clarinet. Another part of my experience growing up in those musical environs in Chicago was learning about the Chicago Teen Ensemble, which was an ensemble made up of kids from the Southside and our conductor, Barry Elmore, would transcribe different works for our eclectic ensemble of winds and strings to perform. We performed in sections all around the city.

That ensemble was really great. I was like the little brother, because I was surrounded by players who were slightly older that I really looked up to in those days.

Most of us were Black, and it was just so inspiring. For the first time I was able to see what it was like to have a life as a performing musician.

We would do gigs in the city, which was such a transformative experience and from that I began believing that anything was possible. I was doing solos with the group at ten, eleven, and twelve years old, you know. It was a small chamber size group: There was a piano, a few string players, my brother on flute, me on clarinet. It was amazing.

Author: So, your brother was in the group too? Fantastic!

Principal Clarinet: Yeah . . .

Author: And he's your older brother?

Principal Clarinet: Yeah he's four years older.

Author: Oh, right . . .

Principal Clarinet: Yeah, so that group was just amazing and then my brother won the Illinois Young Performers Competition at age fifteen and got to play a solo with the Chicago Symphony and I got to watch him, I think, before I even played an instrument.

Author: Oh, I see, interesting . . .

Principal Clarinet: Or I had just started playing my instrument, I don't recall exactly. So that's the kind of stuff that I was around when I was growing up.

Author: Sounds like a solid and supportive background . . .

Principal Clarinet: Yeah and then just kind of fast forwarding from there, I went to this great grade school in Chicago for ninth grade and then at that school, I wasn't sure if I was getting bullied or what. I didn't know what was going on. My parents felt there was something not right and not positive at that school. So, the first thing we did was ask around to see where else I could go to school.

Author: Did you actually get bullied?

Principal Clarinet: Well I think probably, yeah. I think that's what you'd call it. You know, getting into tussles and wrestling with guys in the hallways and stuff.

I think that all happened because I was short, and I played the clarinet. So, I got bullied by my friends a little bit for that, you know. They didn't call it bullying back then, but I think that's probably what it was.

Author: Yeah, for sure . . .

Principal Clarinet: I wasn't getting into serious fights or anything, but it was enough that my parents thought that we needed to examine the dynamics there.

So, I looked at a couple of different schools. One was at the University of Chicago and the other was Interlochen Arts Academy.

Author: Oh, okay.

Principal Clarinet: So I ended up transferring to Interlochen and going there for high school.

Author: Fantastic! How did you like it?

Principal Clarinet: Oh, I just loved it because, for the first time I felt like I fit in.

Author: I understand . . .

Principal Clarinet: I felt like it was cool, you know? Living up in Michigan, in the Northern Woods and I don't know, it was just so much fun and sometimes hard, because of living away from home.

Author: Of course . . . but no bullying?

Principal Clarinet: Yeah, exactly no people teasing me about playing my clarinet. I felt like an artist up there. So, when I got to Interlochen High School, my brother was already at Curtis. So basically, that was like my goal as well, to go to Curtis. Then of course, I wanted to do everything my brother did.

Author: Of course . . .

Principal Clarinet: So, I auditioned in my sophomore year at Interlochen, for Curtis, which was super early and didn't get in. Then I auditioned in my junior year and got into Pre-Curtis. I had enough credits, so I graduated Interlochen High School that year. But while at Interlochen, during those high school years, I was going to Tanglewood, Boston University Tanglewood Institute summer festival, and a couple of other summer festivals. I was in the band first at Interlochen and then the orchestra. That summer, I learned the Neilson Clarinet Concerto while at Interlochen and won the concerto competition. It was just a great clarinet studio and my clarinet teacher, Richard Hawkins, became such a great mentor.

Mike Hawkins was in there, and he was a very young player at the time. It was just a great time in my career. To be at Interlochen and Merit School, with that community of musicians, friends, and great supporters, it was pretty awesome, I was very lucky.

Author: I'll say, and man, you got into all the right places and were timely exposed to all the right stuff, awesome.

Principal Clarinet: Yeah, so I went to Interlochen and then finally got into Curtis. I studied with Donald Montanaro and, you know, I had a really great experience, because, you know, I was kind of the little brother to my older brother, who was at Curtis years before me.

Author: You know, I talked with a Black bass player who went to Curtis, and he said there was a group of Black players there that made it seemed they were like . . . taking over.

Principal Clarinet: [Laughing] By group, I think he might've been talking maybe three of them. [Laughing]

Author: [Laughing] Oh I see . . . was that all? Well in those days I guess three might have seemed like a lot of Black folks in that intimate situation. [Laughing]

Principal Clarinet: Well that's what's funny about people like him who grew up in the South, in places like Savannah. When I look back on my part, the thing that made my racial experience unique and different from his was in my youth orchestra, my brother was there, we had Michael Morgan, who was a Black conductor and a couple of other Black players, you know. But also, I had that entire group, the Chicago Teen Ensemble, we were all Black and even the Merit School was designed to help kids from the "inner city" by being tuition free.

Author: Fantastic . . .

Principal Clarinet: Yeah, Merit was a very diverse school, so I was always around a lot of Black, brown, Asian, and white people who played classical music. However, my youth orchestra didn't lean toward much diversity, but still, it wasn't that unusual for me to, like, meet other Black people who played classical music.

Author: I see . . . nice to hear.

Principal Clarinet: So I had that normalized for me in a lot of ways growing up.

Author: So what years are we talking about here?

Principal Clarinet: Yeah, so 1989 to 2000. Those were my schooling years. From the time I started playing clarinet until I got my first major orchestra job.

Author: Okay. I see . . . yeah, I came along much earlier, boy. I got my job in the LA Philharmonic, June of 1970.

Principal Clarinet: Wow! Yeah, you paved the way. I was born in 1979.

Author: Is that right? Yeah, I was at New England Conservatory during the late 1960s. Boston, where I went to school, was full of all kinds of student protests against the Vietnam War in the Boston Commons.

Principal Clarinet: You went to school in Boston?

Author: I did . . .

Principal Clarinet: Oh my God! I'm scared of Boston right now.

Author: Are you really? Well yeah, I can understand that, because those were scary times. Every weekend there was some kind of protest in the Boston Commons. Once I got a whiff of teargas and once, I got just nicked by a police Billy Club and I decided to go back to school and practice. But that teargas is no joke.

Principal Clarinet: That's what I've heard. I heard a podcast about teargas, about where it came from. I mean it was used on the field of war and adopted by the police of today.

So, on my first major orchestra job, as associate principal clarinet and E-flat clarinet, there was one other Black player, assistant principal cello. He had been the only Black player for what must have been decades. I think he got in the orchestra in the mid-1970s and he's still there. And when he told me the year that he got into the orchestra, that city was, "Whoooooo! Not a place for Black folks!"

Author: What? He's still there? Amazing . . .

Principal Clarinet: Oh, there was one important thing I should mention. When I was at Curtis, I got invited to the Marlboro Music Festival.

Author: Oh! Really? Fantastic!

Principal Clarinet: Yeah, so I started going there when I was eighteen. I went for like three summers, and I think that sort of changed everything about my career, you know? I was getting some training from, like, older players who had major orchestra jobs. Players who were at least ten years older than me.

Some had even studied with my teacher Donald Montanaro, who was associate in the Philadelphia Orchestra.

So I got a lot of lessons, but more, like, coaching from some of those older generation clarinet players while I was at Marlboro. And I think that just helped me understand what it would take to get one of those major orchestra jobs.

So that was super helpful, especially since I got my first major orchestra job when I was in my last year at Curtis.

Author: So, you were able to glean what it would take to get a major orchestra job from those clarinet players who were coaching you?

Principal Clarinet: Yeah, I think I picked up lots of tips and tricks and all these other interesting facts about auditions from them, that sometimes aren't obvious to most players. And those guys were like younger generation players. I was eighteen, and they were probably like in their early thirties."

Author: Oh, so they had just gotten those jobs?

Principal Clarinet: Yeah, exactly.

Author: Oh, so what was the racial atmosphere like at Marlboro. I can't even imagine a Black person being there, which is just my general, perhaps prejudicial, impression of the festival.

Principal Clarinet: Ha! Yeah, that's interesting. I didn't have a perception of what that was going to be like before I got there. Yeah, there weren't very many Black people there. If any . . . [Laughing] as I recall.

Author: Oh, I see . . .

Principal Clarinet: But most of those elite musical festivals were like that in those days, even in the year 2000.

Author: Yeah, for sure, but the thing is, when we started playing in this classical field of music, we weren't really thinking about race, we just wanted to play our instruments. We weren't thinking about who was going to be there and what race they would be. Then, of course, we found out all that stuff later. But aside from race, we found out how expensive it was to pursue your dream in life. To do what you really wanted to do in life. To pursue that special ability that we were endowed with by the creator.

Principal Clarinet: That's a good point actually to go back, for the record. In order to send me to Interlochen, my parents had to get a second mortgage on their house.

Author: Oh?

Principal Clarinet: Yeah, they had to like, sacrifice everything.

Author: Wow! That is fantastic . . .

Principal Clarinet: Yeah, yeah, they were just like, "If you really wanna do something you go for it, and we'll figure it out."

And those weren't easy decisions to be made.

Author: That's so great to hear that you got that kind of support from your parents . . . a lot of support.

Principal Clarinet: You know my dad actually wrote a book titled, *A Father's Triumphant Story: Raising Successful African American Men in Contemporary Urban Times*.

Author: I like that . . .

Principal Clarinet: Yeah, you know, it details my father's and my mother's journey as the parents of my brother and me. So yeah, like a philosophy, my parents really did have like a methodology, a belief system in positivity and in conquering all obstacles. They believed in doing it at all costs.

Author: And they weren't influenced by the popular ethnic dictates that insist, "If you're Black you do this, if you're Jewish you do that, if you're Asian you do this."

Principal Clarinet: No, because they came along in the radical 1960s and they were going into visual arts, following their dreams as artists, you know.

Author: I see, of course . . .

Principal Clarinet: And my dad, speaking of not being in a field you know, when the Chicago Public Schools, and they were both teachers, went on strike, my dad joined the Chicago Fire Department.

Author: I see . . .

Principal Clarinet: And that department did not have many Black people in those days.

Author: I bet!

Principal Clarinet: So, my dad ended up retiring as the deputy commissioner of the entire Chicago Fire Department, ten or fifteen years ago.

Author: Impressive . . .

Principal Clarinet: And my mom was an actress, a dancer, a singer, and a visual artist.

Author: Oh, okay . . .

Principal Clarinet: So, for sure, my parents were the most important part of my story.

Author: Not to digress, but one has to wonder, what it is about a Black fireman that was a problem, a threat, to those white firemen?

Principal Clarinet: Well, it's like anything else, you know. The world's made up of clubs, everything is like a private club, everything is like that.

Author: Or tribal . . .

Principal Clarinet: Yeah, tribal and you want to be in clubs with people who are just like you.

Author: Yeah, and we are also extremely prideful in our tribal-ness.

Principal Clarinet: Yeah, so I was on my first major orchestra job for four years as associate principal clarinet and I had a pretty good time there. I came in the orchestra when the city had its own racial riot because of an unarmed police shooting. So, there was a big protest of rioting and stuff when I arrived in the that around 2000. That was an interesting year. You know you'd think that stuff would've been over back in the 1970s, but in 2000 that stuff was going on when I arrived in the city of my first job. So, it was a strange juxtaposition to be in, joining an all-white orchestra as a Black man during that time.

Author: So, after the riots were over, was there any kind of diversity crusade or any kind of healing activity involving your orchestra?

Principal Clarinet: No, no, that orchestra is doing it now, but not back then. Now that orchestra is doing special concerts for Black History Month and a couple of concerts with a few gospel choirs, but that was about it.

Author: Oh, okay, I see . . .

So, in general, being a Black principal clarinet, did you receive any racial push-back?

Principal Clarinet: Nothing obvious, no . . . if anything, it was more subtle. And I think because the orchestra already had one long-standing Black player, my showing up didn't cause the typical shock that most orchestras have been known to go through and the time was different (2000) than the 1970s when the other Black player joined. However, I did do some interviews early on, at that time, about being young, Black, and new to the orchestra. And I did mention, in those early interviews, that my time was made easier by the Black players who came before me.

Author: So then from this, your first major orchestra job, you went to your second major orchestra job with a major opera orchestra?

Principal Clarinet: Yeah, I went to my second job, a major opera orchestra where I stayed for ten years. So, for my third and final major orchestra job, I had auditioned several times before they actually offered me a position. I even played several trial weeks with them and even had a week where I played on a live broadcast. So the last time I auditioned for them there were just two of us in the finals and we both played trial weeks so they could decide. After those trial weeks, the other guy decided to go back to his old job. So the audition committee, along with the music director, deliberated as to whether they should hold another audition or just, since I was the last qualified person to play in that orchestra, call me up and asked me if I was interested in the job, after I had jumped through so many hoops for that orchestra, and I was like sure, I'll take the job.

Assistant Principal Cello of a Major Midwest Symphony Orchestra

Author: So, how old were you when you were first exposed to music?

Assistant Principal Cello: Yeah, yeah, I started off on piano in like second grade. The director of the church at the corner of my street would let me in after school so I could use the piano. I also had lessons there on Saturdays. The piano was one of those big old upright jobs. [Laughing]

Author: [Laughing] Of course . . .

Assistant Principal Cello: So I did get good enough to where I needed my own piano, but we couldn't afford one. So, after six months or so I stopped playing piano. Then I was singing in the children's choir at church. I had a good musical ear and all of that.

As it turned out, in fourth grade the music teacher from the junior high school, that was right near my house, came to my fourth-grade class and asked who the tallest boy in the class was and I stood up. She had a brand new, ¾ size cello with her, which was really too big for most fourth graders.

So, she asked me, "Would you like to play a cello?" And I said, I don't know, so I looked at it. It had a nice canvas bag, and it was all shiny with a nice looking wood finish. So, I said, "Okay, I'll try it out," and that's how I started.

Author: And how old were you then?

Assistant Principal Cello: I was nine years old.

Author: So, you were tall for a nine-year-old.

Assistant Principal Cello: Yeah, so a ¾ size cello was just right for me. I was about a head taller than a lot of the other kids, ya know so. Yeah, I was an eleven-pound baby with a fat neck. My mother used to call me pumpkin until I started stretching out.

Author: You were born eleven pounds?

Assistant Principal Cello: Yeah, eleven pounds, seven ounces. That's why I don't have any siblings. [Laughing]

Author: Eleven pounds, God! I thought I was big at nine lbs. [Laughing]

Assistant Principal Cello: Yeah, so the school system back then, they provided music lessons. Free lessons all through the summer. They had a repairman on call for any repairs we needed. Everything was going great until I started taking the bus and trolly car down to South Philly, when I was in the seventh grade. Once I had a lesson during rush hour and I had to take the trolly car. Trolly cars don't start and stop smoothly when in tight traffic, and they kind of jerk you around. So, I was seated, and the cello was in the aisle next to me, and I had my arm around it. Suddenly one of the passengers lost his balance and fell on the cello and crushed the top of it, you know.

Author: Ahhhh!

Assistant Principal Cello: So I ended up going to my lesson in tears. I was twelve years old at that point and worried about how we were going to pay for the cello. Fortunately, the man that fell on the cello gave me his phone number and he paid for it. Amazingly it was only forty dollars to repair a cracked top, reset the neck and cut a bridge. [Laughing]

Author: Ah, so you didn't have a hard case?

Assistant Principal Cello: No, no, it was a canvas case.

Author: Canvas? Ahhhh!

Assistant Principal Cello: Oh there were no hard cases around in those days. I didn't see a hard case until I got to college. But, you know, I got through that, but I stopped studying for a while because my teacher kind of turned me off after that episode with my busted cello.

I always wanted to take a cello like his and smash it up against the wall, because he had a nice cello and made fun of mine. So that sort of put a little salt in my feelings toward him over the next year or so.

Author: But you know, it's great to hear that you had a great music program in those days, because after a while, they started to fade out in favor of physical education and science, except in the South, where the early school music programs are the best in the country. So, did your school have an orchestra?

Assistant Principal Cello: Elementary did . . .

Author: Oh really, in elementary school?

Assistant Principal Cello: It wasn't a full orchestra, we had piano, clarinet, cello, violin, mellophone, baritone and that was it. We played a lot of easy tunes. [Laughing]

Author: Easy tunes? [Laughing]

Assistant Principal Cello: But in junior high school, things got more serious, where we had a full orchestra. And back then, the head of the school board music department was Dr. Louis Wursen, a very well-known music educator, who had a lot of clout in the music division. And every year we would have what we called "Schools on Parade" where every school in the city was represented over a weekend, which was held at the convention center. And you would have two hundred kids at a time getting up to play the same music. A good size audience was in the balcony of the convention center and many of the kids sat on the floor. There were also choirs and various other types of ensembles as the kids got older over the years. We had wind ensembles, jazz ensembles . . . it was a whole mishmash of music and musicians, because every school back then had a music program and there was money for it. So, getting back to John Kennedy, he started pushing physical education in the schools and gradually physical education departments gained greater clout and a lot of that money, that would've gone to music, went to developing the physical education department.

Author: Ah, so that's where that trend started.

Assistant Principal Cello: Yeah, and also with the math and science departments. But there was still more money thrown at the physical education department, because the schools could sell tickets to sports events held at the schools and make money.

Author: I see, of course, of course.

Assistant Principal Cello: Yeah, so that's where a lot of those school funds went. And so that reduced and limited any music or arts training to the magnet schools.

Author: So, did you go to Curtis?

Assistant Principal Cello: No, I went to the Philadelphia Musical Academy.

Author: Oh, that's right. You know someone asked me the other day if they were two different schools and I said, of course they're two different schools. Curtis is quite small, isn't it?

Assistant Principal Cello: Yeah, it's very small, it's very intimate, and it's very rich. So, it gives free scholarships to anyone who can get in. But they must have all their stuff together as musicians before they qualify.

Author: Yeah, and there's no tuition, right?

Assistant Principal Cello: Yeah, and it's for protégés, you know. Preferably, young protégés. Actually, I auditioned for Curtis when I was twenty-one and in my senior year at the Academy. At that time, I was kind of on the front line of the whole integration experiment.

Author: Right . . .

Assistant Principal Cello: And as I told you, for my first seven years studying the cello, in elementary school I had a violinist, a clarinet player, and a bass player all teaching me cello in those seven years. In the summers there were a few freelance cellists and the one who taught me was indifferent as well. He would also say just learn that the next etude. All of them were kind of indifferent. Even later, the guy I studied with that graduated from Curtis, was also very indifferent and totally into himself.

Author: Indifferent? Really?

Assistant Principal Cello: Indifferent, yeah, they would just say, "Take the next page," but they wouldn't show me how to do it or explain it, so I had to figure it out for myself. But fortunately, there were lots of graphic illustrations in the cello books, with diagrams showing hand positions and other vital info, so I was able to figure things out for myself and went from there. I knew what it took to produce a good sound playing in the middle of the string.

Even though I wasn't holding the cello correctly, I had a good bow grip because I watched the orchestra director of All-City, Angelo Frascarelli, who was a very fine violinist and who actually ended up coaching our string quartet when I was in high school.

And there was another conductor at the youth center, Sid Rostein, who had something called The Little Orchestra Society that met down at Jefferson Medical College downtown every Friday night. And he would have the orchestra read big works like Bruckner and Mahler.

Author: Oh!

Assistant Principal Cello: And ah, so I would go down there every Friday night and sit in with the orchestra, while I was in school.

Author: What size orchestra was it?

Assistant Principal Cello: It was a full-size orchestra. And they let me play the rococo with them one time.

Author: Really?

Assistant Principal Cello: Yeah! And the principal cellist was Ann Martindale's mom and Ann Martindale ultimately became principal cello of the Pittsburg Symphony.

Author: So, I'm still stuck on "indifferent." So indifferent, meaning they didn't expect you to ever get anywhere on the cello so they wouldn't show you anything? How did that play out?

Assistant Principal Cello: Well, I don't think there was any real push to racially integrate that area of the classical music business in the 1950s.

Author: Oh, the 1950s? Whooooo!! Of course not.

Assistant Principal Cello: Yeah, so I started 1959, right and through the 1960s there was only a smattering of teachers who would bite the bullet and actually reach out to help a Black kid.

And in those days, there weren't a lot of teachers doing that. When we got our scholarship to Philadelphia Musical Academy, the school was on the front side of integration; they wanted to integrate. So, people on the board found corporate money. You know Morey Amsterdam, the comedian who actually played cello in Vaudeville, was on the board of directors at that time.

Author: Is that right?

Assistant Principal Cello: Yeah, and there were other corporate people who put together the money, specifically for our quartet, specifically William Fishman, who was president of the American Retailers Association. And there were other board members that kicked in, which was hiked as a fifty thousand dollar, five-year scholarship for a double degree.

And that was how we were put out in the news, in 1967, when there were race riots in North Philly, race riots in Newark, and race riots in Detroit, you know, and race riots in Watts had happened in 1965. I mean the country was going nuts.

So as a Black classical music chamber group, we were kind of hyped as a means to pacify the community to show them that, "Yes, there are some people who are down with total democracy and want to eliminate this apartheid mindset that we have."

And of course, Philadelphia Musical Academy colleges always seemed to be more progressive than other institutes in those days. But Philadelphia Musical Academy at the time was a rather exclusive conservatory and one of the oldest founded in 1876.

Author: Really? And when did Curtis emerge?

Assistant Principal Cello: Oh, Curtis didn't exist until the 1920s when Mary Loise Curtis and Efrem Zimbalist put together the twenty million dollar endowment that grew financially and allowed that mansion off Rittenhouse square to be eventually become Curtis Institute of Music.

Author: I see, so it's a mansion. I've never been there sounds beautiful.

Assistant Principal Cello: Yeah, the Fleishmann Collection is there, they have a collection of rare instruments there . . . and it's just a grand building with a great staircase as you walk in, you know. As I was saying, I did audition for Curtis, but I was on the front side of this diversity experiment and cello teacher, Elsa Hilger, had to fix a lot of things that seven years of studying cello with those other teachers were not fixed. For example, my end pin was way too short, I was playing in a metal folding chair, so I had to halfway cross my legs to get my knees out of the way. So, I was actually playing the cello, sitting cross legged, nearly vertical and hunched over as well. I was always getting pains in my trapezius muscles in between my shoulder blades. So, Elsa Hilger got an instrument for me, which I still play, and it was quite a surprise when I got it. So on rainy days I would take the trolly car downtown to West Philly for my lessons with her. One rainy day when I took the two block walk to the trolly for my lesson. Her house was about a five block walk from the trolly. That day it was raining cats and dogs, and I got to her house half an hour late because there was an accident at West Philly and the trolly car had to wait for them to clear the accident at the intersection of 42nd and Baltimore Avenue. So, it just sat there. Of course, I got to the lesson late, soaking wet, apologetic, and just totally down about being late, because I really appreciated that scholarship and I wanted to be there on time. So, she settled me down and said, "Don't worry about it. I have something for you." So, I noticed this streamlined cello case in the corner of the room.

And there it was, a cello. She said, "This was willed to me to give to a deserving student, and I've chosen you." And I was just floored you know . . . I got weak in the knees.

Author: My God! She gave you a cello?

Assistant Principal Cello: Yeah, a cello with two bows, a hard case, and all of that. Now it had been poorly stored away and was falling apart, but it was a whole lot better than what I had.

Author: Right . . .

Assistant Principal Cello: So I took care of it. I cherished it and of course, eventually I had to get it restored. So that summer of 1967, I started lessons with Elsa Hilger. I worked very hard, and I picked up on everything she was trying to get me to do. She said she was impressed with my progress and that's why she chose me to have that particular cello. She knew that cello would help me to do more of what she wanted me to do on the instrument. She changed my whole approach to the instrument, changed all my technique, took me back to beginning etudes, placed much higher demands on my musicianship, you know. It was . . . quite amazing . . . and I didn't have an ego in those days. Nobody told me that my shit didn't stink, so I didn't mind going back to the drawing board, like most students would in those conservatory days.

Author: So, did she show you all the stuff your other teachers, that were indifferent, were reluctant to show you?

Assistant Principal Cello: Oh yeah, she fixed all of that stuff.

You know, I knew Yo-Yo Ma, when he was about sixteen, from a string seminar they used to have in Manhattan. The Schneider String Seminar they used to have at Christmas time, which would end with a concert at Carnegie Hall. This was about 1970/1971, Pinchas Zukerman had just finished Juilliard and was beginning his career. I was like in the middle of the cello section and Yo-Yo Ma was playing principal. I remember Yo-Yo Ma and Pinchas Zuckerman playing the

Mozart Symphonia Concertante with the String Seminar orchestra. It was so beautifully done. Yeah, I got to be pretty good friends with Yo-Yo Ma back then.

Author: Oh really . . .

Assistant Principal Cello: Yeah, some of the cellists in the seminar got together in a room and started swapping out their instruments. One of the cellists was Judy Serkin, daughter of Rudolf Serkin, who had a cello with all gut strings. I had never played with all gut strings, so I tried it, and I couldn't play a lick, man. It felt so weird to me. Everything felt different, the bowing and how to use the bow. I mean, I was so flabbergasted! And Judy wanted to try my instrument . . . we were swapping instruments all over the room. We got together and started improvising, we had a little cello party.

Author: So, did Judy Serkin become a soloist? I don't recall ever hearing her name.

Assistant Principal Cello: No, no, she didn't stick with it. But I do recall that her brother, Peter Serkin, accompanied me when I played the Tchaikovsky Rococo Variations at my auditioned for Curtis.

Author: Really?

Assistant Principal Cello: Yeah, that was the reception I was telling you about. My teacher, Elsa Hilger was there, David Soyer, Orlando Cole, the president of Curtis and Peter Serkin.

They all sat there as I played the Rococo Variations.

Author: Okay, nice . . .

Assistant Principal Cello: And, of course, Elsa knew all those people, they were all great people, they were all great players, you know . . . and she wanted to show off what she could do as a great teacher. She was telling all of them that she had this Black kid who could do such and such and such and she achieved it with him in this small amount of time, you know. I remember in my junior year, the summer between 1970 and 1971, she gave me her studio to use when the Philadelphia Orchestra went to Sarasota Springs for the summer. Now mind you, I'd only been studying with her for three years at that time. But the stuff she was showing me was so invigorating, I couldn't put the instrument down and I started growing exponentially as a player. I was so impressed with that.

But that audition I did at Curtis in front of all those important folks was really like a practice audition for a New Jersey Symphony job I was interested in at the time. I never really expected to get into Curtis.

Author: So, Rococo Variations? That's one of your favorite works?

Assistant Principal Cello: Yeah, I got a chance to perfect it after I won that National Association of Negro Musicians (NANM) competition in 1973. It offered the winner one thousand dollars and a Carnegie Recital Debut.

Author: Is that right?

Assistant Principal Cello: So that was cool. The NANM, that had been around for quite a while, preceded the Sphinx Orchestra. The finals were in Atlanta with the Atlanta Symphony musicians as adjudicators and that's where I won the NANM Competition in 1973. Then I played the Brahms Sonata and with the vocal winner we did the Brahms Songs together. She was a mezzo from Los Angeles, I think. A Catherine Ballenger.

Author: Oh yeah, I'll never forget playing their festival in San Diego years ago, when I was with an all-Black brass quintet. I do recall that the numerous gay men in that organization kept inviting all the guys in our quintet skinny dipping after our performances.

A rather strange, sometimes unsavory group of Black folks in general, I might add. Anyway, moving on, so you got your first major symphony orchestra job much later?

Assistant Principal Cello: Yeah, I got that job in 1975, but I wanted to complete my story about NANM. You know, I used that money I won from NANM, in the summer of 1974, to go study at the School for Advanced Musical Studies in Montreux, Switzerland; my esteemed cello teacher and mentor, Elsa Hilger, opened that door and many other doors as well. She got me a grant to study with cellist Bill Stokking of the Philadelphia Orchestra as well as master classes with Slava (Rostropovich). I studied with his assistant, Elena, Slava's daughter, all summer in Switzerland, Zino Francescatti was on the faculty, I had master classes with Demetri Markovich, you know. I mean, I didn't like his interpretation of Bach, I presented my own and then he would dis it, because he didn't like the Pierre Fournier approach. He liked, you know, he didn't like using modern bow technique in that period of music. He was kind of a purist as if we were all playing on gut strings, you know. I mean if I can utilize modern technology to make the music work with modern bow technique, then let me play it that way.

Author: Oh, really?

Assistant Principal Cello: Yeah, right on Lake Geneva.

Author: Oh yeah!

Assistant Principal Cello: And the president of the school was Demetri Markovich. He was a Janos Starke–type, musicologist-cellist, who was into purist Bach interpretations and so forth. He was known for that . . . and the faculty there was amazing. Ah, Thomas Schippers was the guest conductor at the school. Ah, Leon Thompson, associate conductor of the New York Philharmonic back in those days.

Author: That's right, I remember him.

Assistant Principal Cello: He came over there and conducted. He was the adjudicator of the Music Assistance Fund, and I actually got a couple thousand dollars from that fund toward the end of my schooling there in Switzerland. I also had a National Student Defense Loan, which came with some strings.

Author: Strings?

Assistant Principal Cello: Yeah, you had to teach in the school system for three years to get the 1 percent or 2 percent interest rate that they were charging on the loan, so I did that. I taught in the school system for two years and paid off that loan after I got my major orchestra job.

Author: So why was it called Music Defense Fund? Was that associated with the military?

Assistant Principal Cello: National Student Defense Fund. It was for any subject, not just music.

Author: Oh, for any subject.

Assistant Principal Cello: It was a loan of about $850.00 as I recall, which was a lot of money for me back then. So, I used that money from NANM as well, for that Advanced Musical Studies program in Switzerland.

So, in that summer of 1974, President Richard Nixon had his Watergate/ Saturday Night Massacre happening, which caused the dollar to devalue and that affected the European exchange rate, which affected my funds somewhat. I didn't know anything about exchange rates at that time. I only had a Sears Credit, which was totally useless in Europe of course.

Author: Right . . .

Assistant Principal Cellist: So, I had to wire home for money, but back then, you know, I could fly over there and not have to pay for the cello. And nowadays you have to pay full fare for the instrument, you know.

Author: Oh yeah . . . otherwise they check it with the rest of the luggage under the plane and mess it up.

Assistant Principal Cello: So the money I had left over didn't last because of the change in the exchange rate, caused by Richard Nixon's Saturday Night Massacre. The dollar fell about a third against the Swiss Franc. So, I actually lost about a third of my money and didn't have that much left over.

Author: I see . . .

Assistant Principal Cello: But you know, the school provided beautiful meals. Petit dejeuner (breakfast) which was truly petite, and a big dinner. The routine at the school was just hard work six days a week and you had Sunday off to do your exploring. But I only had a couple hundred dollars left to stretch over four or five weeks, so I had to wire home for money.

Author: Did you learn French?

Assistant Principal Cello: Oh yeah, I had two years of French in high school.

Author: Oh, I see, so you were ready.

Assistant Principal Cello: Yeah, my French came back to me quickly, because that was one of my major subjects.

Author: Okay, great that must have made your time in Switzerland even more rewarding.

Assistant Principal Cello: Yes, it did help a lot being able to speak the language. It's an interesting language with a lot of difficult verb tenses. I wasn't that deeply involved with the language and many people spoke English there as well.

Author: So, after Switzerland you came back to the United States?

Assistant Principal Cello: Yeah, I came back, started teaching and freelancing again. So as soon as I got back, I got to play with the Forrest Theatre. I got that job because Renard Edwards, who had been the lone Black violist at the Forrest Theatre for a number of years before he got into the Philadelphia Orchestra, recommended me. And I always appreciated that and of course the contractor, a Polish guy, Jack Reginsky, who knew my teacher. So, one thing led to another, and I got hired for the gig. There was a retiring cellist that I sat with at the theatre the first time named Johnny Petrillo. He had to be in his mid-seventies at that point, so they cut him loose. So, after they cut him loose, they hired me for everything that came through the theatre for the next three years. And I was usually the only cellist there. So, my first show was "Purlie" with Robert Guillaume and Sherman Hemsley.

Author: Oh! So big Broadway folks.

Assistant Principal Cello: Yeah, that was big fun and that was before those actors went to television. I played the "Wiz" with Stephanie Mills and Dee Dee Bridgewater, you know. It was kind of nice, because I was in the orchestra pit against the wall, and I could see the show and play at the same time.

Author: Exactly . . . [Laughing]

Assistant Principal Cello: That was an adventure, you know? [Laughing]

Author: Now at that time they weren't cutting back the size of the pit orchestras for the shows yet?

Assistant Principal Cello: Oh, no, no, those were good gigs, man. They paid $250.00 a week; I think it was and we got paid in cash in a nice envelope.

Author: Cash? Wow!

Assistant Principal Cello: No checks and the name of the production was printed on the envelope. Oh, it was sweet, man. And out of that came other gigs. I remember playing a gig for Alice Coltrane once.

Author: Is that right?

Assistant Principal Cello: I went to her show on a Friday night, went backstage and announced to everyone, "Hey I play cello." (I had no fear back then.) "I attend the Philadelphia Music Academy; can you use another cello?" And there was only one brother on the stage. The rest of the orchestra were white jobbers from Philly and the soloist was a guy named John Blair, who dressed up in this Foo Man Chu huck-up, with the all-black silk outfit, a goatee, and a ponytail. Looking all Samurai and what not. Because, at that time, Alice Coltrane was into this Eastern vibe, you know?

Author: Really?

Assistant Principal Cello: And she was doing her Eastern vibe on the harp with all her pentatonic scales and what not. And John Blair (violin) was screeching and scratching and doing the noise kind of improv. I thought, I could do that. I did that in school with Theodore Antiniu. So, they hooked me up, I went back and did the gig, did my screeching and scratching with John Blair and got thirty-five dollars for the night, you know? [Laughing]

Author: Yeah, yeah, no need to be shy. [Laughing]

Assistant Principal Cello: I was twenty years old, man. [Laughing] I was fear-less, man. . . . Now, when I look back on that, I can't believe I did that.

Author: Yep, fearless . . .

Assistant Principal Cello: But, I had no fear asking for that job. When I got the job, that's when the fear set in, then I was paranoid as hell.

Author: Ha, ha, oh really?

Assistant Principal Cello: I was worried. *Can I keep the job? Am I really good enough?* Things got real then.

Author: Well, you know that fear was a thing that I noticed slowly creeping in. For years, I had no fear, no nerves to speak of when playing, especially solos in the orchestra. However, when you turn about age fifty as a brass player, the first thing to go is your single tonguing. Your main articulator. Then, of course as brass players we learn double and triple tonguing which is a great back-up.

Assistant Principal Cello: Ah, didn't know that.

Author: Then of course there's that pattern of things slowly changing with time. Solos I played with ease and very little nerves as a younger player, gradually got more and more nerve laden as I got older.

Assistant Principal Cello: Right, right . . .

Author: That's why I always say, you want to make it your choice when you decide to retire. You don't want to wait until they ask you to leave, by sending you that fateful letter or the infamous pat on your shoulder and push out the door with the same hand, while telling you how much they love you with a smile. So, I was sure not to let that happen to me. I witnessed too many players struggling to stay on for whatever reason, until they received the fateful hand of dismissal. The plain and simple truth is our playing does not last forever.

Assistant Principal Cello: That's what I'm in the midst of proving to myself nowadays, you know. Now that I've had my operations and had some down time, I've had some time to rest. I believe the eyes need rest, the body needs rest, the spirit needs rest, you know. So, I'm enjoying my practicing now. My hands are not a problem, but my eyes, at my age, are a problem. I can't read music, for example, unless I have enough light.

Author: Yeah, I have the same problem now when reading music.

Assistant Principal Cello: Yeah, but I have glasses now as well.

Author: So, from the time of your playing with Alice Coltrane did your present orchestra job come soon after that?

Assistant Principal Cello: Oh no, I was just twenty years at that time and didn't even know about my present position even existed.

I didn't even know I could be in an orchestra until Elsa introduced me to Bill Stokking of the Philadelphia and got a grant for me to study with him. In fact, she got me connected with that music school in Switzerland. When it came time for the audition of the orchestra position, I hold now, Elsa knew about that and put word on it to me.

Author: Really?

Assistant Principal Cello: She opened that door. All those doors were opened by her. She would say, "I think you should go over there to Switzerland and study." I had master classes with Slava, (Rostropovich) and I studied with his assistant all that summer, Zino Francescatti was on the faculty at that school, I had master classes with Dimitri Markovich, you know. I mean, I didn't like his interpretation of Bach.

I presented my own and he would dis it, because he didn't like the Pierre Fournier approach, he didn't like using modern bow technique in that musical period."

Author: I see . . .

Assistant Principal Cello: He preferred a technique, caressing the string, as if we were all playing on gut strings, you know.

Author: Gut strings, really?

Assistant Principal Cello: I mean it doesn't work, if I can use modern technology to make the music work with modern bow technique, let me play it that way. It worked for Pierre Fournier, it worked for a lot of cellists.

Author: Of course . . .

Assistant Principal Cello: But his thing, he was staunchly purist, you know. His whole approach to playing was kind of like Starker. It was mostly intellectual, with no soul.

Author: Right . . . ya know I was fortunate enough to hear a chamber music concert in Cremona, Italy, of a string sextet of Stradivari instruments from the Stradivari Museum, using gut strings on all of the instruments. God! Such a different sound. And boy, did they tune a lot.

Assistant Principal Cello: We did an opera a couple of years ago in my orchestra that required gut strings. The opera company presented us with the funds to buy the gut strings for our instruments. But they were hybrid gut strings, not the original gut.

Author: Oh, I see . . .

Assistant Principal Cello: They weren't the real deal, but they still felt like gut strings. I didn't like it at all. My instrument played softer, and I had to change my entire technique, by holding my bow differently, you know.

Author: Oh really, that much difference?

Assistant Principal Cello: But it was fun and there was only one cello involved. That was cool, just a small ensemble, a string quartet and some winds and a harpsichord.

Author: So where are we now? You were how old during the gut string opera?

Assistant Principal Cello: Oh, sorry for taking time all over the place on you. I was twenty in my junior year at the academy and that summer between 1970 and 1971, Elsa gave me her studio and that really put heat on me.

Because, that summer I had to practice, and I had to teach people several works of music that I didn't know myself. Elsa knew what she was doing and that was to keep me focused. And I focused, just like those teachers who didn't show me anything early on.

She knew that I would have to learn these pieces based on how she wanted me to think about music and the history of how to play it. She knew that I could scope out any problems a student would have, so she gave me her studio.

I thought, *Okay, thank you, but what if I don't know what to do?* She said, "Well, you'll teach yourself, you'll learn from other great cellist, and you'll teach your students that."

So, I asked her what I should charge my students, and she said, "You'll charge them what I charged them." I said, "Really?" Oh, what an incentive to practice and to earn her rate. So, the students came to my house in West Philly. Mom and I had a three-bedroom house, and the middle room was my practice and teaching area, and Elsa's students would just as nicely walk up the steps, for their lessons, you know. We'd have a lesson for an hour, they'd pay me and boom, you know. This one lady came in from the Main Line rich area outside of Philly.

She was blonde driving a white Lincoln convertible . . . right? She pulled up to the house, this is in West Philly, now. [Laughing]

Author: Right . . . [Laughing]

Assistant Principal Cello: She'd whip her cello out and walk up to the door as nice as she wanted, Mom met her at the door, chatted with her for a moment, and we went on upstairs, had our lesson . . . and she would do that every week! [Laughing] Of course, you know my Black neighbors were talking shit, now. [Laughing]

Author: Of course . . . who is this white woman? [Laughing]

Assistant Principal Cello: They were talking all kinds of smack, man. [Laughing]

Author: And was she a good cellist?

Assistant Principal Cello: Yeah, she was a decent cellist. She was, you know, an amateur.

Author: Oh, I see . . .

Assistant Principal Cello: She wasn't professional, but she listened to what I had to say, and she took Elsa's word, that I was a good teacher. All of Elsa's students had to take her word as well. Elsa put word on and endorsed everything that I did. When I went to Switzerland, she put word on that, she found that grant for me, she found out about the scholarship information for me, saying, "This is where I want him to go this summer" and boom! I was there. I used the money I won from NANM to get there.

And she also found the grant for me to study with Bill Stokking of the Philadelphia Orchestra in December of 1974. I studied with him for about four months and that grant Elsa got me just about covered Mr. Stokking's fee, which was quite high. I couldn't have paid it out of pocket, you know. (Bill Stokking had he accident and injured his finger. Lynn Harold was in the same section with Stokking in Cleveland Orchestra.)

I said to Stokking that I don't see many Blacks making a living in this industry. I mean Booker Rowe, violin, and Renard Edwards, viola, joined the Philly Orchestra in 1970. I knew them and got to play chamber music with them, and they were very encouraging, but they also met with some challenges. You know, the whole orchestra probation period was very stressful for them at that time. Booker had just gotten married, had a child, and wanted to keep his job, ya know. On top of that, the violin section insisted that his spiccato be this way or that way, you know. They took him through a bunch of changes.

Author: I believe it . . .

Assistant Principal Cello: I knew about what he was going through, so I asked Booker, what's it like . . . could I actually do that? And he said, "You can, all you have to do is believe." After he told me his story as a Black classical violinist, he got the principal job in the Philadelphia Orchestra. My jaw dropped to the floor. I was just overwhelmed with appreciation for his tenacity, desire, and willingness to overcome. I thought to myself, there are a lot of things I can overcome, but I shouldn't overcome this musical gift from God.

Author: Absolutely . . .

Assistant Principal Cello: I should honor this gift from God and let everything else take a hike, you know. And that's how I kind of treated my gift from that point on.

So, when I did the audition here for my present position, it didn't seem like an audition. It seemed like I was giving a recital. I felt like I was playing everything stylistically correct. You know how some people just play the notes?

Author: Yes . . .

Assistant Principal Cello: When I played Mozart, it sounded like Mozart, when I played Brahms or something romantic, it sounded like that. When I played Stravinsky, it sounded like that, you know. When I did Impressionist, it sounded Impressionistic. So, I understood how to present all the composer's styles.

Author: I see . . .

Assistant Principal Cello: And, that got me over. And when I got into the finals, Thomas Schippers, whose face was on the brochure of the school I had gone to in Switzerland, I didn't know Thomas Schippers was the music director when I went to audition for my present position. I was so green I didn't even check the stats for the orchestra.

Author: Really? [Laughing]

Assistant Principal Cello: Yeah, I just went there and played, and I thought, I probably won't get this gig anyway. I'd heard that the town of my present orchestral position was an uptight town, perhaps not being a place I'd want to be. I came to town with all kinds of defenses and what nots about, being so close to the Mason-Dixon line and the South, you know.

It was all that racial baggage that I'd learned from the 1960s. [Laughing] I brought my own philosophical and mental baggage with me. After I got the job, I had to get out into the community and learn what to excise and what to keep.

Just as American culture as well as classical music culture was going through its own growing pains as to whether it wanted to accept Black people's humanity, doing what we do in any field of endeavor. And in the process of getting out into the community, I met some beautiful people who had already been through what I had experienced in their respective disciplines. I met other professionals, and we had our own special kind of bond. There were some guys I got involved with who were Proctoids. That was the slang for Proctor and Gamble middle management people. There were people from Zerox, there were KAPPAs, Qs (a billiard club), or ALPHAs, you know. Even though I never joined a fraternity, but I had a relationship with fraternity brothers. So, without going through the hazing and everything, I still got the benefit of their brotherhood and fellowship along the way.

Author: And what was the position that was open in the orchestra?

Assistant Principal Cello: That was for the tenth chair in the cello section. That was just to get in the orchestra. I moved up to my present position, assistant principal, when I was age forty-nine.

Author: Oh, I see . . . I see . . .

Assistant Principal Cello: Yeah, I started in the back of the cello section, but I was one of the better players in the back of the section. Plus, they wanted to get me out there and let the community know what the orchestra was doing for diversity. So that meant I ended up playing a lot of church jobs in the community; I ended up doing house concerts and chamber music with other players in the orchestra. Just getting out there, mixing with their doners, sponsors, and so forth."

Author: You were the only Black person in the orchestra at that time?

Assistant Principal Cello: Well there was a brother in the orchestra from Suriname a John Helstone, violinist, he was here for my first year and a half. Then he moved to Holland and became assistant concertmaster in the Rotterdam Philharmonic. Yeah, he went to Juilliard; he was a very fine violinist and a great chess player too.

We played a lot of chess together. We actually had a chess team in the orchestra, about six of us, and we competed in the town's local chess league. That was another place where I met people in the town that were serious interesting people, usually around the university area.

Author: I see . . .

Assistant Principal Cello: Then I also met other people, schoolteachers, and other businesspeople from the Hood. So, getting out in the community, I managed to put together a group of kids to do concerts, while I was teaching at the performing arts school in the city. I would take those kids to do gigs. Some of my students wanted to play jazz along the way.

One of my cello students also played the bass. His father was a jazz violinist, and his grandmother was a doctor in the LINKS organization. So, she opened doors for her kids, their friends, and me. You know, one thing led to another and in my first twenty years, I had actually done a whole lot for diversity in the community. So, in the interim around 1995, the orchestra and the community put together what they called the Multi-Cultural Awareness Council, which was an advisory group of a diverse group of professionals who were interested in the arts and the diversity of the orchestra. They devised ways to promote diversity in terms of concert repertoire, support staff in the music hall, where we played, which was a whole different ball of wax, the management of the orchestra and diversity of players on the stage, the whole nine yards.

Author: Great to see how you embraced the city that you were so skeptical about at first. But how was your experience in the orchestra as the only Black member? Did you receive any push-back?

Assistant Principal Cello: No, no, John the violinist from Suriname had already broken that mold. I mean, he wasn't American, but he was a person of color. And there were other Black players who were hired as substitute musicians. One brother, Ron Crutcher, a very fine cellist who went to Indiana University, a few years older than me, got his doctorate and he became an administrator at that group of colleges down in North Carolina . . . ah, University of North Carolina, Raleigh, Durham that area."

Author: Right . . .

Assistant Principal Cello: So he became an administrator down there and then he was provost at Miami University in Hamilton, Ohio. Miami University, Oxford, the main campus, is right up the road. Then from there he went to a college right outside of Boston, Wheaton. I heard him play in a trio here. I don't think he was fully contracted in this orchestra. They would call him in as a freelancer. They still did that when I was here. They would call in players from the college. They'd call a Black player to play percussion or something. They did it ad hoc.

Author: Ad hoc, right . . . [Laughing]

Assistant Principal Cello: I called it à la carte.

Author: À la carte, right . . . [Laughing]

Assistant Principal Cello: I had a legitimate audition for the orchestra, so I became a full-time member.

Author: Right, of course . . . so did you get any racial push-back from your colleagues in the orchestra?

Assistant Principal Cello: Well, of course, they try you. Their racial bias requires that they test the mettle of the person that they are objectifying. I got little petty stuff, but nothing of any consequence that I couldn't handle, you know.

Author: Of course . . .

Assistant Principal Cello: I had more street knowledge than they thought I did. I think they assumed that if I was a Black classical musician that I was light in my loafers and scared to death of the consequences of not saying yow-za to the white man.

Author: Right . . . that you'd be a yuck-yuck nigger. [Laughing]

Assistant Principal Cello: Yeah, but once we got past the fact that I wasn't going to give them all that and that I wasn't light in my loafers then they changed up the grove.

Author: Yeah, they do test you.

Assistant Principal Cello: Then they realized . . .

Author: Don't mess with him. [Laughing]

Assistant Principal Cello: Yeah, don't mess with me. [Laughing]

Principal Tuba of a Major West Coast Symphony Orchestra

Author: So where are you from originally?

Tuba: I was born in Jamaica Queens, New York City, back in 1975, but I only lived in New York for about a year after my birth, technically speaking. Then my mother moved us back to Hartsville, South Carolina, where she was born and grew up. That's where my mother, grandmother, and great-grandmother all lived, so we moved back there.

Basically, that's where I grew up and did my college undergrad work, so for me, South Carolina is where I truly consider home.

Author: Interesting . . . so you were born in 1975?

Tuba: Yes . . .

Author: Oh God! Ya make me feel old. I was already five years in my orchestra that year. [Laughing] So what were your experiences growing up in the South?

Tuba: Generally my experiences were good. I was an only child; it was just me and my mother. My father wasn't in the picture. Actually, it was me, my mother, grandmother, *and* great-grandmother. I grew up in a household with three generations of mothers. I didn't call them grandmother or great-grandmother, but they were all different forms of mother. So, my mom was Mom, my grandmother was Mother, and my great-grandmother was Ma.

Author: And I bet they were all telling you what to do. Boy do this and boy don't do that.

Tuba: That's right . . . but they kept me outta trouble for the most part. I needed a little discipline here and there [Laughing], but I wasn't a problem child per se. I did my homework and earned good grades in school. You know, I was actually valedictorian at my elementary school.

Author: Ah really? Didn't know they used that terminology in grade school.

Tuba: Yeah, they did, and I believe when I graduated high school, I ranked about fourteenth in my class out of maybe four hundred graduating seniors that year. So, I did pretty well academically. I started with music, back in seventh grade, which was when most students became eligible for band. It was interesting that no one talked or pushed me into music. Something inside me said, *I want to play an instrument. I wanna be in the band.*

Author: I see . . .

Tuba: I found out later that my mother played clarinet when she was in high school.

Author: I was about to ask you if someone in your family played an instrument.

Tuba: Yeah, Mom played clarinet . . . and I heard she was actually first chair in her band at her high school.

Author: Ah, so you had music in your family and didn't realize it until you took up an instrument or when did you find out that your mother played clarinet?

Tuba: Yeah, she might have mentioned it when I joined high school band. But she said she still had her clarinet, although a wooden instrument of that age, even though it was in a case, probably disintegrated. [Laughing]

Author: That's entirely possible. [Laughing] So, did you really start playing tuba in seventh grade?

Tuba: Yes, like most of the kids at the time, I really wanted to play the saxophone. That was the popular and coolest instrument to play, in my school days. Kenny G was starting to come into his own on soprano sax, but I was thinking more like playing tenor or alto sax. I went into the junior high school band room and met with the band director, Miss Penny Rodgers.

She had me try all the various brass instrument mouthpieces, woodwind reeds for the saxophones and clarinets. She even let me try a couple of percussion instruments. That way she could quickly assess my general aptitude and potential on each instrument. Eventually, she handed me a tuba mouthpiece to buzz on and upon hearing my first notes, her eyes kind of went wide and she exclaimed, "Now this could be a good fit."

Author: Ha, really . . . so you just buzzed the mouthpiece, and she was impressed?

Tuba: Apparently. You know, at the time, I had no real affinity for the tuba. After the instrument tryouts, Miss Rodgers gave every beginning band student a form to list their top three choices of the musical instruments that they might want to play. I wrote saxophone as my first choice, tuba as my second choice, and I think trombone was my third. I ended up having tuba assigned to me. It would be many years later when I was made aware of an infamous band director axiom that states, "If you have any kid that shows the least amount of interest in playing the tuba, you put em on tuba right away." [Laughing]

Author: [Laughing] Is that right? I've never heard that one.

Tuba: [Laughing] Yeah, I bet you haven't! It's pretty unbelievable, mainly because the tuba is such a hard sell to high school students.

Author: Oh, because of its size?

Tuba: That's certainly part of the issue. But even if the kid says, "I'm not opposed to it and might want to try it," ya give em a tuba and that's the way it works. [Laughing] At least that's how it was for me.

Author: [Laughing] Really?

Tuba: Of course these days they have these small ¾ sized instruments for smaller kids.

But at that point I was a pretty big kid for my age, and they had only full-size tubas at the junior high so I started my tuba playing on what I would call a 5/4 sized instrument. The old King model 2341, with a detachable bell.

Author: A C-tuba?

Tuba: No, a BB-flat tuba, but I remember it was in two separate cases. One large case for the body and another for the (upright) bell.

Author: Right, did your band director try to put you on sousaphone for marching band?

Tuba: I didn't do any marching until ninth grade, but Miss Rodgers did allow me to take a sousaphone home to practice during my two years in junior high.

Author: Okay.

Tuba: I guess they didn't have enough actual tubas at school to allow me to take one home.

Author: I see . . .

Tuba: So I had this sousaphone at my house, and me being clever yet lazy, when I did practice, I would just leave the bell off! I figured out that I could play the bottom half without putting the bell on. And while the horn was easier to handle and way less awkward, I was probably playing an instrument in B natural instead of B-flat without the bell. Fortunately, I didn't ruin my ear by playing an instrument roughly a half step higher in pitch.

Author: Indeed, a half step sharp tuba. [Laughing]

Tuba: But you know, looking back, I would tell anybody, as soon as I could crawl and walk, that in terms of a career, I wanted to be a doctor. I was really attracted to medicine and biology. I'm still attracted to it. I'm just scientifically minded in general.

Author: I see . . .

So, did you get any kind of resistance like, kids laughing at you for carrying a big tuba home every day?

Tuba: No, no teasing, I think at that point my Uncle Theo came and picked me up at school with the instrument or later on, my mother. Actually, I kept the sousaphone at home for a couple of years, and upon starting high school, I returned it and just did all my practicing at the high school on the real tuba.

Author: I see . . .

Tuba: Because what would often happen on the weekdays, after school ended, was marching band practice, but not right away. So, I would practice in between the end of school and marching band practice, do homework, or both. Typically, band practice lasted about an hour to ninety minutes.

Author: Okay, I see . . .

Tuba: So later when I was in eleventh grade, I reached a crossroads about where I was headed in terms of my career. I still had a great desire to pursue medicine. But at that point, I had enjoyed great success as a young tuba player and was playing in All-State Band, Solo and Ensemble Festival, University of South Carolina Honor Band, and I had even started to play a few gigs here and there. In fact, my very first gig was a wedding. We had a student brass quartet, two trumpets, trombone, and tuba. I think the location was somewhere near (rural) Spring Hill, South Carolina.

Author: All right . . .

Tuba: So the one player who had the car picked all of us up for the gig. We drove out to the wedding, a nice event, about a fifty- to fifty-five-minute drive. We played, and I remember we got paid a hundred dollars. So, to split up that hundred dollars, we went to a store, and each of us grabbed a soda or a beer and paid with that hundred dollar bill.

Author: Oh, oh, so a hundred dollars for the entire group?

Tuba: Ah . . . Yes! [Laughing]

Author: Okay, I see . . . [Laughing] well, ya gotta start somewhere. That is beautiful.

Tuba: Yeah and the wedding was outside. I don't want to say it was in a ditch, but it was a forested outdoor setting, like a grotto. There was a pond and a short bridge to an island where the couple to be married, tied the knot. I just remember vividly the coordinator was lighting these candles and putting them in bags up in the trees to kind of set the scene and atmosphere. But he would light a candle, pick it up from the top, and put them into bags. We thought, he must have had asbestos for palms because otherwise he'd be burning his hands.

Author: Amazing the things we remember.

Tuba: Yeah that memory just popped into my head. So, that was my first official paying gig as a brass player.

Author: Right, and to actually get paid for playing, that was a big deal. I remember those days.

Tuba: Yeah, I thought, *wow, we can get paid to do this*. Also, that was the beginning of my realization that through music, I would also get to travel.

Author: For sure . . .

Tuba: In my small town I couldn't really study tuba with anyone at all, let alone anybody of prominence.

My first real tuba lessons were actually during the summer between my junior and senior years in high school. I auditioned for and was accepted into what was known as The Governor's School for The Arts. In South Carolina, we had these schools for different disciplines and concentrations such as arts and mathematics, etc.

Author: The Governor's School? Was that a state institution?

Tuba: Yes, they had them in different places throughout the state. For the arts it was at Furman University in Greenville, South Carolina. I went there for six weeks, which to me seemed like a long time to study just tuba. There were two brass teachers, a trumpet teacher, and a French horn teacher.

The trumpet teacher taught the trumpets, and the French horn teacher taught all the other brass instruments. So, I took six weeks of tuba lessons with the French horn teacher, Robert Pruzin, who was principal horn with the South Carolina Philharmonic. Does that name sound familiar?

Author: Not at all . . .

Tuba: Well, unfortunately, he's no longer with us. I heard not too long ago that he had passed in 2013. But he was a great musician, great horn player, and like I said, he taught all the brass players except for the trumpets. So those six weeks of lessons with that French horn player were my first real private lessons from a top brass professional.

My last two years in high school, I also participated in what was called the Columbia Youth Symphony of Columbia, South Carolina. There were three of us from my high school. A trumpet player, myself, and a trombone. The trumpet and trombone player both had their own cars and took turns driving the three of us to the rehearsals every Sunday.

Author: Was this like an honor orchestra that required an audition?

Tuba: Well, for the most part it was just a youth orchestra, and as I recall, it did require an audition. But the funny thing I remember about it was, they used three or four tubas in the orchestra.

Author: Extra tubas in an orchestra, why?

Tuba: I'm not sure why they wanted extra tubas. Perhaps it was just to be sure that at least one player would show up to every rehearsal . . . [Laughing] Or maybe it was to supplement the overall bass sound, but honestly, who knows?

So, a funny story: The first piece I got to play with that orchestra was the Dvorák New World Symphony. Now if you know anything about that symphony, you'll recall that it has only fourteen notes in the entire tuba part.

Author: Of course, of course . . . [Laughing]

Tuba: The notes are all in the second movement. Seven notes in the beginning of the slow movement and seven notes at the end, and they are all in unison with the bass trombone.

Author: Yup . . .

Tuba: So in that orchestra, the part that was in front of me was a string bass part, not a tuba part. They told me to just play what I could play of the string bass part.

Author: Really?

Tuba: [Laughing] So, I'm looking at the part and I'd never seen anything like it. A string bass part, which, of course, I later found out, sounds an octave lower than what's written in the part. So, I'm thinking to myself, "Wow! This part goes up high I've never seen that many high notes in a part." [Laughing] Somehow, I got through it and made something out of it. To think that was how I started my professional career.

Author: So, that orchestra didn't have enough string basses?

Tuba: I guess not (I'm remembering maybe four or five) and maybe because of only fourteen notes for tuba in the New World Symphony, they figured they should give us more to do since we drove all that way.

Author: So, was there like an All-State Band or orchestra in your area?

Tuba: Yes, there were both but I only played in the All-State Orchestra once during my senior year in high school. However, I was in All-State Band for three of my four high school years.

Author: Okay. Were you first chair?

Tuba: I was never first chair though. In my freshman year I took first in Regional Band. There are five regions in the state. If you made regional band, then you would qualify to audition for All-State Band.

Author: I see . . .

Tuba: And if you got into All-State Band, then you gave up your spot in Regional Band so the alternates could then move up.

However, in my freshman year, after getting first chair in Regional Band, I became lazy (again) and I didn't really practice/prepare for the All-State Band audition. I guess I got a little complacent and ended up not making All-State Band. That was a good lesson for me. [Laughing]

Author: Ah ha!

Tuba: But in my sophomore year I got third in All-State Band and in my junior and senior year, I was second chair.

Author: Not bad . . .

Tuba: Yeah . . . I think it wasn't until my senior year in high school that I finally got into the All-State Orchestra.

Author: So, by then you must have realized that you were an exceptional musician and good enough to play professionally? Were you looking to major in music and play professionally at that time?

Tuba: Well, it was in my junior year that I started to realize that I had to make a decision about which way I wanted to go, music or medicine. When I finally made my decision, I had a serious talk with my mom, because I was so scared and worried about what she might think. I wondered if she would support my decision to go into music.

Author: Right, of course . . .

Tuba: So when I told her I wanted to go into music she said, "Well, you know, I saw this coming. You've been involved with music for a while and having a lot of success. If this is what you want to pursue, then just go be the best at it."

Author: Yeah, she knew. Ya can't fool mama. She knows you better than you know yourself. So, was the doctor thing still in the cards?

Tuba: After telling my mother I wanted to go into music, the doctor thing definitely took a backseat. But everyone in my family was supportive of my wanting to go into music. However, I do remember a certain dissenting opinion at the corner barber shop, where I got my haircut, when I still had hair.

Author: What, you don't have hair?

Tuba: Well, I shave my head bald. Anything left at this point is pure luck or stubbornness. Ha!

Author: I see, okay, so what were you saying about the Black barbershop?

Tuba: Well, at the barbershop, there was one barber who was the oldest of the four that worked there. In my earlier youth, I had shared my desires and dreams with all of them about studying medicine. When I told them all that I decided to pursue music, he was the only one who said, "Man! I wanted to see you become a doctor."

Author: Oh really? Interesting . . .

Tuba: Yeah, well he was being honest with his disappointment in my change of direction.

Author: Sure, that's typical of folks in our backgrounds, because being a doctor always appears to be a more reliable and surefire choice for a career to most people. When you say you're going to be a musician everyone blurts out. "Oh, no, you'll starve to death, it's too much of a risk!"

Tuba: That observation is reminiscent of what a bandmate of mine told me one day when he heard me practicing scales and such for All-State Band. He said, "Why do you practice so much? You can't make any money doing that."

Author: Isn't that the worst, as if they knew what they were talking about. Everybody was an expert in my community as well. People had that crazy logic as well. They would ask, "Have you seen anybody else around here playing a French horn in a symphony orchestra?" Of course, I would say, no and their response would be, "There's your answer, don't do it."

Tuba: Oh my goodness!

Author: That response gave me the worst feeling in my gut. I thought I was hearing that beautiful French horn sound and all that amazing orchestral music written for it, that just captivated my musical soul and this naysayer of my community was telling me not to pursue such beauty, not to pursue such an amazing artform simply because I hadn't seen anyone else, in my little dipshit town, where no one had the remotest idea about what I was dreaming to pursue.

Tuba: If that was the litmus test for doing or pursuing anything, then we'd all still be slaves.

Author: Yeah, I'm telling you. There was always a lot of that kind of fear, do what's safe and keep out of trouble. My father was a trumpet player and he told me that my lips were too thick to play the French horn, that it was an instrument for thin-lipped white boys.

When I went to take up the French horn at my high school, the band director also told me that my lips were too thick. "Most of you colored fellas have the thick lips, ya know, and you'd be better off playing a trombone or tuba because they have larger and wider mouthpieces."

But for you, you have to look at what you actually did in your situation. You stood up for yourself. Every musician seems to get some push-back from their hometown, community. Then of course, we understand that most of that push-back was actually a form of concern, but it was still discouraging to hear it and process it as a young person.

Tuba: Yes, and ironically, like you said, it was all coming from a good place, like the barber who said he wanted to see me become a doctor. Well, when I started thinking about becoming a doctor, I realized that I would need a lot schooling, then more schooling and even more schooling and that was going to cost a lot of money.

Then there was internship, then residency and I'd probably be about thirty before I would even start to truly be a doctor. And then, how much debt would I be in after all that education?

So honestly, looking at the alternative, music seemed to be the thing. Besides, I had already gotten a few gigs here and there. Music, it just seemed easier. [Laughing] I enjoyed it more and I wouldn't have to get into huge amounts of debt. But little did I know what the cost of a good tuba would be, which was another story.

Author: Oh, I know that story. But getting back to the doctor thing, did you participate in anything equivalent to like an All-State Band, but in the medical world? How interested were you really, or was it just something that was in your head?

Tuba: I would have to say that it was mostly in my head. I remember there was one medical book, with a lot of photos, dealing with the different systems in the body. The endocrine system, lymphatic system, etc. God! I must have checked out that book from the library over twenty times. You'd see my name over and over in the library card catalogue.

Author: Of course . . .

Tuba: Yeah, but I never did anything official along medical lines. If I would've taken any course along the medical lines, it most likely would've been biology. The problem was that Advanced Placement biology was a two-period class. The second period took place at the same time as wind ensemble, which was the best musical ensemble in our high school. And since I wanted to play in that ensemble, I would've had to drop down to the lowest of the high school ensembles in my high school program in order to take that Advanced Placement biology course. So right there was the first battle. Was it I going to do medicine or was I going to do music? So, I pretty much decided I was not going to take Advanced Placement biology.

Author: And so, the music won out.

Tuba: Yeah, and in all honesty, I don't think my band director would've let me take that Advanced Placement biology course, if it meant leaving the top wind ensemble. [Laughing]

Author: I don't think so . . . [Laughing]

Tuba: Although I never brought it up to him. I just made that decision on my own.

Author: So, were you thinking, at that time, while still in high school, where you wanted to go to music school, a conservatory or college?

Tuba: Well, you know, it's funny when I think back. I was the first one in my family to get a four-year college degree and I was the first to get a master's degree. So many firsts in my family, so you can imagine, I wasn't able to get experienced advice at home as to where to go for college. So, I applied to the University of South Carolina; I got in and got some scholarship money.

Additionally, because it was in the State of South Carolina and because my mother was 100 percent non-military service connected, disabled veteran (Army) I would have my tuition paid by the Veteran's Administration.

Author: Oh? Okay.

Tuba: I think that was one of the biggest things that motivated me to stay in my state. Also, as far as I could tell, the University of South Carolina had a pretty good music program, and it wasn't too far away from home. I had already been traveling to Columbia, where the university is, for youth orchestra so that felt familiar already. It made sense that I ended up going there for my undergraduate. Again, no one advised me to go there, it was just the only place I auditioned.

Author: I see . . . but you also didn't end up with any student debt.

Tuba: Ultimately, I did have some student debt, but nothing like the medical field or like the students have these days, which is unbelievable.

Author: Absolutely . . .

Tuba: I had my share of student loans, and it was a very good feeling to make those last payments. I was very fortunate to be able to do that because of my present symphony orchestra job.

Author: Remember that news story about the Black billionaire, who was the commencement speaker at one of the Historically Black Colleges and Universities, who announced at the end of his speech that he had paid off all their student loans? That was such a great story, because so many students these days have serious debt after college.

Tuba: So wait, this speaker paid off every one's student loans in the graduating class?

Author: Yes! Amazing! His name is Robert Smith; he's a Black billionaire. All the students went crazy hugging each other and jumping for joy.

Tuba: Oh, that's an amazing story.

Author: And to him, you have to understand, if he's a multibillionaire, he saw that as a tax deduction, a tax-deductible donation. I think those loans totaled over sixty million dollars.

So, who was at the university teaching tuba when you attended?

Tuba: Oh, so at the University of South Carolina the tuba/euphonium teacher was Dr. Ronald A. Davis.

Author: Okay. Don't know that name.

Tuba: Well, he was raised in southern California, and I believe he studied with Tommy Johnson in Los Angeles. At the time he was probably the fourth or fifth person ever to earn a doctorate degree in tuba performance.

Author: Did he go to the University of Southern California?

Tuba: Yes, I believe he did. I don't remember exactly, but he had these three degrees on his studio wall.

Author: I'm sure Tommy Johnson taught at the University of Southern California.

Tuba: If Dr. Davis didn't study with Tommy Johnson at the University of Southern California, I'm pretty sure he studied with him privately.

Author: I see, so did you ever meet Tommy Johnson?

Tuba: I talked to him once over the phone.

Author: Great guy . . .

Tuba: Yeah, he was extremely nice, a real gentleman. I think I was asking him about tuba equipment questions, and he was very generous with his time and very accommodating. I would've loved to have had a chance to work with him.

Author: Yeah, he was great to work with as well. Often, he and I were the only Black faces on a recording or film scoring session and he would always give me that Tommy nod.

Tuba: Right . . .

Author: And you know, Tommy played everything in town. He was on all the big sessions all the time.

Tuba: Yeah, I remember hearing that incredible story of him playing on a BankAmericard commercial. He showed up at the session and there was no music stand set up for him in the back of the studio. He alerted the contractor who then told him, "No, no, Tommy, you're up here today, in front of the orchestra." The commercial featured the tuba player as a stick figure, so he had to sit up front as the soloist.

Author: So, did everything go okay with your tuba teacher at University of South Carolina? Did you get along? And, once you got into that university, studying with that teacher, you must have realized, at some point, that you were going to major in music and play in a major symphony orchestra one day?

Tuba: Yes, Dr. Davis and I got along pretty well. He was fairly strict yet supportive and gave me a good foundation on the instrument. As to your second question, well it would be great for me to pretend that I had it all figured out, but that simply wasn't the case. I actually started out as a music education major.

Author: Oh boy . . . that!

Tuba: Yeah, everybody I told about my musical aspirations said I should get a music education degree, because if it doesn't work out for you in music, you'll have something to fall back on. You could teach high school band.

Author: Ahhhhh!

Tuba: At the time it made sense because, I imagined at most schools your first two years of a performance degree or an education degree, were virtually the same.

Author: Not true!

Tuba: Well maybe it just seemed true for me. In my sophomore year at university, I remember going to the trombone professor and just asking straight out what I should be looking for as far as good brass music performed in symphony orchestras. So, he let me have it, mentioning the likes of Mahler, Bruckner, Strauss, and Wagner.

Author: Of course, of course . . .

Tuba: I remember going to a Best Buy, back when they had a pretty good classical music section. Of course, this was long before YouTube, where you could get online and pull up virtually anything. There was no Spotify or iTunes yet, so I had to literally go and buy CDs when I was in college.

Author: Amazing, how things have changed.

Tuba: I remember purchasing a CD of Bruckner Symphony number 8, Chicago Symphony, with Georg Solti, conducting during a live recording in Leningrad. I remember listening to that recording front to back and then immediately turning around and listening to it again front to back. After that I told myself, that's what I wanted to do. I wanted to be an orchestral tuba player. That was the end of my sophomore year and in my junior year I decided to change my major and go into performance.

In fact, I remember going to one of my music education classes where the teacher laid on an intense lecture about how we should not be pursuing music education as a fallback option. "Teaching is a serious business, and one should be totally dedicated to it." I think she laid it on a little heavy, but I didn't mind, because I already knew where my heart was. I wanted to be a performer.

Author: Ah ha . . .

Tuba: That's also why Anton Bruckner and his symphonies have a very special place in my heart, in particular, for helping me make my life's decision.

Author: Yeah, that Bruckner 8th symphony, in particular, holds a special memory for me as well. When I was still a student at Conservatory, I got a chance to sub with the Boston Symphony. I was hired to play assistant first horn to principal horn, James Stagliano. Of course, I was very excited to be hired and I practiced that horn part every day.

I played all the rehearsals with the orchestra, but at the dress rehearsal, the day of the concert, the principal horn didn't show up. He had gout and often had trouble walking when it kicked in. So, believe it or not, I was asked by the conductor, Eric Leinsdorf, to move over from the assistant first horn position into the principal chair and play principal horn for that entire Bruckner 8th rehearsal. My teacher was sitting right next to me on second horn. He appeared more nervous than I was. He kept telling me to rest my lips on the big loud Tutti passages where all the brass played, because I didn't have an assistant to spell me. He kept telling me to save my lip for the big solos and there were lots of big solos. I nailed all the big solos, because fortunately, the solos in that symphony were right up my alley. It was the type of playing I did best; it was my forte.

The conductor made a big deal about thanking me for filling in for the rehearsal. "So, we want to thank the boy from the Conservatory, whatever his name is, for filling in this morning."

To my great surprise I got a standing, shuffling ovation from the entire orchestra. During the applause, a French guy in the orchestra turned to me and asked, "From where do you come, my boy, you are an artist." [Laughing]

After that rehearsal I was taken into a room were the assistant conductor of the Boston symphony, Michael Tilson Thomas, reviewed the tempi of the symphony with me, in the event I had to play principal horn on the concert that night.

Tuba: Oh wow!

Author: Yeah, so I went home from that rehearsal wondering if I was actually going to be playing principal horn with the Boston Symphony that night and what was that experience going to be like? I took a nap and got a call around 4:00 that afternoon. It was the Boston Symphony personnel manager, telling me that, "The principal horn will be playing the concert and thank you for filling in at the rehearsal this morning. It will surely reflect on your paycheck." I thought, "Okay, good news all around." [Laughing]

Tuba: [Laughing]

Author: As I walked home after the concert that night, it was hard to believe all that had happened that morning. Yeah, that Bruckner 8th is a beautiful work of art and has a special place in my heart as well.

Tuba: Wonderful story! Yeah, I finally got my chance to play that symphony professionally with the Detroit Symphony.

Author: And you recently got to sub with the Los Angeles Philharmonic? When was that?

Tuba: Yes, that was last week.

Author: Oh, really? Who was conducting, was that with Zubin Mehta?

Tuba: Ah, it was supposed to be Semyon Bychkov, but he had a shoulder injury, so David Robertson came in as a last-minute substitute.

Author: Hmm . . . I wish I'd known; I would've attended the rehearsals to hear you play with that brass section.

Tuba: When I got into graduate school at University of Cincinnati College Conservatory of Music, where I did my master's degree, I had to borrow an F-tuba that belonged to the school. One of the grad students in my junior year of undergrad (University of South Carolina) had a CC tuba that he allowed me to borrow to start learning CC tuba fingerings.

However, eventually I was able to purchase my own CC tuba because, because my grad professor wrote a letter to the university loan department, which enabled me to borrow the money for it.

Author: So, what does a decent instrument, like the one you borrowed money from the university for, cost these days?

Tuba: Well, I paid around ten thousand or eleven thousand dollars for my CC tuba back in 1977, but these days the same instrument would probably be closer to twenty thousand dollars or more.

Author: I see, okay, well, there are some French horns that are costing close to twenty thousand dollars. The German horn maker, Engelbart Schmidt horns, of course depending on the model, cost close to that and you wait almost a year for delivery.

When I think about the horns I grew up with, I never thought about what they might've cost. They were so old, especially the Elks band instruments that my father played on for years. They would just leave those brass instruments on a shelf without a case for months. No one in those days could've imagined an instrument costing what we pay these days. My first French horn cost three hundred dollars, but that was in 1965.

Tuba: In fact, I will tell you when I took my first symphony audition, which was my fourth major orchestra audition, I was using my PT6P, which was the one that I bought, with borrowed money, from the university during my first year in graduate school. But the F-tuba I was using belonged to the university and I remember thinking, I hoped the symphony wouldn't ask me at the audition if that F-tuba was my personal horn, because I wasn't going to lie to them, but I just hope that question didn't come up. Because I was afraid that maybe they wouldn't give me the job if they knew I didn't own an F-tuba. And sure enough, in the finals, after all the solo excerpt playing was done, there were a few questions from the committee and one of the questions was, "Tell us about your equipment." [Laughing]

Author: I see . . .

Tuba: So I remember telling them that my CC tuba was a PT-6P and the F-tuba was a PT-10 and it was a university instrument.

Author: And who was asking you these questions? One of the brass players on the committee?

Tuba: Ah . . . In fact, I think that question actually came from the associate concertmaster.

Author: Really? That's odd . . .

Tuba: And I think that concertmaster was known for always asking those kinds of questions at all auditions, especially at string auditions. I think he was always curious about different violins and other string instruments, but I don't think he meant any harm in it. I believe it was just something they were asking everybody.

So, at that point I was still in graduate school . . . and you asked me earlier about orchestra auditions.

Author: Yes, I did . . .

Tuba: So my first audition was for The Presidents Own Marine Band in Washington, DC, and that was in 1998 and I was runner-up to Mark Thiele in that audition. I came back home and took my second audition, which was the Rochester Philharmonic . . . and I had a good first round. The last excerpt was Petruska when I missed a note. I was going to ask for a do over, but they asked me to play the excerpt again and I missed the same note and then I missed another note.

Author: Ah!

Tuba: Then they said thank you so I didn't advance, and I was told that if it wasn't for those missed notes in Petruska, I would've advanced. But they gave me a chance to fix it, so, no complaints. My third audition was the South Carolina Philharmonic.

Author: I see . . .

Tuba: Yeah and there were a whopping five players that showed up to take that audition.

Author: Five?? [Laughing]

Tuba: [Laughing] Well, it was a per service job in a small regional orchestra with a limited playing season. This was in 1998 or so, and the only reason I was thinking about taking that audition was the bass trombone player in that orchestra was also my roommate when I was at University of Cincinnati College Conservatory of Music. In those days he and I would have had services for a few days every month, and I could ride with him, because I still didn't have a car.

Also, the principal trombonist in that orchestra was from Cincinnati. So with the commuting for that job, I already knew two people I could ride with for sure.

Author: So, you didn't get the job?

Tuba: Well, in the finals it was me and my old undergrad tuba professor, Dr. Davis.

Author: Really? Wow!

Tuba: [Laughing] You know, I can now appreciate what my undergrad tuba professor must've felt like, having to go up against one of his students.

Author: I understand, but don't you think he had to feel some degree of pride seeing that he got one of his students to that level in the music world?

Tuba: True! But I also know that for many years he coveted that tuba position in the South Carolina Philharmonic.

Author: Oh, okay, I see . . .

Tuba: Also, the guy that had just left the tuba position, my professor didn't respect very much. Let's just say, they had issues between them. For example, I remember at one point, my professor told me that the South Carolina Symphony reached out to him to play second tuba on the Rite of Spring. My professor told them, in no uncertain terms, that if he were to play with them at all, it would have to be on first tuba.

Author: Oh really? [Laughing] That's pretty pushy, don't you think? I mean, come on!

Tuba: Agreed, just the same, Dr. Davis, told me that I may get a call from the South Carolina Philharmonic to play second tuba, if they didn't agree with his terms.

He wanted to give me a heads up. Ultimately, I ended up playing second tuba on the Stravinsky, Rite of Spring, with the South Carolina Philharmonic.

Author: So, I imagine that had to piss off the orchestra's principal tuba player, don't you think?

Tuba: There's no way to know how much of the details got back to him, but when I did get the call and played with the South Carolina Philharmonic principal tuba player, he treated me fine, even though I did pass on a suggestion from my tuba professor. When I told the principal tuba player, he said to my great surprise, "That sounds like a Dr. Ron Davis idea."

Author: Ah ha! Really? [Laughing]

Tuba: And, I said, "Well yes, it is," and he said "Okay," but we still didn't do it. [Laughing]

Author: That was so insightful, the fact that the principal tuba knew it wasn't coming from you. So, those two tuba players really had a rivalry thing going it seems.

Tuba: Oh yeah, for sure, but my point in all this was, when that principal tuba retired and the audition came up, I knew that my former professor really wanted that job.

So, it was very, almost strangely, interesting when I took that audition, and ended up in the finals with my former tuba professor. As I recall, the audition committee for that audition was the principal horn (Pruzin), the principal trombone, the bass trombone (my graduate school roommate), and the music director. In total, a committee of four people. So, the principal horn liked my teacher's playing and the bass trombone liked my playing. I think the principal trombone was leaning toward my teacher. I was told later by the bass trombone that the music director, more or less, stayed out of it. He chimed in a couple of times to make comments on my behalf but, ultimately, they decided to go with my former tuba professor, Dr. Ron Davis. And of course, I had nothing against that, but some of my friends who were at the audition said my professor was pacing up and down, listening to me when I was auditioning. They said he was extremely attentive. When someone tried to talk to him, he was like, "Don't talk to me, don't talk to me!" [Laughing]

Author: He was really that uptight?

Tuba: He was a little nervous. And there were some things that came out after the fact as to whether my being out of state should or would have any bearing on my being chosen for the job. I had been told by the personnel manager that it would not. Admittedly that upset me to a degree, but I channeled my frustration and focused on the next upcoming audition, which was for the job I have now.

Author: Okay.

Tuba: Sometimes, ya gotta let the small things go to make room for something bigger and better down the line.

Author: Right . . .

Tuba: And everything happens for a reason, especially true in this case, because the very next audition was the one that I won for the job I have now.

Author: For sure, so how did the audition go for that major orchestra job? Were there a lot of players?

Tuba: Ah, yeah, about ninety-six players.

Author: Ah!

Tuba: Yeah, and I survived the ninety-six and I have a little funny story: Cincinnati Airport, Cincinnati Northern Kentucky International Airport, is notoriously one of the most expensive airports to fly in and out of for some reason. I actually saved money by renting a car in Cincinnati, driving to Louisville, Kentucky, parking the car at that airport and flying from Louisville to my audition destination city round trip and then flying back to Louisville and driving back to Cincinnati.

I actually saved money instead of flying directly out of Cincinnati to my audition destination city. So that's what I did, it just made sense moneywise.

So, at the audition I played the preliminary audition, got to the semi-finals and I think my tuba got knocked around on the airplane flight. Because I noticed that my first valve started hanging up and sticking periodically. Typical of that model tuba.

Author: Which was?

Tuba: Ah, Perantucci-PT6P. P-stands for piston, a four-piston horn. The PT6 is a rotary horn, but the PT6P is a four piston one rotor horn."

Author: Where is that horn made?

Tuba: Ah, Perantucci is German.

Author: German, okay.

Tuba: Yeah, it's a blend of two tuba makers. It's Dan Perantoni and Robert Tucci. They collaborated on a few tuba designs in the late 1980s, early 1990s, and yeah, it was 1988 or 1989, when I took that audition.

Author: Oh, I see . . .

Tuba: So I remember telling the personnel manager, "I just want you to know that I've been having a little trouble with my instrument's first valve sticking. So, if a problem comes up while I'm playing my audition, I'll look at you to let you know it wasn't me. It was the instrument."

Author: And did that valve stick?

Tuba: Yeah, it did hang up a few times. I got her attention, and she went and explained it to the audition committee.

Author: So, the personnel manager was on stage with you listening?

Tuba: Yeah, she was on stage as the proctor.

Author: Got it . . .

Tuba: So in the finals, the committee said to me, they understood that I was having some trouble with my instrument. So, I laid my horn on my lap and showed them how the valve was sticking, so they could see for themselves.

Author: So, this was in the finals when you were talking to the committee . . . and the screen was removed?

Tuba: Yes, in the finals the screen came down.

Author: Oh, okay, I see . . . so you won the audition?

Tuba: Yes, well six of us were in the finals, eliminating two, they had a section round with just the four of us, where we played with the trombone section of the orchestra. I was the last of the four to play. The committee conferred and then the music director, James De Priest, came out in a wheelchair.

Author: Yeah, okay!

Tuba: He thanked the four of us for playing, looked at me and said, "Mr. Clark, congratulations."

Author: Wow! So, you got the job! How did it go at the first rehearsal, was it a comfortable feeling with the other brass players, especially the trombone section?

Tuba: Oh, yeah, so I came out to the new job a little bit early actually, because there was a student, I knew from University of Cincinnati College Conservatory of Music, an oboist, playing in the symphony and who was from that area.

When she found out that I had gotten the job, she offered me a place to stay until I got settled. Of course, I took her up on it because I didn't know anybody in that city.

The first day on the job, we were rehearsing for what was called The Waterfront Park Concerts. The orchestra would play free concerts for the public in several different parks around the city. We started rehearsing Gershwin, An American in Paris.

I had already met with the orchestra bass trombonist a couple of times. He came over to where I was staying, and we just played duets and got used to playing with each other. That was really helpful and right away we started to develop a relationship.

Author: Okay, good, good . . .

Tuba: So, at that first rehearsal, I was just playing my part as I normally would and I couldn't help but notice that whenever I played, several of the orchestra players would just turn around and look at me.

Author: Yup . . . yup . . . oh yeah, I remember that kind of thing.

Tuba: Even as a young player, just starting a new job, I knew there was a code of orchestral conduct that says you don't look a people when they play.

Author: Of course . . .

Tuba: It's just not good orchestra etiquette. But still, people would just whip around as if to say, "What's that?" When I asked the bass trombone player what was going on, he said, "Don't worry, they just haven't heard a good tuba player here in a long, long time." [Laughing] I heard my predecessor had been on that job for fifty-two years.

Author: Oh God, I see, so you shocked them, I see, I see . . . [Laughing] so this is what a tuba sounds like, folks.

Tuba: So, when we got to the famous solo between the concertmaster and tuba toward the end of the piece and I played it . . . oh, and it was our resident conductor, Murry Sidlin, not De Preist. After I played through the famous tuba solo. He just cuts off the orchestra, looks at me and he says, "Tuba! Can you do that again?" And I said, sure what would you like me to change or adjust and he said, "No, no, nothing, just play it again." So, he starts again with the concertmaster's solo, and I play my solo again, and he looked at me and said, "Thank you." And we kept going on with the piece.

Author: What do you think that was about?

Tuba: [Laughing] Well, I think he just appreciated what I was doing and wanted everyone to hear it, because he had a big smile on his face. I came to look at him as a friend and I really enjoyed his tenure with the orchestra. He had very good musical ideas.

Author: I think he was showcasing you, that's all. Yeah, we've got a good tuba player here, folks.

Tuba: So you asked about my first day playing in the orchestra, that was it.

Author: So did the bass trombone player tell you much about the previous tuba player, because he must not have been much of a player.

Tuba: Yeah, I got the sense pretty quickly that it was clearly a case where a person had stayed too long on the job.

Author: Sure, sure . . .

Tuba: You know, what they say, "You're only as good as your last note."

Author: Yes indeed . . .

Tuba: You can have a brilliant career, but if those last few years are not so great, it can tarnish your legacy.

Author: Absolutely . . .

Tuba: I heard he was a bit of a character, but he was also the orchestra librarian as well as being the principal tubist.

Author: What? God! That's insane, really?

Tuba: And they said, no one could go up to the orchestra library. If you wanted a part, he would bring it down to you, but no one from the orchestra was allowed up there. It was like his private world. He kept horns up there, and there was a legend that he had thousands of instruments of every kind, that he owned all over the state.

Author: I see . . .

Tuba: He was known as a huge educator all over the state. He taught at Lewis & Clark College, which is one of the positions that I currently hold, as far as teaching tuba.

Author: Quite the character. Oh, great to hear that you have a teaching position at Lewis & Clark College.

So, were there any other African American players in the orchestra?

Tuba: Just me and maestro, James De Preist, but at the time, there was like a permanent substitute viola player. I think his name was Cleo.

Author: Oh, okay.

Tuba: Yeah, he didn't have a permanent position, but he played often with the orchestra. Ah, trying to think, if there was anyone else. I can't remember.

Author: It's okay, but I just have to ask you if De Preist ever had you over to his house for dinner. I heard he made great barbecue ribs.

Tuba: Ah! Yes, at his condo, he did have me over for dinner a couple of times.

Author: Oh, that's great.

Tuba: Yeah, and Jeanette, his wife, put a couple of pieces in the oven for us.

Author: Oh, he was just a great human being. I'll never forget playing the Tchaikovsky 6th Symphony with him. Just looking at his face during the performance. You could tell he really got the music.

Tuba: If I can say anything, I just remember playing things for him and to just see that smile he had when you did something that he liked. You just felt so good when he did that.

Author: Oh, for sure, he was the absolute best to work with on any music.

Tuba: Okay, I do have a few stories about Maestro De Preist, if you wouldn't mind.

Author: Not at all.

Tuba: The first one was when I mentioned earlier, that when I auditioned for the Symphony, I was using a school F-tuba.

Author: Right . . .

Tuba: In one of my meetings with the maestro, like when I was over for dinner. He asked me, at one point, if everything was alright in the orchestra, was there anything I needed. So, I said, well, honestly, I do need to get an F-tuba, because in order for me to cover this job properly, I need a smaller instrument for certain pieces in the repertoire where the C-tuba is too big and not the right sound. And he said, "Okay, how much does one of those cost?" So, I based my answer on the price of the horn I'd been using, which was a PT-10, a Perantucci 10. So, I said about ten thousand dollars. And he said, "Okay, let me work on that."

Author: You see, man, that's what I liked that about him. Nothing was unobtainable.

Tuba: Yeah, so what happened was, Gretchen Brooks, an orchestra donor, had made a sizable donation to the orchestra, which was earmarked, that in the last five years of his final contract he could do recordings of his favorite works. So, Gretchen Brooks gave millions to the orchestra to do that. Then she came to one of the orchestra rehearsals. He introduced her to the orchestra and then called me up to meet her. He told me that he talked to her about the F-tuba, and she agreed to cut off a little sliver of her donation to the orchestra to allow me to purchase the F-tuba.

Author: Really nice . . .

Tuba: Of course, it was made clear to me that the orchestra owned the tuba, but I was able to choose when I wanted to play it and, of course, had unfettered access to it, but it wasn't my instrument in terms of ownership. Having that instrument was a huge help to my playing that orchestra job and a huge help to my career.

Author: I'm sure . . .

Tuba: Oh! The other thing I want to say about Maestro De Preist is, one day, when we were sitting down talking, he asked me, "So how did you get started playing tuba?"

And I was like, "Well, I originally started out thinking I wanted to be a doctor. And one of my doctor role models, as a young man, was watching *The Cosby Show*. I loved watching Dr. Huxtable and how successful that Black family was. I remember one particular season of *The Cosby Show*, when they played a calypso tune for the opening music, with all the cast wearing island shirts and dancing to that calypso style music. At the time, as a high school tuba player, I thought to myself, *why can't we play that tune in my high school band?*" And the maestro said, "Ya know, it's funny you mentioned that, because I wrote that tune."

Author: What, what? Really?

Tuba: [Laughing] Yeah, so apparently, he and Bill Cosby knew each other as youngsters in Philadelphia. The maestro went onto tell me that in the same year he composed that calypso music for *The Cosby Show*'s theme song, that piece was also recorded by this orchestra.

Finally, I told him that he's the reason I'm here as a tuba player and he's also the reason I'm here, from way back, when I wanted to be a doctor, and was inspired by Dr. Huxtable on *The Cosby Show* that featured his calypso tune as their theme music. Ya can't make this stuff up. We had a big laugh about that tune.

Author: I bet.

Trumpet of a Major East Coast Symphony Orchestra

Author: So where did you grow up, sir?

Trumpet: Prince George's County, Maryland, which is about half a mile from the Washington, DC, border.

Author: And how did you get started in music?

Trumpet: My interest in music started because my parents were musical. My mother played keyboards for our church, because we went to church, now. And my mother at one time wanted me and my sister to take piano lessons, which we did. While I was in the midst of doing that, one day my sister and I were playing in the closet of our small bungalow near our house, and we found this black box. We opened it and it happened to be my father's Conn 22B trumpet.

Author: Ah ha!

Trumpet: I didn't know that my father even played the trumpet until I found that instrument. So, I flipped out man . . . and I was trying to figure out how to play that son of a gun.

Author: And were you successful?

Trumpet: Yeah, I tried, and I really had a burr up my butt about wanting play it too. So, I found the mouthpiece, put it in the horn, but I didn't know what the hell to do with it. [Laughing]

Author: [Laughing] Really?

Trumpet: Yeah, so I told my parents that I wanted to learn how to play the trumpet and they said, "No, you're not ready to learn trumpet yet, you have to get a keyboard background first." I was like in the third grade and eight years old at that time.

Author: I see, so were they hiding the trumpet from you?

Trumpet: No, no, it was just that my father wasn't playing it anymore and it was kept in that closet.

Author: I see . . .

Trumpet: So what happened, when my sister and I actually went to take piano lessons with the piano teacher my mother had chosen for us, God saved us.

Author: How so?

Trumpet: The piano teacher wasn't there. We were told that she had just passed away.

Author: Okay, so, no piano lessons?

Trumpet: Exactly, so that opened the door, which enabled me to twist my both parent's arms to allow me to pursue playing the trumpet. And way back then, early 1960s, in Prince George's County, Maryland, believe it or not, the schools were still racially segregated."

Author: Of course . . .

Trumpet: So we had in that area, right outside of Washington, DC, a gentleman who was the band director of the all-Black Belmont Heights Junior-Senior High School. That high school had almost three thousand kids in it, many of whom were bused past a whole bunch of white schools to get to this one Black junior-senior high school, in Prince George's County, you know.

Author: Sounds like the early 1960s, yup.

Trumpet: This was like, well, let's see, I graduated from high school in 1962.

Author: Okay.

Trumpet: So we're talking about, late 1950s, early 1960s man. So, this band director came over to my school to start an elementary school band program. Of course, I got to be in that band program that he started and come to find out, he was a trumpet man.

Author: Oh, okay.

Trumpet: So I worked with him in that elementary band program. I think he came over to our school once a week. By the time I graduated from elementary school and got to the seventh grade (grade school went from grade one through six), I wanted to be in the band, because that band director/trumpet teacher had a really good band.

So, my best buddy, a clarinet player who was the son of the high school principal, he and I attended a special music program at Catholic University of America in Washington, DC, every Saturday morning. It was kind of advanced music therapy for us. We took music theory and harmony, and I became quite solid in music theory, even though I was still pretty young. But I tell you what, that Saturday morning music theory class, at that university, was great.

Consequently, in my seventh-grade school year, I busted my ass studying music theory and trumpet. So, in the seventh grade, I graduated to the high school band.

Usually, players don't graduate to the band until ninth or tenth grade and even then, they had to pass a test where they had to play arpeggios, scales, and a whole bunch of other shit, man. Ah! So, I remember now, Ivick C. Cook was that band director's name.

Author: I see, so you made it into that band in the seventh grade?

Trumpet: Yeah, I even played the high school commencement that year. And man, there was a trumpet player, playing first trumpet, who was graduating that year, Leslie Newsome.

He was one of those guys that just had a natural embouchure; he could play anything and never practiced. Don't know what happened to him, but I tell you, he could've been incredible.

In fact, there was this gorgeous trumpet solo in the Pomp and Circumstance graduation march, that he used to play beautifully and after he graduated, I got a chance to play that solo and actually, that was my indoctrination into that amazing high school band.

So anyway, I was in that band up until junior high school. However, I was still traveling to Catholic University studying music theory and harmony on Saturdays. When I got to ninth grade, I started playing in the American University Orchestra in Washington, DC.

I used to get on a bus, and at that time, I had to walk seven-tenths of a mile with my two trumpets on Sheriff Road (once I started driving, I clocked it), exactly seven-tenths of a mile to get to the bus line that took me to play in that university orchestra.

Author: So where did you get your other trumpets?

Trumpet: Well, I had my father's B-flat trumpet.

Author: Oh, right . . .

Trumpet: In high school, I got some other horns from a guy named Tony Zavarello, whom my father used to deliver mail to when he was a postman. He had a shop called Zavarello Music.

Author: I see . . .

Trumpet: Yeah, so I was grooving with trumpets. But I tell you what, I tell people, man, if I had to walk that seven-tenths of a mile to that bus today, at night, like I always did, I'd probably be dead by now, because some drug person would've probably killed me just to get my trumpets for drugs, you know.

Author: Yeah, damn!

Trumpet: You know, because I had to walk to the bus seven-tenths of a mile and then ride the bus from northeast Washington all the way downtown and then by bus out to American University. It would take me sometimes two hours to get to that orchestra rehearsal.

Author: And you'd be walking at night sometimes?

Trumpet: Yeah, I'd be walking from the end of the bus line and then seven-tenths of a mile back home carrying trumpets and shit.

Author: But at night, right?

Trumpet: Oh yeah, always at night, when I was done with those rehearsals, man.

Author: And carrying how many trumpets?

Trumpet: Oh, I'd always be carrying at least two trumpets all the time. And yeah, people would surely knock you in the head and take whatever you were carrying to buy drugs. But you know, I think the drug issue today, would be much worse than it was back then.

Author: You have a point . . .

Trumpet: Yeah, so I did that routine for a few years. I played in the American University Orchestra and the Catholic University Orchestra when I was in the tenth grade. Then the conductor of the American University Orchestra got the conducting job at the George Washington Symphony Orchestra. So, he took me with him as principal in the George Washington Symphony Orchestra, where I got a lot of experience playing principal trumpet. I played in that orchestra for the rest of my years in high school, even up until my first year in college, I was still playing with him; Doctor George Steiner was the conductor's name. He was also a violinist . . . but he made me principal trumpet, man.

I continued to play in that orchestra after college, until I joined the US Navy Band. (I have a lot to tell you later about the military bands in general.)

Author: Oh, really? So then, tell me about your experiences with the military bands.

Trumpet: So when I went to audition for the military bands. . . . I could write a book about that shit.

Author: Oh really, do tell, do tell.

Trumpet: Okay, first of all, the Marine Band had no bootcamp requirement.

Author: You don't say? I thought for sure the Marines would require bootcamp.

Trumpet: No, the Marine bands had no bootcamp. So, when I was still in high school, I auditioned for something called the Friday Morning Music Club, which was one of those high- brow, Sa ditty music clubs up near the embassies of Washington, DC. So, on Friday mornings they would have concerts and stuff.

Author: Is that right, never heard of it.

Trumpet: So as a student member, I auditioned playing the Hindemith Trumpet Sonata.

Author: Okay.

Trumpet: And man, I played the hell out of that sonata, so the music club wanted to know, since it was 2:00 o'clock in the afternoon, if I could stay and play that same sonata on a recital scheduled at 4:00 o'clock, that same afternoon. Apparently, there were some cancellations. So, I asked my accompanist and she said sure. While I was waiting, I asked one of the judges of the audition when would I find out if I got accepted into the Friday Morning Music Club and he said, "We only have club members play on these recitals."

Author: Ha! Nice way to tell you that you got in. And you were in college at that time?

Trumpet: Yeah, I was in college then. But let me tell you what that concert led to.

At that concert was Lieutenant Colonel Dale Harphram of the US Marine Band, okay?

Author: I see . . .

Trumpet: His son played cello in the Philadelphia Orchestra and his wife was a cellist in the National Symphony in Washington, DC, where my trumpet teacher, Lloyd Geisler, played. So anyway, this Colonel Harphram comes to the concert where I'm playing the Hindemith.

Author: Okay . . .

Trumpet: So, a little bit later when I graduate and I call the US Marine Band to audition, I found out that I had to talk to this Colonel Harpharm, so I leave my name. Now there aren't too many blonde, blue-eyed brothers with a name like mine. [Laughing].

Author: No . . . [Laughing]

Trumpet: You get where I'm going with this? So, when I got this Colonel Harpharm on the phone, this is the way he answered the phone: So, I said, "I'd like to speak with Colonel Harpharm," and he said, "Yeah, this is Lt. Colonel Harpharm, what can I do you out of?"

Author: Do you out of . . . ?

Trumpet: Yeah, that's what he said. So, I told him I would like to audition for one of the Marine bands. And he said, "Well, we don' have any openings until 1969." It was 1966 at the time and that was just a bold face lie he told me.

Author: What, he was giving you a hard time?

Trumpet: Yeah, I mean, the guy knew that I could play, because he heard me play the Hindemith concerto right in front of him at that Friday Morning Music Club recital.

Author: That's right . . . I mean, so what was the problem?

Trumpet: He just wasn't gonna give me a chance. So, I auditioned for a few more military service bands. Oh, I can tell you a few things about that scene in a minute?

So, I found out from some of the players who got in the service bands after I did, in 1966 and 1967, that they did indeed have openings in 1966 when I applied. Plus, I played in the Kensington Wheaton Philharmonic, which was conducted by one of my trumpet teachers, John Stephens, who had connections at Catholic University, that I used to attend on weekends.

So, you know, a lot of the service band players would come and play in the Catholic University Orchestra to get a break from those service bands and play in an orchestra. One guy named Tom Knox, who was a really good arranger for the Marine band, told me, "Man, you sound incredible, you should come audition for the Marine band, we've got three openings." Yet, I knew that, but according to this Lt. Col. Bell Harpharm, there weren't any openings in the US Marine Band for three years.

Author: Yeah right . . . so he just didn't want you around, because you played way too well for his comfort.

Trumpet: Exactly!

So, my high school buddy James Goldson, who I went to Catholic University with, when we were in high school, and whose father was principal of our high school. He went to Michigan State University and after college we both auditioned for the Navy band together and got in.

My mother knew someone at the Pentagon, a Mr. Ford, so she arranged our Navy bootcamp orders so I could attend at the same time as my buddy.

And that was great to have a friend in a situation like bootcamp, with all the crazy stuff that happens, people committing suicide and shit.

Now the other group I auditioned for was the Army band. So, what happened with the Army band was, I had an audition set up and when I got there, I waited forty-five minutes. Forty-five minutes! I was about to leave; I was so pissed off, man. So finally, Bob Ferguson, who was the head of the trumpet section, comes in wearing an undershirt with a brown crewneck sweater over that, some khakis, white socks, and some brown shoes, to audition me. I remember that like it was yesterday.

So, there was a Black guy I knew, Ambrose Jackson, trumpet player. You ever hear that name?

Author: Ah, yes . . .

Trumpet: Well, Ambrose went to school at Catholic University and studied with my teacher, Lloyd Geisler. I knew him because he became one of my teachers in my third year of college. So, Ambrose had been in the Army band, and he went through the same prejudice bullshit that I did, man. For example, every time they had trumpet openings in the Army band, Ambrose would audition, and he would hear nothing back from them regarding how he played. The next thing he heard was, one of Bob Ferguson's students had been hired. So, when I went to audition for the Army band, I knew everything I was going to have to play, verbatim, because Ambrose Jackson, who had been in the Army band, told me. He said, "You're gonna have to play two Charlier Studies, No. 2 and No. 16. No. 16 is all double tonguing, very fast and technical."

So, when I auditioned, I played a solo, the Paul Vidal Concertino, a really fine French piece, man. Then at the audition the guy told me that the Army is going to ask me to play Taps. Then they're going to tell me that there are no openings in the concert band, and I'll have to play in the ceremonial band. And that's exactly what happened. That was the Army band, that was Bob Ferguson, head of the trumpet section in the US Army Band.

Author: Oh, right, that guy again.

Trumpet: But then eventually, I auditioned for the Navy band, got in, and that's the band I played in for four years.

Author: Got it . . . Whew!

Trumpet: Now, while I was on the bus going to the Great Lakes bootcamp, for the Navy band, I found out from my mother that two important pieces of mail had come for me at home. One was my 1-A draft notice for the US Army, which would've had my ass fighting in Vietnam, with a rifle in my hand, and the other piece of mail was from the Army band telling me that they wanted me to play in the concert band. So, they must have smelled a rat, because they knew I had enlisted in the Navy band, so it was safe to offer me that position then, knowing I wouldn't be there anyway, so they covered their asses.

Author: Wow, amazing . . .

Trumpet: Yeah, that was how that bullshit went down, man! So, I went to the Navy bootcamp, came back home on leave, and then the Navy called me back, because there were so many funerals, because of Vietnam, that they needed extra trumpet players to play Taps. I didn't have my correct uniform with me, but they said if I came back and played Taps, they'd give me some extra leave. So, I said, hell yeah, I was right near home anyway, so why not.

On my first job playing Taps, when I arrived at the Arlington Cemetery and was getting out of the car to play, I heard somebody yell my name. So, I thought, who the fuck, is calling me, waking up the dead, yelling my name. So, I found out that it was a guy who used to play in the American University Orchestra with me.

Author: I see . . .

Trumpet: And I found out that he had enlisted in the Army band to keep himself outta Vietnam too. So, he gave me the lowdown on the Army band. He said, "Man, I'm glad you didn't come into the Army band, because the same thing that happened to Ambrose Jackson would've happened to you. You would've been in there wanting to get into the concert band and they would've had you come, audition, and then tell you there were no openings, and you would never get in." But I never told this guy that the Army sent me a letter saying that they wanted me in the Army concert band, knowing that I was already enlisted in the Navy.

So, this guy, who was white, told me that he's glad I didn't enlist in the Army band, because he had personally heard, Bob Ferguson, principal trumpet in the Army band, say he wasn't having any niggers in his trumpet section. So, the Navy band was the only band I auditioned for and I didn't audition for the Airforce band, but the Marine and the Army bands were definitely bad scenes. They were totally unfair situations, man.

Author: Amazing . . .

Trumpet: So then, of course, I did the Navy bootcamp, and I made the best of it. When I got there, they asked us, "Is there anybody here who's a musician and can conduct?" So, I blurted out, "Yeah, I can conduct!"

Author: Ah ha!!

Trumpet: So I became the conductor for the boot camp band.

Author: Look at cha!

Trumpet: So that conducting kept me out of a lot of not so pleasant training parts of bootcamp. I went into George, the gas house, survival training. You had to grab your gas mask to keep from dying. Well, I did have to learn how to shoot guns and all of that. But when I first got there, I was a non-qualified swimmer, and you gotta be able to swim in the Navy.

Author: Oh, so you couldn't swim when you got there?

Trumpet: No, I wasn't a white boy who learned how to swim at the Boys Club, man. But I learned how to swim quite well in the Navy. In fact, I had a buddy in there, G. James Goldson, the clarinet player, who gave me the nickname of Tuna. [Laughing]

Author: [Laughing] Tuna? So, you swam that well?

Trumpet: Oh yeah, man. So, that was the boot camp crap and when I got to Washington, DC, I was in the Navy band. I did well when I first got there, man. Shortly after I got there, Ted Allen, who was the lead cornet player in the band, was retiring and there were three of us that they tried out his spot. So, what happened was, one guy, his name was John Emrich, was replaced by a guy named Frank Scimonelli, who could play the hell out of the post horn. They also tried out John Taber who was a really great player and then they had me try out. So, when I played, I think, Ted Allen, the lead cornet player, really liked me, because I came in on a Friday morning and they told me that they wanted me to play in the concert band that evening. So, I agreed and at that rehearsal I sat right next to Ted Allen.

He played everything, all the solos and lead stuff at the rehearsal. However, at the concert that night, at the Continental Auditorium, downtown at the Department of Commerce, again, I sat right next to Ted Allen, but he didn't play a note. He sat there the entire evening with the trumpet on his knee. He had me play everything. All the solos and shit that came up, that I had never even played in rehearsal. He kept giving me little gestures with his hand, "You play, man, you play." That shit went on all night, so I played everything, I was scared to death, but I didn't miss shit, man, not one note!

Author: Why did he do that, was that some kind of, on the spot, audition?

Trumpet: Yeah, that was like an audition, that's how they put you through the test. I guess they wanted to see what I could do under fire, but I did it, no problem. So, when the band came back in on Monday at the rehearsal, Anthony Mitchel, the conductor, started to conduct, but then put down his baton, looked at me and said, "You did an incredibly fantastic job on principal trumpet at Friday night's concert." And I said, "Yes sir, thank you sir." You know everything was yes sir, no sir, military style.

Author: And this was the Navy band?

Trumpet: Yes, it was . . . and you know that Anthony Mitchel was one of the most celebrated conductors they had in the Navy band. Then at that same rehearsal, he asked me if I was nervous at that concert on Friday. And I said, yes sir. [Laughing] The entire band broke up, laughing, man.

But despite how I played on that one Friday night with Navy concert band, they weren't going to make me lead cornet.

Then not long after that particular concert with the concert band, they formed a ceremonial band, which had some really great players. Of course, that band played all the funeral services in the military cemeteries and shit, but I tell you what. It was a honken band, man. They called it the honors band and I counted about eighteen players in that band, who, when they got out of the Navy, landed major symphony orchestra jobs.

Author: Oh, okay, they were that good?

Trumpet: Oh yeah! So that was basically my music scene in the Navy. Meanwhile, I was still playing for George Steiner at George Washington

University Orchestra. And I had a brass quintet that I formed called the Potomac Brass Quintet.

Author: Okay, busy, busy . . .

Trumpet: We played quite a few celebrated events with that quintet around the DC area and . . . Oh, while I was still in the military, I got my master's degree from 1967 through 1969 on Uncle Sam's dime, known as the GI Bill. And man, I had to play a recital and a whole bunch of other shit for that master's degree.

Author: I bet . . .

Trumpet: I left the Navy band in 1970 and auditioned for my major symphony job, but I still had ten years left to utilize the GI Bill after I left the military.

The way I found out about my major symphony orchestra job was from trumpet player, Wilmer Wise, who was playing assistant principal in the orchestra. He called me on a Monday evening and left a message on my phone, telling me that he was leaving the orchestra and coming back to New York. I called him back, even though it was 1:00 AM in the morning, and he said, "Here's the orchestra personnel manager's name and phone number. Call him up because we're going to have two trumpet auditions here on Thursday." Now, that was Monday evening that we were talking.

Author: Holy shit! [Laughing]

Trumpet: You see what I'm saying, man?

Author: Wow! Just a few measly days to prepare?

Trumpet: Yeah, so I called the personnel manager of the major orchestra that Monday night. His name was George Aranow. He told me the date and time of the audition, but something told me to ask if there was a list of audition repertoire, because he wasn't going to tell me, man.

Author: What? . . . Really?

Trumpet: He never said a word about the audition repertoire list. So finally, I said, excuse me, is there a list of audition repertoire? Then he told me, and there was a whole bunch of shit on that list too, but I had a strong feeling that if I hadn't asked him, I wouldn't have known.

Author: I see, I see. . . . Wow!

Trumpet: And back then, we didn't have all the computer stuff that they have now, like Trumpet Excerpts.org and all that kind of shit.

Author: Right . . .

Trumpet: So the next day, Tuesday, I went to the Library of Congress and stayed there getting the music and again on Wednesday and almost got my damn car towed. In Washington, DC, they start towing at 3 o'clock in the afternoon.

Author: I see . . .

Trumpet: So I studied all the repertoire on that audition list.

Author: Between Monday and Thursday, you did all that?

Trumpet: Yes sir . . . I stayed up all night practicing, organizing, and just preparing for that audition. What happened then was, the Navy band didn't want to let me off to do the audition. But fortunately, there was one guy in the Navy band who covered for me, so I could take that major orchestra audition. They actually had two openings for trumpet: assistant principal and third trumpet, and second trumpet. So, Rob Roy Mc Gregor won the assistant principal and third job.

Author: Really? Of course, I knew him from my orchestra.

Trumpet: And the day I drove up there to take the audition, it was raining like cats and dogs. I had all my trumpets in a shopping cart. And of course, people were laughing and giving me a hard time, seeing me pushing a shopping cart full of trumpets.

So, I played that audition and apparently, I did okay because a few days later the personnel manager of the orchestra called me and said, "We'd like you to be our second trumpet player." And I said, "No shit?"

Author: Ha! [Laughing] Did you actually say that?

Trumpet: Yeah man, I said, no shit!

Author: Okay, did they have preliminaries, semi-finals, finals, and all that stuff?

Trumpet: No, you just played the stuff, and they made their decisions. It was just a one-shot deal, but it lasted about forty-five minutes, though.

Author: Quite long, for a brass player . . .

Trumpet: I think there were four of us auditioning. It wasn't like they do now, with screens, preliminaries, semi-finals, and finals. I think it was fairer then than it is now, with all these sophistications they have today.

Author: And who was conducting the orchestra then?

Trumpet: Ah, Sergiu Comissiona.

Author: Of course, of course . . .

Trumpet: Yeah, he's the one who hired me. I'll never forget, I've got a friend in the Oklahoma Symphony that I've never actually met. She called me up one day and said something really weird happened. Now at that time, she didn't know that Comissiona had conducted my orchestra. He was guest conducting her orchestra and that's where he died.

He conducted one rehearsal, took ill, and never made the next rehearsal. They found him dead in his hotel room the next day.

Author: Wow, never heard that story. So, once you got into the orchestra, how did things work out with the players in your trumpet section?

Trumpet: It was okay, but the principal trumpet made it obvious that he had never been around Black people. Some of the things I had to put up with, that he would say, were ridiculous, you know.

Author: He would say things like what? Oh boy, I can only imagine.

Trumpet: Like, "all Black guys have big dicks, right? . . . Is that right?"

Author: Oh really, he would ask you that kind of shit?

Trumpet: Yeah, all kinds of ridiculous racist shit like that, man. But you know, as time went on and as I became more respected by others in the orchestra, I would talk back and come down hard on him. It wasn't until then that his kind of racist shit began to diminish. However, if I had come down hard on that racist shit in my first year, I might have been kicked out of the orchestra for being insubordinate, you know what I mean. Even though he was being disrespectful and racist, you gotta pick your battles.

Author: Of course. . . . So how was the orchestra, was it a good group?

Trumpet: Oh yeah, it was a dynamite orchestra and trumpet section. We toured Europe and Asia, and there were times some of the reviews would say that the orchestra was comparable to the top five major orchestra symphony orchestras in America.

Author: Oh, okay, impressive. So, were there any other Black players in the orchestra at that time?

Trumpet: Yeah, we had a female cellist and one other player, who passed away. And when I first joined the orchestra, there was one other Black person, a bass player, but he left and joined the Philadelphia Orchestra. But he was very light skinned so you would never know he was Black, but you could tell by his hair though.

Author: Oh, of course, of course . . .

Trumpet: Yeah, so it was a pretty good situation overall and as time went on, I gained solid respect of the orchestra. As a matter of fact, there was a group in the orchestra called the Artistic Advisory Committee. I was the chairman of it for several years, until my last years in the orchestra.

Man, I was crazy enough to talk to the executive director of the orchestra, telling him that he ought to get his ass down to the stage and see what's going on in the orchestra. That's how I talked to him. I didn't give a shit.

Author: I see . . . damn!

Trumpet: I also had a big blow up with Broadway composer Marvin Hamlisch. You know Marvin Hamlisch, right?

Author: Of course, played under him several times.

Trumpet: Well, one week we did four pops concerts in a row: Thursday afternoon at three o'clock, Friday night at 8:15, Saturday night at 8:15, and three o'clock on Sunday afternoon.

At the first concert on Friday night, as the orchestra was arriving, I was warming up and shit, and man suddenly, I heard my name over the loudspeaker, "Principal trumpet! Go to the conductor's room!" I thought, *oh damn, what do these people want, I was trying to warm up for the concert, man.*

Author: Of course . . .

Trumpet: So, I went to see the conductor and he told me that we needed to make a change in one of the pieces. I said, "Change what? What are you talking about changing?" Once you start a series you don't be making no changes. That was a union rule, you can't do that shit.

Author: What did he want to change?

Trumpet: He wanted to change something that we never rehearsed, and it involved the trumpets, that's what bothered me. And if it got fucked up on the concert they'd wanna blame the trumpets. I said, shit man I'm not gonna risk doing that.

Author: What piece was it?

Trumpet: It didn't matter, it was some commercial piece, but if you don't make the change at the rehearsal, you're risking a fuck up on the concert. I said, "You are not making a change!" I yelled at his ass! And that's it, that's final, forget it!

Author: Why did he want to make a change, was there a problem?

Trumpet: I don't know, didn't care. You don't do no shit like that where you can't rehearse it first, man.

Author: Not a good idea.

Trumpet: Definitely not a good idea. After that, I was so affected by that kind of shit, it wasn't long before I left the orchestra. I was also the head of something called the CDC committee. It was like a community development committee sponsored by the orchestra. It was all about getting the music out to "The People," you know what I'm saying.

Author: Oh yeah . . .

Trumpet: Getting the music out into the community and making a connection for the orchestra. So, I told them in the committee meetings, that as long as I've been in the orchestra, they've never featured any of the African American musicians of the orchestra as soloists. I said that's ridiculous, you know.

You've got Bruce Wade, you've got Ester, and not to mention myself. The next thing I knew, Ed Hoffman from management came to me and asked, "What are you going to play for your concerto with the orchestra?" I said, "What are you talking about?" So, apparently the principal trumpet and the assistant principal trumpet had been consulted by the orchestra management about my playing a freaking concerto with the orchestra.

In other words, management wanted to make sure I wasn't going to be stepping on no toes in the trumpet section by being asked to play a concerto.

Author: So, they asked your two trumpet player colleagues.

Trumpet: Yes!

Author: Fair enough . . .

Trumpet: In fact in 2019, during that damn pandemic, I did a big recording project. I'll send it to you. I did a whole bunch of shit, man.

Author: I see, alright, can't wait.

Trumpet: One of the pieces I included on that recording project was a real high register trumpet concerto that I performed with the orchestra. I did that Molder Concerto, that Wynton Marsalis did on one of his Grammy recordings.

Author: Oh that piece? Difficult!

Trumpet: But I stood up and played that shit live, with my orchestra when they asked me to play a concerto.

Author: I'd love to hear that!

Trumpet: I did a lot of great shit on that big recording project. I did the Neruda, three concerti, I did the Haydn, the Hummel . . . just a whole lot of shit, I'll send it to ya.

Author: Please do . . . so, did you know Wynton?

Trumpet: Oh yeah! I'll tell you how I met him. I was playing with a group called the Left Bank Jazz Society.

Author: Okay.

Trumpet: Wynton happened to be in town and a student I had was the son of a big jazz saxophonist. That student called me up and said, "Wynton's in town, you wanna go to the concert with me?" I said, "You want me to go with you? I'm not really a jazz player, are you sure you want me to go?" So, we get there at the Left Bank Jazz Society. When we get to our seats, I asked the usher to give a note to Wynton. So, I told Wynton in the note that I'm a trumpet player in the symphony here. I'm in the audience and I'd love to meet you, man.

Author: So, what happened?

Trumpet: So Wynton comes out onstage . . . and before he played a note he said to the audience, "Where's the brother who plays trumpet in the symphony orchestra here?"

Author: [Laughing] That's Wynton! Oh yeah . . . he is fearless!

Trumpet: He said, "I've known about this brother for some years now and he's playing trumpet in your symphony orchestra and y'all should go hear him play."

Principal Tuba of a Major West Coast Symphony and Opera Orchestra

Author: So how did you get involved in music?

Tuba: Well, growing up in a family of six children, with divorced parents, we were always looking for something to occupy us and explore or curiosities. For me, I was always interested in the sciences, collecting rocks, catching bugs, climbing trees, you know, getting dirty. My exposure to music was primarily from my three older sisters, who were making up dance routines to popular R&B tunes with neighborhood friends. Our parties and celebrations always revolved around "serious" dancing. From my earliest memories, we always had an old upright, out-of-tune piano in the house that my sister played on and took a few lessons. There was a very limited amount of formal musical training in the house. I always managed to lose myself in the piano sound as I plunked on a few notes at a time while pressing the sustain pedal. That said, my mother did give me a cassette tape of Dvorak's New World Symphony, that I would tuck under my pillow and softly play as I fell asleep.

Author: Okay, but were you playing an instrument at that time?

Tuba: No, at that time I had no real musical interest. It took the public school system, James Lick Junior High in San Francisco, to get me playing a musical instrument.

One day my sixth-grade friend said, "Hey, when you go to junior high, you should join the band!" So, I just thought, let me join the band, because my friends were there. I first tried the trombone because it had a pretty cool look about it and I liked the slide action it had.

Author: Yeah, okay. [Laughing]

Tuba: You know, I had long arms, so I said, let me try this thing and out of the blue, I was playing on that trombone. And I happened to be sitting next to this kid, who was a troublemaker. I remember his name to this day, as the band teacher said to me, "Hey, well there's a tuba over in the corner of the band room, anybody wanna try it?"

Author: Ha!

Tuba: So my hand went up and I said, "Let me try it!" So I went over to it and climbed into this little special chair holding the tuba. I guess I was about thirteen years old at that time.

Author: Oh, only thirteen, great . . .

Tuba: Yeah, you had to climb into this little chair that was kind of holding up the tuba. So, I tried the tuba and I stuck with it. I got to be my own tuba section. Back then the public schools, including my junior high, had an orchestra. My band director was Mr. Smith. He was a great inspiration, an African American and a tenor saxophone player. So by gravitating to playing tuba I got to go on field trips and experience new adventures with my friends outside of school.

The tuba then became part of my life. I got so good at it that I started playing around San Francisco in music programs like the park and rec. bands, the All-City Orchestra, the Summer Music Workshop, continuing right on into high school.

Author: I see, so what was your high school experience like?

Tuba: I went to Lowell High school, a public school known for its academic prestige. But what was really great about Lowell High School was that it had a solid music program. Their orchestra had a reputation for touring abroad. It was just a nice, vibrant crew of teachers and students. So, back then, I guess I was considered a nerd or music geek. Then that's how most of the people in the music department were considered.

Author: I see, well we didn't have those words back when I was in high school. Geek?

Tuba: You know, what was interesting, I would ride my bike up and over the hills to the high school, which was way across town near the Ocean Beach. I didn't realize until later in my career that riding my bike up over those steep hills actually got me in great shape to blow that tuba. It helped me make music out of that big hunk of metal.

Author: So, I guess I should ask, was that big hunk of metal an upright tuba or a sousaphone?

Tuba: It was just an old upright tuba.

Author: Oh, okay.

Tuba: You know, in those days, I always considered myself a tuba snob, in that I never had to march with my instrument. In San Francisco, the high schools didn't have big marching bands. We had only pep bands that sat in the stands for sport events.

Author: Oh, so you didn't have to march with a tuba, okay.

Tuba: To march was rare for a tuba player. In high school, I got into All-State Honor Band, held in Redding, California. What was funny about that experience was, they said I had to bring my high school band attire. I thought, *Oh cool*. We wore these stylish red blazers with a white shirt and tie and black slacks.

Author: Oh yeah . . . sharp!

Tuba: So when I showed up to Redding, I was one of several tuba players and they were all wearing these embroidered military-type marching band outfits. I had no clue it was going to be like that, so I stuck out as the odd one.

Author: And you had on a red blazer, white shirt, and black tie?

Tuba: Yes, I was like . . . cool. The whole thing about marching was foreign to me. I mean, we had to learn how to march in high school, for a parade. I think one year it was for a Saint Patrick's Day Parade.

Author: But, but, for marching, you didn't use a sousaphone?

Tuba: No sousaphone!

Author: What? I can't believe it! [Laughing] How do you march with a regular upright tuba?

Tuba: Well, there's a solid leather strap that you connect to rings on the tuba and then you put the strap over your shoulder.

Author: Oh, oh, I see, I see, okay. [Laughing]

Tuba: I didn't have a clue! I thought it was normal to carry that upright double C tuba. I would take music lessons holding that horn with the strap around my neck. I would sit and do concerts with that tuba strapped to my shoulder. We had a dance band, a big band, an orchestra but I still used that shoulder strap. But a big step for me was toward the end of high school. The San Francisco Symphony had just built Davies Symphony Hall, before that they were sharing the War Memorial Opera House with the opera company.

Author: Oh really? I see, and . . .

Tuba: Yeah, so they were able to start the first San Francisco Youth Orchestra. And I had just started to study with Floyd Cooley. He was my first real formal tuba teacher one on one. He recently passed away last week, sadly.

Author: And he was the principal tuba of the San Francisco Symphony?

Tuba: Yeah . . . but he got me into the youth orchestra and encouraged me to audition.

I was the first principal tuba in the San Francisco Youth Orchestra, with Jahja Ling conducting.

Author: Nice . . .

Tuba: That was so great, we got to break in the new Davies Symphony Hall. We were part of the brand-new hall's acoustical tuning. And back then, the Musicians' Lounge was not yet off limits to kids.

Author: I see . . .

Tuba: So I would sneak down there during the rehearsal breaks and play on that pool table. And of course, being a tuba player, I didn't have to play every piece on the concert, so I learned how to play pool.

Author: Of course . . .

Tuba: But, it was a great experience playing in that youth orchestra. That was my senior year in high school and into my first year at San Francisco State.

Author: Okay, what year was that?

Tuba: That was like, 1981/1982 and that was my first youth symphony. We set the bar really high for great music.

Author: So, was it a good orchestra?

Tuba: Oh yeah, it was one of the best youth orchestras I'd ever played in for sure.

Author: Okay. Sounds like a rich experience.

Tuba: And what was always interesting, the orchestra being so brand new, it always got a lot of media attention. I think I was one of the few Black kids in the orchestra. There were a lot of Asians and a few Latinos. I was the only Black player in the brass section, as I recall. Ah! Trish Grima, a good friend, she played trumpet. So, the media was always interviewing us kids for the newspaper. It seemed like that orchestra was always getting media attention, you know.

Author: Great, why not?

Tuba: And they'd always bring in these guest artists. Oh, like Isaac Stern.

Author: Isaac Stern? Really?

Tuba: Yeah, and what was so interesting, I didn't have any idea about the orchestra world. I couldn't understand the delay of sound in a professional orchestra after the conductor gave the downbeat. It wasn't like in my high school band, where the sound would start right at the conductor's downbeat. So, after one of our rehearsals, we had a little question and answer session, and I had a chance to ask Isaac Stern about this delay. And I don't think he understood what I was asking.

Author: Was he playing or conducting?

Tuba: Conducting.

Author: I thought so, he was quite a character.

Tuba: So at that time, as a young man, I was just trying to learn and figure out the whole world of classical music. I was in my first year of college, so I invited my college friends to come check out this concert I was playing in at the San Francisco Symphony's Davies Hall. I was so excited. So about six of my dorm room buddies came and they said, "Yeah, man we sat there at your concert waiting for you to play!" [Laughing]

Author: Oh, they didn't understand that you had rests in the music, I see, they didn't understand that you didn't play all the time. [Laughing]

Tuba: But, beforehand, going back to like junior high school. The school district had this summer music workshop where they invited all the bands from around the district, from all different high schools, to play during the summer. And David Ramadanoff, the assistant conductor of the San Francisco Symphony and later promoted to associate conductor under Edo De Waart, was the conductor of the orchestra. They brought in professional instrumentalists to coach each instrument. That's where I met Zacharias Spellman of the San Francisco Opera, who later became my tuba teacher in college after Floyd Cooley of the San Francisco Symphony. But what was really hilarious was, several years later as an adult, I was talking to my old teacher Zacharias and he said, "Julian, I remember coaching at the Summer Music Workshop here and there was this one little kid who had his tuba in a sleeping bag, and he was rolling it around on a skateboard . . . a little kid." And I said, "Oh really, that's interesting, who was that kid?" And he said, "That kid was you!"

Author: Ha! And you had your tuba in what kind of bag?

Tuba: A sleeping bag because the regular tuba case was too heavy.

Author: [Laughing] Amazing . . .

Tuba: Yeah, I bundled the tuba up in that sleeping bag and rolled it along on a skateboard.

Author: I see, on the skateboard, genius!

Tuba: You know, you're a kid and you don't think anything's wrong with rolling your big heavy tuba around on your skateboard. It worked for me, so problem solved. My father said if I was willing to carry the tuba up and over that hill, he'd let me play it.

Author: I see, and how old were you then?

Tuba: I was like thirteen.

Author: Were you big enough to even carry a tuba? How tall were you? [Laughing]

Tuba: I was just a little kid. But my tuba was kind of small, a small three valve deal. But I didn't know there was any stigma around it.

But, jumping back to college, my first lessons with Floyd Cooley were getting more intense, because there were things about tuba playing that I just wasn't getting. Back then, he didn't have the patience for a young kid.

Author: I see . . .

Tuba: I mean, he was involved in teaching at the San Francisco Conservatory and playing in the San Francisco Symphony, so in one of my lessons he got fed up, lost his patience, got up, and walked out. So, I was left sitting there thinking, *What am I doing with this thing, this tuba?*

Author: Your tuba teacher walked out? Really?

Tuba: Yeah, he walked out of my lesson. He came back after a few minutes. I think he went out to smoke a cigarette. So, I was sitting there debating with myself, if I should continue playing the tuba or not.

Author: What was the issue that made him walk out?

Tuba: I just wasn't getting the right sound, he said. I think back then he just didn't have the patience to communicate with someone on my elementary level as a tuba player.

Author: So, he didn't have the patience? Interesting.

Tuba: However, I learned later in life, decades later, when I attended the International Tuba and Euphonium Conference in Denver, that Floyd Cooley had stopped playing because he apparently had contracted focal dystonia.

Author: I see . . .

Tuba: Yeah, he had stopped playing and retired from the symphony, but he continued teaching. When I bumped into him years later and he saw that I was still playing, he said something I guess was the closest thing to an apology. He said, "You know back then, Julian, I didn't really appreciate teaching."

Author: So, it wasn't really your playing in particular, that made him walk out of your lesson?

Tuba: No, I think only in his later years did he really appreciate the value it was to be a really good teacher. And I heard that other tuba students had similar experiences with him in his early years of teaching, where he'd get really frustrated and walk out . . . he just had a temper.

Author: And he was quite young to be playing in the San Francisco Symphony and teaching at a major conservatory.

Tuba: Yes, and he was the youngest tuba player ever to play in the San Francisco Symphony.

Author: I guess it does take some amount of maturity and experience to teach. Then, of course, some musicians have never taught a day in their lives and suddenly, they end up winning a major orchestra job and are then almost automatically hired to teach at a top music conservatory, but they have no idea how to teach.

Tuba: Exactly but I only studied with Floyd Colley my first year at San Francisco State. Then Zachariah Spellman came in from the San Francisco Opera. He was young, hip, and cool, and we had the best time. He had me thinking outside the box. He was all about being a nontraditionalist, he'd go camping with his tuba. [Laughing] I think, as I recall, he'd go camping with his tuba on a motorcycle. Then he'd take his tuba out of the sleeping bag so he could sleep in the tuba case.

Author: How's that??

Tuba: Then, he'd put the tuba back in the "case" and travel on his motorcycle. He was like a nomad. Zachariah was really creative, and he got me thinking really musically and broadened my approach to thinking in general. He was really a breath of fresh air and to this day he remains a great inspiration to me. He would wear a green streak in his hair.

Author: And he was playing in the San Francisco Symphony then?

Tuba: No, the opera.

Author: Oh, the opera, right . . . a green streak in his hair? Ha!

Tuba: Yeah, and I thought, Oh, so it's okay to be different.

Author: Is that what you thought?

Tuba: Yeah, and I felt quite comfortable with that kind of openness. You know, we were coming out of a very radical time, the late 1960s, early 1970s.

Author: Right, right, of course . . .

Tuba: My tuba teacher and I both lived not far from the Haight-Ashbury district and Golden Gate Park, where, at the time, it seemed people weren't afraid of each other. You know, there were concerts in Golden Gate Park and people would be dancing with each other. They had like Game Day, Earth Day.

Author: You mean people weren't afraid of each other racially, different groups, gender, young, old?

Tuba: Exactly! Racially, people were like, really open. My mother had a lot of friends who had lots of kids, different people coming in and out of our lives, that we would kind of hang out with . . . it felt kind of like a commune. I could even go to the local Parks and Recreation centers where they had activities for folks. My mother got us going to the De Young Museum, where you could sign up for art classes. They had these community centers, where my sisters were doing theatre and dance. I have to really thank my mother for exposing us to all those different opportunities.

Then by the 1980s, when I was still a kid in junior high, on some evenings, I would go over to San Francisco City College music department and on weekends over to the city's Park and Recreation Community Band nearby. Folks there would say, "Hey, come and play!" And I would sit in the band and play with more experienced, older players. Actually, I got to meet Joe Allessi Senior, the father of Joe Allessi Junior, who's the principal trombone of the New York Philharmonic.

Author: Okay.

Tuba: Joe Allessi Senior, founder of Allessi Brass Mutes! He invited me to come and sit in with the City College Band. I was just this junior high school kid looking for another outlet to play my horn, and I didn't have to sign up or register to play with them. It was just part of that whole open-minded period. There were just opportunities to get out and play and participate. To play music and be a part of something. It was just fun.

Author: You know, that was always the image people had of that area, San Francisco, Haight-Ashbury, Golden Gate Park, Castro District, during that quasi-radical, free period in American history.

Tuba: And that particular free-spiritedness really influenced me about being more community oriented. And being six kids, we had to always find ways to keep ourselves busy. And outside of music I was into the sciences and hanging out in my backyard, where I built a clubhouse and a walk-in aviary with doves and pheasants. At age fifteen, sixteen, and seventeen, I got to go to a biology camp in the East Bay. I'd jump on public transportation, go to the East Bay, and hang out at Tilden Park and go on hikes. By that time my music was really beginning to take off. I was playing at Marriot's Great America, where I formed a brass quintet from that group. That was great, because I love small brass ensembles, playing chamber brass music.

That love grew from San Francisco State, where my former tuba teacher, Zachariah Spellman, pulled us brass students together into a brass quintet. I thought that was great! Brass quintets, I thought were cool! We were gigging around the city, five of us, and we didn't have to follow a conductor.

Author: Ha . . . no conductor, indeed . . .

Tuba: Yeah, playing all around the city, playing in the Dickens Christmas Fair, playing in parks, but in my junior year in college, I was still trying to do the sciences. I took classes in zoology, geology of national parks, and I even took bio-calculus.

Author: How's that?

Tuba: I was like, my God! This is hard! [Laughing]

Author: So, there's a calculus that applies to biology? I didn't know that.

Tuba: Yes, there is, and I was hitting that stuff hard. I felt like I was going to crash and burn, when an opportunity came up from a friend of mine. He said, "Hey, man they're looking for a tuba player down in Disneyland." It turned out that it was an audition for Disneyland, Tokyo. My friend said I should go audition. They want to form a Jamaican Police Band. So, I jumped on a bus to Disneyland, Anaheim, California, where there were all these Black brass players doing a group audition, playing through all these Latin, Calypso Disney tunes.

Author: So, that was what they really wanted?

Tuba: Yeah, so they wanted a Jamaican Police Band to play in Adventureland at Disneyland, Tokyo.

Author: Ha! Really? Look at cha, that is crazy. [Laughing]

Tuba: Yeah, so I went down to Anaheim for a morning audition and by the end of the day, Stan Freese, contractor for the gig, came up to me and said I had won the audition and he wanted me to go to Tokyo. So that meant I would need to take off from school, disrupting my four-year college plan that I'd set up. But, on the other hand, when would I get a chance to live in Tokyo, Japan, and get paid to play my tuba?

Author: So, so, did you take the gig?

Tuba: Yeah, I did! So that meant I had to get a tuba case.

Author: Right! [Laughing] But not a sleeping bag? Just kidding . . . [Laughing]

Tuba: But by that time I had bought a decent tuba.

Author: Oh, okay, good . . . [Laughing] And what size tuba did you buy?

Tuba: Oh, it was a four-quarter Hirsbrunner.

Author: Oh! Nice . . . Swiss, and that's a good-sized instrument, isn't it?

Tuba: Yeah, but Disney hooked me up. They got me a huge flight shipping case, an "Anvil" trunk that had to be shipped separately, without my tuba. Arriving later in Anaheim, Disneyland we basically rehearsed for about, maybe a week before Disney flew us to Tokyo. Now what was great about that gig was, it was basically an all-brass band.

Author: Right . . . okay.

Tuba: So for Disneyland, Tokyo, we were supposed to be a police band in Jamaica, wearing police outfits. Now one might see that image as non-politically correct, but we were all Black musicians with an opportunity to play in Japan. Three trombones, two percussion players, a trumpet, an alto saxophone, and myself.

Author: You said it was not politically correct, what did you mean?

Tuba: You know, an all-Black group, Disney (and its racial history) and back then Disney, Tokyo had an amusement park called Dutch Land where all the Japanese folks were wearing blonde wigs. Our being there as an all-Black, Jamaican Police Band had racial overtones, you know, "Look, we've got an all-Black brass band from the Caribbean." I don't know if Disney Tokyo still has such a band today.

Author: But you got the gig!

Tuba: Oh yeah, and that was like the grand opening of the Tokyo Disneyland Park. I was there for six months.

Author: Oh! Is that right?

Tuba: Six months living in Tokyo, and I wasn't even twenty-one years old yet.

Author: Did it pay well?

Tuba: Yes, it paid well, I saved some cash, bought another tuba, and a camera.

Author: Oh, the best place to buy a camera, for sure.

Tuba: The guys in the band were buying like, Yamaha, DGX-670 electric keyboards.

Author: Right, I remember those.

Tuba: It was interesting. There I was, in my early twenties, immersed in Japanese culture and at the time, I think it was 1984.

Author: Ah, 1984? Did you learn Japanese?

Tuba: Oshi-nihungo-oshi masta!

Author: Ah ha!

Tuba: I learned enough to get around by myself and get back to my apartment.

Author: Okay.

Tuba: What was most interesting culturally was, we were Black musicians in Japan. Michael Jackson was big at that time. Also, at that time, the Japanese were not used to seeing people of color, especially Black folks. So, when they'd see us, the only way they felt they could relate was to say, "Ah so, Michael Jackson, Hai!"

Because it was the opening year of that Tokyo, Disney Park, they had a lot of entertainers from the United States to help fill out the array of performers. So, we were an all-Black group, but they also had an American rock group that had a few blondes that couldn't handle being singled out. They were getting a taste, I might add, of what it's like to be Black. They were singled out, gawked at, followed, and just had a big deal made about their blonde whiteness. They just couldn't deal with the tension of being viewed as different, of being other rather than the majority.

Oh, the Japanese had an interesting description of our Jamaican Police Band that we translated. In the program of our concerts they had, "Jamaican Police Band, very fine and exciting. All the young girls yearn for them."

Author: I see . . . and what uniform did you wear?

Tuba: Oh, we wore a uniform of navy blue pants, white coats, and white safari helmets. And we also wore tan safari shorts and shirts just for the performance or should I say the parade. We were doing seven shows a day and the middle performance of the day was an actual parade. Half-hour on and half-hour off. But it was an intense gig and I grew up a lot and really got down deep into myself about being a professional musician. We had a dozen tunes in the book that we had to memorize.

Author: Oh, I see, right . . .

Tuba: So, what was pivotal about that trip was, the Empire Brass Quintet was on a tour through Japan.

Author: Really?

Tuba: I had met their tuba player, Sam Pilafian, briefly at a concert in Berkeley, California. I had an epiphany when I saw what they did in performance. I wanted to do what the Empire Brass Quintet did. So, when they came to Japan, I just had to go to their concert. The trombone player of the Empire Brass was Larry Isaacson, who was my coach when I was playing in the San Francisco Symphony Youth Orchestra. He was playing second trombone in the San Francisco Symphony at the time.

Author: I see . . .

Tuba: So, when I see the Empire Brass Quintet come on stage in Japan, I know two of the faces, Sam Pilafian and Larry Isaacson. So later they said to me that there were over three thousand people in the audience, and they saw only one Black person and they thought, "Hey! We know him." So, I blew them away by being the lone Black person, whom they knew, showing up in a Japanese audience.

So, a couple of days after their concert we had a little pow-wow, where Sam Pilafian introduced me to a lot of the local Japanese musicians, who were playing in theaters, the symphony, and doing freelance work in Tokyo. Then out of the blue, Sam asked me if I wanted to come out and study with him at Boston University when I was done with the gig in Japan. I said, "Hell yeah."

Author: And you were barely twenty years old then, right?

Tuba: Yeah, I wasn't even twenty-one yet, just a junior in college then. And what was especially amazing about Japan being pivotal for me, was getting to know Kubo, one of the jazz tuba players in Tokyo. He said to me, "Hey man, Howard Johnson is coming to town."

Author: Wow! Okay. What a treat.

Tuba: He said, "You should come hang out with him, he's a jazz tuba legend and he plays baritone sax too." I said sure. I would love to hang out with him, he's a legend. He even had a Miller Lite Beer television commercial.

So, I went to the hotel to meet Howard Johnson and Kubo wasn't there yet to introduce us. I went ahead and knocked on Howard's door, we met, and he said, "Let's go wait in the lobby for Kubo." So, I got to know Howard Johnson and I thought, *Wow! This guy is one of the greatest jazz tuba players and I was having a great conversation with him, Wow!*

Then all of a sudden, Howard looks up and he says, "Hey, Bobby, how you doin'?" Bobby McFerrin walks into the lobby.

Author: Holy shit, really?

Tuba: So, there I was, sitting there in that hotel lobby with Bobby McFerrin and Howard Johnson. Me, this little twenty-year-old, Black kid tuba player from San Francisco. Hanging out with these great musical artists.

Author: Yup!

Tuba: It was so comfortable, so beautiful that they knew each other, and I was there listening to them catching up. And oddly enough, Bobby McFerrin later moved to San Francisco, living a block down from where I grew up.

Author: Is that right?

Tuba: Yeah, Howard Johnson was so warm and supportive to me, and later when I moved to the east coast, we kept in touch, and he helped me out a little bit. Yeah, and so Boston, was a whole different vibe.

Author: For sure . . .

Tuba: The east coast was a whole different life for me. But it was great, I started the Atlantic Brass Quintet, and this quintet was being mentored by the Empire Brass Quintet. We would play with them in brass chamber music festivals and seminars in the summer at Tanglewood. My brass quintet was the staff quintet for Tanglewood. I got to hang out there as a staff member on the faculty. And of course, the Boston Symphony was there and the Tanglewood Fellowship Orchestra as well.

I just remember fondly the hanging out at Tanglewood with all these great up-and-coming, future classical artists. We also hung out with Marin Alsop; she coached my brass quintet. Yeah, a bunch of folks were there at Tanglewood that year. So, the great thing that happened, to keep a long story short, I was a founding member of the Atlantic Brass Quintet, a group that got picked up by Columbia Artists Management, we were following in the footsteps of the Empire Brass Quintet.

Author: Really? Impressive . . .

Tuba: Yeah, I was living the life that I really wanted. I got to achieve the professional level that I really wanted. My quintet got to perform with the Empire Brass Quintet in Carnegie Hall, a series called The Empire Brass and Friends; we performed on their holiday concerts.

Author: Okay, nice . . . so the Atlantic Brass Quintet, I heard quite a lot about you guys.

Tuba: Yeah, things were happening. So, by the time the Empire Brass Quintet was starting to talk about retiring, my quintet was available to fill that gap, you know. And you know, right around that time, we got to play for Art Garfunkel's wedding.

Author: Ah ha, really?

Tuba: Yes . . . so after all that success with the Atlantic Brass Quintet, the group disbanded, and I got a call from a trumpet player about the new brass ensemble that was forming. My first rehearsal with that group was in Los Angeles, where I met you. That group was so refreshing after playing in Tokyo with the Jamaican Police Band. The playing was on a whole different level. However, while I was still in Boston and after playing with the new brass ensemble, my playing fell apart. So, for some five years, I couldn't hold a note. I got focal dystonia.

Author: Holy shit! Sorry . . .

Tuba: It happened, like, overnight and during that time, I was playing in several brass quintets in town: I was playing in a Klezmer band, I was getting calls, playing like crazy, gigging everywhere, mostly school concerts for young audiences of Massachusetts. I was on their roster with two other musical groups.

Author: And all that playing was after the focal dystonia?

Tuba: No, that was right before the focal dystonia, and one day, all of a sudden, all of that wonderful playing I was doing, had to stop.

Author: Wow, what a shame.

Tuba: In fact, just before the focal dystonia hit, I was planning to leave the east coast and audition for the Los Angeles Philharmonic. So I was putting together audition tapes for that and suddenly, I thought, how come I can't play this excerpt like I used to just last week? There was not much pain, you just don't have control.

Author: Right, I see . . . damn!

Tuba: The focal dystonia happened like in November and by New Year's Eve, I played my last concert with my Klezmer band. And so then, I had to find a way to survive.

Author: God! So, what did you do?

Tuba: Yeah, well I looked in the newspaper and found a job called roaming operator. It was a customer service job for the cellular industry. Remember roaming? So, like if you crossed the street, your phone would switch to another service and if you kept walking it would switch to another and another. Also, it mattered what area code you were dialing, ancient!

So, a roaming operator was a service that would connect your call. You'd give us a credit card number and we'd connect you.

Author: But that doesn't happen anymore, thank God. I remember those days.

Tuba: Oh no, it's totally changed now. I was carrying a brick-sized phone in those days.

Author: A what kind of phone?

Tuba: You know those phones that were as big as a red brick or two, that had a padded shoulder strap so you could hold the phone up to your ear, you remember, 1990? We don't even think about that stuff now. So, I became supervisor right away for my phone company job. They were opening new offices. . . . I mean, things were really happening fast in the cell phone industry.

After a while, I was thinking I had to get back to the west coast. I wasn't doing any music. I tried teaching a lesson or two and I decided it was too depressing thinking about music.

Author: Of course . . .

Tuba: So when I came back home to the west coast, after five years, I started to successfully rebuild my playing.

Author: What did you do to rebuild your tuba playing?

Tuba: Well, in 1995, I was still working in the cellphone industry with Air Touch, when pagers began getting phased out and cellphones were quickly emerging. While I was doing the cellular stuff, I started to get back into playing. I was just playing simple stuff, like playing in the Green Street Mortuary Band.

Author: A mortuary band? Okay!

Tuba: Christian Hymns, a ten-piece band that would march around Chinatown playing for all the Chinese funerals, which was a big tradition in the North End, Chinatown.

So, I managed to get my playing back to the point where all of my buddies from San Francisco State and my early college years were saying, "Hey! You're back in town and you're playing again!"

Author: So how did the return of your playing ability manifest itself? Was it an extremely gradual process, and did it test your patience?

Tuba: My recovery was basically one note at a time.

Author: I see . . . amazing . . .

Tuba: That's pretty much my story. I still had to figure out what was happening because I didn't know what that focal dystonia was.

Author: Of course, nobody knew, really.

Tuba: I had no clue. I went to one workshop; I think her name was, Jan Kagarice. She was doing workshops on the condition in the Bay area. I would do long tones to see if I could get a sound. I even tried to rearrange my approach to playing. It was about making music, making a beautiful sound, and not about trying to make a living.

Author: Right . . . but you know, I don't know many people who recovered from this focal dystonia.

Tuba: Yeah, very few but, some players have recovered. I learned that Warren Deck and Floyd Cooley both had it in their later years. I talked to Warren Deck, and he said he could get about 80 percent of his playing ability back, but he thought that amount wasn't worth it for him.

Author: So those guys had it too?

Tuba: And you know, for me, I still feel it somewhat, but I managed to get back into freelancing. I was able to play with the Freeway Philharmonic, where you drive and play with all these regional orchestras. So, I started getting back into shape. Honestly, I thought I'd never be able to make it in music again.

Author: And when did you begin to pursue the position you have now?

Tuba: Yeah! So, Verizon Wireless had a place up in Folsom, California, near Sacramento. And at the time California State University, Sacramento, had a position open for teaching tuba and from there I started subbing with the Sacramento Philharmonic. The Sacramento Philharmonic started up after the Sacramento Symphony folded. Michael Morgan conducted the Sacramento Philharmonic. The Sacramento Philharmonic kind of shared Michael Morgan with the Oakland Symphony Orchestra.

Author: I see . . .

Tuba: It was so great working with Michael Morgan. I was subbing with the Sacramento Philharmonic and performing with the Sacramento Opera when they needed a tuba player. I was also teaching at Sacramento State, so I thought, you know, I'm gonna relocate to Sacramento from San Francisco, it's about an hour and a half away.

Author: Good idea . . .

Tuba: By that time, my playing was much stronger, and I finally felt like I was contributing to the music and not being a burden to the music anymore with that dystonia. I was comfortable performing again, and the dystonia experience really informed my approached to teaching. So, I got that job teaching at

Sac State going. I really built up that tuba studio there. During the pandemic, I had like a dozen students and formed a brass chamber music class as well. The Philharmonic was great, oh, the Sacramento Opera and the Sacramento Philharmonic merged.

Author: Ah, that's what I was going to ask you about.

Tuba: So what was great, there was a tuba vacancy in the Sacramento Philharmonic and when they merged with the Opera I got merged right into the position, since I was playing with both orchestras anyway.

Author: You didn't audition for the position?

Tuba: Not officially. I played for the music directors of both orchestras. I was really fortunate, being in the right place at the right time and playing well. It just worked out for me.

But being with the Sacramento Philharmonic . . . Ah! There always seemed to be this thing about being one of the few Black people in classical music world. And Teresa King, a Black woman, she's our keyboard player for the Sacramento Philharmonic. She and I are the only two Black players in the Philharmonic and occasionally a few Black players might be hired as subs, but very few. Lynn Richards, viola, she's amazing, she freelances in Los Angeles as well. There were very few of us that could be seen playing in the Sacramento Philharmonic.

You know, growing up in San Francisco in a Catholic school system and the only Black family in the Saint Paul Parish, I think in a way, was preparing me for the classical music world. [Laughing]

Author: Now that's interesting . . . [Laughing]

Tuba: You know, my mother is from Trinidad and Tobago, and my father is from Baltimore. Our families came from big family Catholic traditions. We were like the only Black families in that whole parish of Catholics growing up. And true to most semi-first-generation immigrant families, we strived to be successful.

Author: Are you saying that parish of Catholics prepared you for dealing with the white people in the classical music world?

Tuba: Yeah, it was like being in the classical music scene, you know, standing out, everybody knows you!

Like being constantly under a microscope. Everything I did was noticed! And I had great musical experiences, but after a time in that scene, you develop a set of skills that enable you to navigate that world. You learn to straddle the two worlds that you live in. And there was a constant weight on your back, always, of always having to be, on.

Author: Hummm?

Tuba: You know, I've had only a few very outright racist experiences, but in the classical music word, it was kind of the opposite of out and out racism.

You become the go-to person, the token, the one who must always represent the Black race. There's a fine line when your Black face shows up in just about every photo involving the orchestra's public image.

Author: Right . . . [Laughing]

Tuba: I was on every program the orchestra published, and they recruited me to be the community engagement manager.

Author: Is that right?

Tuba: But I'm good with people.

Author: Oh. I see . . .

Tuba: They had me narrate Peter and the Wolf.

Author: Oh really? Ah ha! [Laughing]

Tuba: I was the front man for a woodwind quintet we had in the orchestra called the Wolfgang Woodwind Quintet. That's how the orchestra noticed how well I managed an audience. Me as a good people-person-frontman and so, get this, I actually became a member of the orchestra staff. I was asked to be their community engagement manager.

A year later, I teamed up with Gail Winney, the orchestra's amazing education director. We worked great together getting the orchestra's musicians out and into the schools and community.

Author: Oh, great . . . So that was like a second job for you.

Tuba: Yeah, exactly, I became a staff member. So, principal tuba and an orchestra staff member.

Author: Wow! Unheard of, impressive!

Tuba: Yeah, so I was pulling double, triple duty, where I would be setting up all of these community events, community concerts, creative concerts for the Philharmonic. I'd be the front person on setting them up and then I'd be playing in the brass section of the Philharmonic.

So, I'd be performing, talking, and creating and setting up those events. I did that for ten years. And just before the merger of the Sacramento Symphony and the Sacramento Opera, we, the Philharmonic, established the Carnegie Hall Partnership for "Link-Up" an education program for third through fifth graders. We built that up to about five thousand kids a year participating. Carnegie Hall developed the curriculum. Then I'd get out into the schools and get school partners and then the orchestra would do a culminating concert, where all the kids would have that as a big field trip with dozens of buses, thousands of kids. The kids would play along with the concert on recorders the songs and tunes they learned. So, the Sacramento Philharmonic established the Carnegie Hall Partnership in our area, but that concert series was national.

Author: I see . . . wow!

Tuba: So my being a person of color, even though the music was great, I still had to intentionally create a welcoming experience, to bring communities of color into classical music and into the classical music world.

Author: And you were like the ombudsman for that, but you got paid?

Tuba: I got paid! Well . . . I got paid, but for that amount of work, you're never paid enough.

Author: Right, right, of course . . .

Tuba: But it did get kind of strange, a bit over the top even, my being so popular. Everybody in the organization knew me or knew about me, I should say. I'd show up to all the post-concert receptions because I'd be escorting our guest artists who engaged for and attended our community events. At our post-concert receptions, I was familiar with all the guest artists, board members, and staff. I was always one of the few people of color in the room. It began to feel weird to me every time someone would exclaim, "Oh, you've gotta meet our principal tuba, he's so great!" [Laughing]

Author: I get it and I remember that. They just made over you something annoying.

Tuba: I felt like I was on a leash, the way they carried on, parading me around like a pet.

Author: Were there any other Black players in the Philharmonic at that time?

Tuba: Oh, very few, just one or two.

Author: You said there was a viola player and . . . ?

Tuba: And an orchestra pianist . . . yeah, Theresa Keene. Oh, and there were a few Latinos and a few Asians, but they weren't necessarily members.

Author: Oh, they were substitute musicians?

Tuba: Yes! And you know, after a while, you kind of realize that you no longer have the energy for being their token Black person, their ombudsman, just for the sake of their world image.

Author: Of course, I understand.

Tuba: Everyone was always coming to you, so you always felt like you were under the microscope, you always had to make sure you were doing good work, well represented, making sure you were dressing the part, looking your best.

Author: So, then you didn't have any of the usual racial push-back from players in the orchestra at large?

Tuba: No, not the racial push-back, but the opposite side of that was they always came to me regarding Black or racial issues.

Author: So, you were the go-to guy for any and all things Black.

Tuba: Yes! You know, I was the go-to for being the minority representative. The go-to to show that the orchestra was being openminded and diversified.

Author: Right, of course . . .

Tuba: So, Michael Morgan was our conductor, a Black conductor. And the thing about that was, they didn't really harness the fact that Michael Morgan, a Black conductor, could branch out and connect to the Black community. I don't think the board of directors took full advantage of what this orchestra could've been as far as diversifying the field. We would bring in some guest soloists that were diverse, but there could've been more.

Author: Its funny that they saw you as someone to reach out to the Black community, but not Michael Morgan, the Black music director. I wonder if they thought Michael would be uncomfortable with such an idea.

Tuba: You know, Michael would've been great for that. He would've been great for fundraising because the Sacramento area is very diverse. It's been diverse since the Gold Rush times. And there are several military bases, McCullen and Travis are in the area, which are extremely diverse.

The orchestra just missed out, because if you go to an orchestra concert in that area today, the audience would still be extremely white and not representing the diversity in the area.

I eventually stepped down from that staff role in the orchestra because I got tired of bringing folks to their table to help, and then having my hands tied because the orchestra didn't really want to make the financial commitment to such diversity endeavors.

Author: Sounds like the orchestra could've used a more progressive management that would've achieved the diversity and inclusion they claimed they so desired.

Finale

The conversations in this book represent the present-day number and status of most African American classical musicians playing in major American symphony orchestras. All of these players, more than half a century earlier, would've been absolutely forbidden from auditioning and certainly not hired by *any* major American symphony orchestra. A question I have been asked countless times during my career is: Why? Black people have always been great in every other musical genre.

During my several decades playing in a major American symphony orchestra, I couldn't help but notice that most white American classical musicians I encountered and worked with, and the white American classical music world in general, seemed to always be on their knees culturally before Europe and European classical music as an artform. They seemed to *desperately cling to Europe*, as if it was their artistic and cultural identity.

As if it were some kind of desperately needed, cultural touchstone available exclusively to them, and that only *they* truly understood its intrinsic value. Even though for many white, American classical musicians, their European ancestry would be, at best, obscure.

Even the founding fathers of this country were on their knees culturally before Ancient Greece. Many of them actually spoke Greek and some of them were advocating for many years the idea that classic Greek become the national language of these United States.

Before American-born conductor Leonard Bernstein became music director of the New York Philharmonic in 1958, it seemed almost every major American symphony orchestra just had to have a sixty-year-old, white, male European as their conductor and music director. Again, always the reaching out and looking up to the European paradigm.

Consequently, in my experience, I couldn't help but notice that when a Black classical musician emerged on the stage of this highly coveted European/American classical music scene, performing totally on par, or better, with anyone in the field, the very presence of said excellent Black classical musician always seemed to invade or infringe on the white American classical musician's sense of cultural identity. That this European classical music was somehow *their* music, despite their often-remote European ancestry.

Therefore, I've come to believe that more than a half century ago in these United States, the aforementioned state of mind of the white classical music world is the main reason Black classical musicians were, for so many years, absolutely barred from performing in major American symphony orchestras.

The reasons were numerous, though some were totally unfounded and just simply racist. Two of my favorites being: 1) Black classical musicians, even those trained at major conservatories, lacked the necessary training and pure white musical insight to play in a major symphony orchestra; and 2) Black classical musicians were unable to depart from the "jazz feel" when they played music and therefore were unable to produce the pure, white European classical music style needed for a major symphony orchestra.

Then what about Black classical musicians who trained at major conservatories and playing traditional orchestral instruments and never attempting to play jazz? Would they have trouble departing from the jazz feel?

Perhaps there was something deeper at work in those dark days. Perhaps a deep, culturally pathological fear that Black classical musicians would bring the same level of musical excellence to the classical music stage that they did in so many other musical genres? Or was it the fear of having to witness firsthand excellent Black classical musicians performing in the symphony orchestra to such a superior level that they musically belie the deeply imbued racist fantasy that Black classical musicians somehow lacked the white artistic, musical insight to play classical music? Regardless of their love and passion for the music?

Then, given that time in American history (1920–1969), the racial resistance to Black classical musicians playing in American symphony orchestras fit in quite snugly with all the other racist paradigms present at that time in the United States.

So, what exactly was this fear of Black in classical music that seeped into the American music psyche over more than half a century ago?

Was it a fear that African American classical musical giants, like Leontine Price, Grace Bumbry, Jesse Norman, Kathline Battle, André Watts, and so many others, would emerge as time passed?

Was there a fear that one day a Black principal clarinetist of the New York Philharmonic would appear in all his excellence? A Black associate principal French horn of the New York Philharmonic or solo trumpeter, Wynton Marsalis, winning a Grammy in both classical and jazz would emerge? Would the many great Black maestros, Henry Lewis, James De Priest, Dean Dixon, William Grant Still, Thomas Wilkins, Jeri Lynn Johnson, Anthony Parnther, Coleridge-Taylor Perkinson, and many others, cause that fear?

Or was it simply the classical music world's denial and resistance to admitting how Black Americans had excelled in so many other fields, like science, medicine, sports, politics, literature (producing literary giants like James Baldwin, Toni Morrison, and Maya Angelou), and in countless other areas of human endeavor besides music? Was the classical music world to be the last hold out? It's almost as if the white classical music world was saying: *Black people may have achieved success in countless other fields, but they are not going to excel in our European classical music. They are not going to have this.* As if they want to say, "As American, white, second-class Europeans, this is *also our music.*"

Although, I must say, given the many condescending exchanges with white classical musicians in my many years working with them, if they did in fact feel like white, second-class Europeans and were therefore accepting of a kind of, dare I say, second-class Europeanism, then that would explain why so many of them tried to talk down to me, as if they expected me to a accept some kind of insulting third-class status that would have me looking up to them regarding European classical music.

When I contemplate the overall history of Black people in the United States, one enormous multi-part question constantly and almost hauntingly screams into my Black male psyche: How in God's name was it possible that a group of people, who experienced such a deeply insane history in these United States, make such amazing, upwardly mobile, superhuman strides, despite being untimely ripped from their native countries and cultures, survive centuries of chattel slavery, to make a country great, and *still* aspire to be American citizens?

And despite resistance to that, by experiencing, from their fellow white Americans, everything from public lynching and burnings as entertainment where refreshments were sold, to having their beautiful Black toddlers stolen and used for alligator bait, to electing supreme court justices, members of the senate and congress, and finally, a Black president of the United States? How??

And because of said historically brutal obstacles overcome by Black people, in the United States, I am today extremely optimistic that the state of the young, future, Black classical musicians that I've observed in the top music schools and who have obviously been historically deputized by their forefathers, to strive, flourish, and proliferate for generations to come in the classical music world, especially in the United States.

Finally, given my many rich experiences living in the United States, especially witnessing the miraculous African American existence here for all my years, I can hardly resist the temptation of deeply believing that, though being the first to inhabit it, despite all beliefs to the contrary, there is still no one walking on this God's green earth quite like the Black human being.

Fine

Index

About the Author

Robert Lee Watt studied French horn at the New England Conservatory of Music with Harry Shapiro of the Boston Symphony. In 1970, he was hired by the Los Angeles Philharmonic as assistant first French horn under maestro Zubin Mehta, making him the first African American French hornist hired by a major symphony in the United States.